JOURNAL FOR THE STUDY OF THE NEW TESTAMENT
SUPPLEMENT SERIES
179

Executive Editor
Stanley E. Porter

Sheffield Academic Press

Texts Reading Texts,
Sacred and Secular

Alison M. Jack

Journal for the Study of the New Testament
Supplement Series 179

This book is dedicated to the memory of Carol Kellas,
friend and scholar

Copyright © 1999 Sheffield Academic Press

Published by
Sheffield Academic Press Ltd
Mansion House
19 Kingfield Road
Sheffield S11 9AS
England

Typeset by Sheffield Academic Press
and
Printed on acid-free paper in Great Britain
by Biddles Ltd
Guildford, Surrey

British Library Cataloguing in Publication Data

A catalogue record for this book is available
from the British Library

ISBN 1-85075-954-5

CONTENTS

PREFACE

The language, themes and imagery of the Bible have been read and re-written in texts across time. In the Revelation of John, the Hebrew Bible echoes and is reinvented, just as, in James Hogg's *The Private Memoirs and Confessions of a Justified Sinner* (1824), many explicit and implicit readings and interpretations of the Bible are offered. In this book, these readings of the Bible, and the ways in which Revelation and Hogg's *Confessions* have themselves been read, are considered from two postmodern perspectives.

The validity of reading the Bible as literature is defended in the Introduction to the book by demonstrating that many of the problems that might prevent such a reading, such as the multiplicity of available manuscripts and the undefined role of the author/editor, also have to be overcome by those working in the field of literary studies. In the following chapters I suggest that postmodern ideas of marginalization and deconstruction offer new contexts in which to read both Revelation and Hogg's *Confessions*. In Part 1 (Chapters 2 and 3), I argue that readings of the *Confessions* that are sensitive to the 'ex-centricities' of the text enable new readings of Revelation from the same perspective. In Part 2 (Chapters 4 and 5), I suggest that readings of Revelation from the perspective of deconstruction open up new possibilities for readings of the *Confessions*.

Chapter 2 argues that Hogg's understanding of the Bible and its interpretations may be regarded as marginal in a postmodern sense. Readings of the Bible offered in the *Confessions*, and in other examples of Hogg's work, demonstrate this 'ex-centricity'. When, in Chapter 3, Revelation is read in a way that highlights its marginalized status within society, its readings of the Hebrew Bible take on new significance. Both texts are shown to offer readings that are subversive and sceptical of the claims of the dominant master narratives of their time. The insights of postmodernism illuminate these previously silenced 'ex-centricities'.

In Part 2, various modern readings of Revelation and the Confessions are discussed, and their inadequacies are demonstrated from the perspective of deconstruction. In Chapter 4, a reading of Revelation from the perspective of the 'abyss' makes possible a reading of the *Confessions* in which Robert's assumed culpability is questioned and Gil-Martin's role is redeemed. When the burden of explanation of every ambiguity in the novel is lifted, the horror of the text stands without any natural and supernatural explanation, and is placed within the locus of everyday experience. A new reading of Revelation is offered in Chapter 5 which foregrounds the nightmarish aspects of the text, and reconsiders the conflicting roles assigned to the Christ character. When Revelation is read as a nightmare, the text is robbed of its status as Scripture. When the text's apparent message about the necessity of choosing God over Satan is deconstructed, the boundary between the lost and the saved is blurred.

Out of the context of postmodernism, new ways to approach texts have arisen. Two of these, a sensitivity to a text's marginalized status and deconstruction, have offered new ways to read both Revelation and the *Confessions*. Reading the two texts side by side in these ways disturbs and challenges traditional readings of them both.

ACKNOWLEDGMENTS

Many people have helped to bring this book to completion. I could not have hoped for a more interesting and interested PhD supervisor than Dr Douglas Templeton of the New Testament Department at New College. Dr Templeton's comments were always thought-provoking and to the point. In the English Literature Department, Professor Ian Campbell was hugely helpful and supportive, and pointed me in the direction of James Hogg. In Professor Campbell's sabbatical year, Dr Penny Fielding offered constructive criticism and lots of encouragement. Dr Timothy Lim was a willing sounding-board while I was working on the Qumran section. As always, Professor John O'Neill showed much kindness and scholarly concern.

I should like to thank my parents for their belief in my abilities, despite their horror at the topic I eventually chose. My husband, Paul Davies, has been supportive, caring and interested throughout, even when I was in danger of losing interest myself. Many other friends have helped by talking and listening: my thanks go especially to Catriona Morrison, Arul Dhas and Abigail Clark.

I was assisted by a scholarship which enabled me to spend a week at St Deiniol's Library, Hawarden, and I should like to thank the Trustees of the Library for their generosity.

ABBREVIATIONS

ABD	David Noel Freedman (ed.), *The Anchor Bible Dictionary* (New York: Doubleday, 1992)
Bib	*Biblica*
BJRL	*Bulletin of the John Rylands University Library of Manchester*
ExpTim	*Expository Times*
JBL	*Journal of Biblical Literature*
JJS	*Journal of Jewish Studies*
JSNT	*Journal for the Study of the New Testament*
JSOT	*Journal for the Study of the Old Testament*
JSP	*Journal for the Study of the Pseudepigrapha*
JTS	*Journal of Theological Studies*
RB	*Revue biblique*
RevQ	*Revue de Qumran*
RHPR	*Revue d'histoire et de philosophie religieuses*

Chapter 1

INTRODUCTION

...τί ἐστιν... καινὴ κτίσις.

...a new creation is everything! (Gal. 6.15)

καὶ λέγει μοι, Μὴ σφραγίσῃς τοὺς λόγους τῆς προφητείας τοῦ βιβλίου τούτου, ὁ καιρὸς γάρ ἐγγύς ἐστιν.

And the angel said to me, 'Do not seal up the words of the prophecy of this book, for the time is near' (Rev. 22.10).

There is not an error into which a man can fall, which he may not press Scripture into his service as proof of the probity of (Hogg's *Confessions* [1824: 107]).

Although literary theory is becoming an acceptable perspective from which to approach the Bible,[1] its postmodern aspects are rarely wel-

---

1. In the last two decades there has been a two-way interaction between the fields of literary and biblical studies. Many literary critics have taken a renewed interest in the Bible as a literary text, and many biblical critics have begun to apply some of the tools of literary criticism to their readings of the biblical text. Kermode and Prickett are two examples of literary critics who have brought their knowledge of literary theory and texts to bear on biblical scholarship. Good examples of their work are Kermode's article 'The Argument about Canons' (1986: 78-96), and his edition, with Alter, of *The Literary Guide to the Bible* (1989); and Prickett's *Words and the Word: Language, Poetics, and Biblical Interpretation* (1986) and, with Barnes, *The Bible* (1991). Prominent among the many biblical scholars who use literary theory is Jasper, who is editor of *Images of Belief in Literature* (1984), author of *The New Testament and the Literary Imagination* (1987), and editor of the 'Studies in Literature and Religion' series. His introductory volume to the series, *The Study of Literature and Religion* (1989) applies different strategies, philosophical, hermeneutical and literary, to explore the relationship between imaginative literature and theology. Hays and Petersen are two examples of traditional New Testament critics who have found different aspects of literary theory illuminating. In *Echoes of Scripture in the Letters of Paul* (1989) Hays offers a reading of

comed in the wider world of biblical studies.[2] Suspicion and dismissiveness characterize much of the reaction to those works which attempt to read the Bible from a postmodern literary perspective.[3] The aim of this book is to participate in the current debate and to explore the possible dialogue between postmodern literary theory and sacred texts. Central to the topic is the reading process. Specifically, readings of the Bible across time and in several different contexts will be considered, and readings from the perspective of postmodern literary theory will be

Pauline texts that is informed by the work of Hollander *The Figure of Echo* (1981) on Milton and other poets; and Petersen's sociological aims are accomplished in *Rediscovering Paul: Philemon and the Sociology of Paul's Narrative World* (1985) through the use of a literary analysis of Paul's narrative. Many other examples could be given, some of whom will be referred to in the course of the book.

2.   The antipathy to postmodern ideas is often expressed in terms of support for the claims of historical criticism. In his recent commentary on Revelation, Roloff (1993: 13-14) asserts that 'as far as its composition as a whole is concerned, Revelation should be seen as a uniform, consistently constructed work that from beginning to end reflects the theological intention of the author... Whoever wishes to understand a text of the distant past must try to determine what the writer wanted to say to his or her readers at the time and in what sense those readers could understand the writer's message'. Such a statement could hardly be more opposed to postmodern literary critical concerns. Postmodern readings of the Bible, particularly in New Testament studies, continue to be marginalized. In a review of Pippin's (1992) deconstructive discussion of Revelation (which is considered in Chapter 5), Russell (1993: 282) comments that the book 'perhaps says more about the convictions and prejudices of the author than it does about those of John himself', thus completely missing the point of such a reading. Ashton's (1994) critique of deconstruction and his arguments for historical criticism will be considered below.

3.   Of all New Testament scholars, Moore has written the most extensively on the interface between postmodern literary theory and biblical studies. His books, *Literary Criticism and the Gospels: The Theoretical Challenge* (1989), *Mark and Luke in Poststructuralist Perspective: Jesus begins to Write* (1992) and *Poststructuralism and the New Testament: Derrida and Foucault at the Foot of the Cross* (1994), have helped to bring the concepts of postmodernism into the field of the literary study of the New Testament. Other examples include Detweiler and Robbins, 'From New Criticism to Poststructuralism: Twentieth-Century Hermeneutics' (1991), Malbon and McKnight (eds.), *The New Literary Criticism and the New Testament* (1994) and the Bible and Culture Collective, *The Postmodern Bible* (1995). In *A Myth of Innocence*, Mack (1988) relates Derrida's ideas in *Of Grammatology* (1976) to a reading of Mark's Gospel. The journal *Semeia* frequently publishes articles written from a postmodern literary critical perspective.

offered. The focus of interest will be the book of Revelation. Revelation's reading of the Hebrew Bible will be considered, as will some of the ways that Revelation has been read in this century. This reflection on the reading process will be facilitated by a comparative consideration of readings of James Hogg's novel, *The Private Memoirs and Confessions of a Justified Sinner* (1824).

At first sight, the choice of Hogg's *Confessions* as a comparative text seems arbitrary, even perverse. However, at the most basic level, the *Confessions* is a literary text and as such enables a consideration of whether or not the same methodology can be used for both literary texts and Scripture. It offers a context in which to discuss the Bible as a literary text. The *Confessions* has been chosen specifically because of the similarities between it and Revelation. In both, interpretations of the Bible play a central role. In terms of content, both deal with the issue of eternal destiny and the struggle between good and evil. In terms of their genesis, both texts arose in contexts of alienation: Revelation was apparently written at a time of persecution by the State; Hogg's position in Edinburgh literary society, it will be argued, was both tenuous and ambiguous. Most significant, perhaps, is that both have been the subject of countless and contradictory readings. A wealth of literature exists that tries to explain the two texts, but Revelation, like the *Confessions*, seems to be resistant to the sort of closure many readers seek. In the following chapters it will be argued that because of the latter two similarities in particular, Revelation and the *Confessions* respond well to postmodern literary-critical readings such as the two offered here.

In one sense, there is no such thing as 'a literary reading of the Bible'. Literary criticism is a not a unified movement, but an umbrella term for a multiplicity of approaches. Many of these different approaches have been applied to readings of the Bible, and critics and advocates of the movement alike have often tried to claim that all literary readings share characteristics in common. For Alter and Kermode (1989: 1-2) a literary reading is interested 'in the virtues by which... [texts] continue to live as something other than archaeology'. They suggest that a reading that uses methods developed in the criticism of secular literature breaks the previously accepted link between the text and history. Literary readings are more concerned with the text's rhetoric and discourse than with the history of the text's creation or with the clues it might offer about its historical context. Alter and Kermode's (1989: 5) stated interest lies in the literary criticism of the Bible that 'stresses the role of the critic as someone who helps make possible fuller readings of the text, with a particular emphasis on the complex integration of diverse means of communication encountered in most works of literature'. However, literary criticism is a much more diverse activity than Alter and Kermode are willing to accept,[4] and postmodern reflection upon this activity is critical of attempts to cancel out the differences between ways of reading or the range of their interpretations. Postmodern literary theory challenges both the sort of literary criticism Alter and Kermode employ, and the assumptions of historical biblical criticism which this literary criticism had begun to undermine. Literary criticism that takes account of postmodern thought makes problematic all methods of interpreting texts which bolster a text's unity over its multiple or dissenting voices. For this reason, cherished notions of the text, the author and the reader are disturbed by postmodern literary critical readings. For some biblical critics, the Bible is an unsuitable candidate for any literary reading in the first place because of the particular nature of its text, writers and readers. It is anachronistic to define the Bible as literature. For these critics, the Bible is doubly unsuited to readings from a postmodern literary critical perspective. In the following section, the arguments for this position are considered, and the effect of postmodern literary theory on all readings of texts is debated in greater detail.

Reading the Bible as Literature: The Problem of the Text, the Author and the Reader

One of the central issues in the debate about readings of the Bible from a literary critical perspective is the role and identity of the author of the biblical text. Can biblical texts be thought of as having authors who are responsible for the texts as we have them, and, if not, does this mean that they cannot be considered as literature? Were the gospel writers not editors and collectors of existing traditions rather than authors? Moreover, what is 'the text', when so many different versions of the text of the same verses exist? Once these questions are dealt with, the equally trenchant objections of traditional biblical critics who hold 'the epistemological conviction that the text has a determinate meaning, that the

---

4.   The seven chapter headings of *The Postmodern Bible* (Bible and Culture Collective 1995), each dealing with a different critical practice, cover only a fraction of the varieties of literary criticisms.

text is a transparent window to an extra-textual referent, and that the referent can be discussed with some degree of accuracy' (Burnett 1990: 53) are still to be faced by those attempting to read the Bible as literature in a postmodern literary critical context. For many traditional historical scholars, any literary reading that emphasizes the text's indeterminacy, the role of the reader in the production of meaning, or that separates the text from its assumed theological or historical context, fails to read the text 'properly'. In his article in the edition of *Semeia* dedicated to postmodern literary issues, Burnett concludes that 'thinking in (post)modern terms about the text, referentiality, and discourse is one way to begin the deconstruction, and thus the reclamation, of our discipline' (1990: 70). This conclusion remains to be defended.

The indeterminacy and lack of unity of the available texts has caused some critics, for example Ashton (1994: 140-42), to question the possibility of reading the Bible as literature. From the multiplicity of the manuscripts available, which text should any literary critic interested in the Bible accept? Should the work of deciding which is the best text be left to historical critics alone, while readers who use narrative criticism, for example, occupy themselves with 'higher' things? Of course, this is not a problem faced only by readers of the Bible. In the study of literature both ancient and modern, there are many different kinds of textual indeterminacies to be resolved: the author's words are corrupted by the printer or the censor; several different texts are available, either all approved by the author although written at different stages of his or her life, or only one approved by the author, perhaps the one that most readers find inferior to the others; a text exists that is the result of the named author's collaboration with others; or a text is found that the author did not consider to be publishable or finished. Debate about the role of bibliography, the various rules governing the resolution of these difficulties, continues in the field of literary studies, and many of its features will be familiar to biblical scholars.[5] Indeed, literary biblio-

---

5. The classic bibliographical debate between those who argue that the author's manuscript should form the editor's base-text (e.g. Bowers 1959) and those who stress the importance of the social, collaborative context in which the work was written and produced, arguing for the first edition as the base-text (McGann 1983), is not relevant to biblical studies, in which nothing approaching an author's manuscript survives. Textual critics of the Bible are well aware of the issues raised by McGann's argument that decisions about the edited form of the text need to be embedded in the text's broad cultural context, taking into account the history of the

graphy acknowledges a debt to biblical and classical scholars who have struggled to formulate rules for deciding between the many texts available (as, for example, McGann admits, 1983: 7). This is very much an area in which literary and biblical studies overlap.

The parallel concerns of biblical and literary studies, and in particular the literary study of the Bible, are exemplified in the Statement of Textual Policy offered to editors of the Edinburgh Edition of the Waverley Novels (Hewitt *et al.* 1996: 2-4). The aim of the editors is 'to restore Scott's novels to a form which reflects his original intentions and which is freed as far as possible from the various errors and non-authorial interventions that arose in the course of their publication and successive reprintings' (p. 2). To do this, editors are instructed to collate all extant pre-publication material, together with the earliest editions of the text, and from this collation to restore readings 'lost in the production process through accident, error or misunderstanding' (p. 3). All authorial or editorial alterations to the chosen base-text ('the earliest fully articulated and coherent form of the text' [p. 2]), except typographical and copy-editing errors, are to be acknowledged in the critical apparatus of the edition. This process of collation and decision-making between several possibilities on specified grounds is very similar to the work of biblical text-critics. In both fields, there is a shared aim of producing a text 'close to what the first readers would have read had the process of writing and production been less pressurised and more considered' (p. 4). The text-critical problems raised by the multiplicity of biblical texts, particularly of the New Testament, do not make literary critical readings impossible: such literary criticism continues in the field of literary studies, in which very similar textual issues arise.

However, in both fields there is an undeniable tension between some textual and literary critics: many textual scholars working in biblical studies share with their colleagues in literary studies a concern about many literary critics' unquestioning assumptions about the nature of texts. Bowers argues that '[t]he literary critic must become sophisticated, and leave his childish faith in the absoluteness of the printed word' (1959: 34). Parker (1984) offers a more strongly-worded attack against those who fail to consider the history of the production and transmission of a text, but who nevertheless feel qualified to comment on its meaning. Parker argues that 'non-meanings, partially authorial

text with regard to the related histories of its production, reproduction and reception.

meanings, and inadvertent, intentionless meanings co-exist in standard literary texts with genuine authorial meanings' (1984: 10). However, some critics either over-ride the inconsistencies this co-existence produces in their compulsion to make sense of what they read: '[c]onfident that their aesthetic goosebumps are authorially planned, critics are lured into seeing authority where the passage they are reading contains nonsense' (p. 11); or they abstract the influence of the author and unknowingly find meaning in a corrupted text:

> It seems that treating the author as an abstracted, Olympian power frees critics to celebrate nonsensical texts and adventitious meanings in texts where the words, but not all the meanings, are the author's; and treating the text the author created as if it were merely hypothetical, a metaphysical concept, freeing them to identify 'the text itself' as the published text or the revised and republished text (Parker 1984: 15).

For Parker, textual meaning is the intention of the author, with the acknowledgement that any text may be distorted in the writing, revision and publishing stages of its transmission. Where information about the history of the text is available, such as manuscripts or proofs, the evidence they offer should not be ignored. It is to fall prey to a 'new ignorance' to avoid questions of the history of what is already inscribed in the given text as, Parker argues, many deconstructionists do. Parker (1984: 240) suggests that textual history may explain many of the marginal elements that are of such interest to the postmodern literary critic. However Hewitt *et al.* (1996) comment, deconstruction has highlighted for literary critics what textual critics have always been aware of: that 'texts cannot/ should not be trusted' (p. 8); and that all readers need to be aware of the difficulties of the textual edition used and the assumptions of its editor(s).

Certainly in the field of biblical studies a knowledge of the transmission of a text affects the way that text is read. This is particularly obvious in readings of the Synoptic Gospels, in which it is usually assumed that Matthew and Luke read and adapted Mark. Textual variants exist that offer contradictory meanings of the same text, and these should not be ignored in any reading of the text, whether of a literary nature or not. Textual criticism is less marginalized in biblical studies than in literary studies, and a literary reading of a biblical text would be impoverished if it did not take any of the major textual variants into account. From the perspective of deconstruction, textual variation offers another level of 'différance' to consider. Significantly, the presence of wide textual variation need not make literary criticism of the Bible impossible. Within the field of literary theory, issues of textual variation also have to be confronted and their hermeneutical implications faced.

In his polemic against the literary criticism of the Bible, Ashton (1994: 142-48) has argued that most literary critics of the Bible arbitrarily smooth out the difficulties of the text's diachronic development out of laziness or ignorance. He comments that 'there can be no doubt that in most respects the smooth [synchronic] approach is much *easier* than the alternative, which in the nature of the case promises a very bumpy ride' (p. 143). However, as Ashton himself at times admits, this is a criticism of specific literary readings of the Bible,[6] rather than a fatal argument against the use of any literary critical methods in biblical studies.[7] It is important for biblical scholars who seek to read the Bible as literature and for their critics to be aware that issues of the genesis of texts are problematic not only to them. These are issues for all branches of literary criticism, not just the literary criticism of the Bible as Ashton seems at times to imply. Texts other than the Bible have complex textual histories that may or may not be taken into account. For Ashton, there is strong evidence that the Gospel of John was not written in one sitting, and that therefore its present coherence (or incoherence) is less important than the processes by which it came into being. Any criticism that operates on the assumption of the text's unity can have little to offer. In taking this view, Ashton is himself representative of one group within literary studies. Hawthorn, writing about literature in general, comments:

> The issue has divided twentieth-century literary critics down the middle, between those who demand that the literary work be treated as independent and free-standing, and those who insist that unless it is seen as the

6.   In his chapter on Narrative Criticism, Ashton deals most extensively with the work of Culpepper (1983), Staley (1988) and Mlakuzhyil (1987). He labels the work of these critics as examples of narrative criticism, distinguished 'by a consistent vision of the Gospels as, above all, *stories* and the desire to reach a better understanding of how these stories are told' (1994: 141).

7.   Ashton criticizes the work of Powell (1993), who argues for a reading that considers the history of a text to be irrelevant to the work of the narrative critic, on the grounds that Powell 'is not thinking in general terms of literary criticism as it is actually practised (unless he happens to be an adherent of the tenets of New Criticism, a school that went out of fashion more than thirty years ago); rather he is thinking very narrowly of the exclusively *biblical* understanding of narrative criticism' (1994: 144).

final and visible stage of a long and complex process of creation then it cannot properly be understood (1993: 64).

The issue at stake is the role to be assigned to the author(s) in the creation of a text's meaning. The movement away from a belief in the author's control of the text was articulated most forcefully in the context of New Criticism by Wimsatt and Beardsley (1946). They argued that the intention of any poet is both unknowable and irrelevant. The poem only has meaning on the level of the poem, and there is no need to step outside the text in search of an author. Later critics were to make more fundamental attacks on the role, or even the discrete identity, of the writer in the creation of meaning. Famously, the death of the author was proclaimed by Barthes:

> We now know that a text is not a line of words releasing a single 'theological' meaning (the 'message' of the Author-God) but a multidimensional space in which a variety of writings, none of them original, blend and clash. The text is a tissue of quotations drawn from the innumerable centres of culture (1984: 146).

Significantly for this study, Barthes argues that the death of the author fulfils much of the function of the death of God movement in the late nineteenth century. The author had filled the theological void left by the death of God, and had taken on God's role of ensuring meaning in the absence of any other metaphysical certainties. When the author 'dies' to his work, a departure from belief in authority, presence, intention and omniscience is signalled, just as it had been signalled by those proclaiming the death of God. Burke (1992: 23) summarizes the view of the author Barthes rejects:

> The author is to the text as God, the *auctor vitae*, is to his world: the unitary cause, source and master to whom the chain of textual effects must be traced, and in whom they find their genesis, meaning, goal and justification. The author thus becomes, in Derrida's words, the 'transcendental signified' and attains the supernal privilege of being at once the beginning and end of his text. Accordingly, criticism accepts the role of passive exegete to the author's intentions.

For Barthes, the author has been made incarnate in his or her text, granted omniscience, and given the role of guarantor of the text's singular meaning. Therefore, to liberate the text from its author is the equivalent of liberating the world from God. Once the text is delivered from the false control of the author, it is free to become a playful affirmation of indeterminacy.

Barthes's pronouncement of the death of the author, and his use of the analogy of the author and God have sometimes have been accepted in postmodern literary criticism without further consideration. However, as Burke argues, Barthes's attack on authorship is not particularly relevant to modern authors who rarely claim omnipotence or univocal mastery over their texts. Similarly, Anglo-American literary criticism of this century, aware of the intentional fallacy and narrative constructs such as the implied author, could scarcely be accused of promoting the idea of authorship Barthes claims to have annihilated. Burke suggests that in Barthes's essay, '[a]ll author-positions are subsumed under an essentially nineteenth-century theocentrism' (1992: 26) which does not relate to the literary situation of today. Barthes's concentration on the need to lose the author in order to allow the text freedom is misguided: the key issue is that of closure of representation, the validity of the text's claims to refer to an external world, rather than the death of the author. The author need not be viewed as the possessor of meaning, through whom the language of the text is linked to a reality outwith the text: '[i]f a text has been "unglued" of its representiality, its author need not die: to the contrary, he can flourish, become an object of biographical pleasure, perhaps even a "founder of language"!' (Burke 1992: 47). The possibility of reinstating that author within such a literary context will be considered further below.

Derrida is also invoked as a critic who rejects the notion of the author's control over the text.[8] An indication of his views is given in the essay 'Signature Event Context' (1977). Derrida's objections to authorial control are epistemological: he is sceptical of any imputation of properties of presence or representation to texts. He questions the determinative power of the author's intention over the communicative act, and suggests that language at times resists or wanders away from the author's determinate or intended meaning. Derrida proposes a new way

---

8.   Although it is not possible to explore the issue further here, it should be noted that Derrida's views on authorial intention have provoked much debate, such as Searle's reply to Derrida in which he accuses Derrida of having a 'distressing penchant for saying things that are obviously false' (1977: 203). Fish (1989: 65) makes a helpful contribution to the debate in which he discusses Derrida's assertion that '"the quality of risk" is internal to the very structure of language'. As Fish (p. 57) points out, however, this does not mean that Derrida believes that written or communication does not occur: rather, Derrida accepts that such communication occurs 'with a "relative" certainty that ensures the continuity of everyday life'.

of interpretation in which 'the category of intention will not disappear; it will have its place, but from that place it will no longer be able to govern the entire scene and system of utterance' (1977: 192). This refusal to give the author's intention a privileged place is not the same as New Criticism's rejection of the author's intention as irrelevant and unknowable. If the author's intention is to be deconstructed, it may be accepted that intention is relevant and recognizable. As Burke (1992: 141) comments: 'It is only in terms of this reconstruction that the deconstructor can begin to separate that which belongs to authorial design from that which eludes or unsettles its prescriptions.' The intention of the author, in so far as it may be reconstructed, may act as one level of hierarchy to be deconstructed. Derrida, then, occupies the middle ground with regard to the role of the author. Although he reads against the author, he does not argue for his or her disappearance or demise. The critic is given priority over the author on the Derridean premise that the author does not have full control over his or her language.

Clearly the relationship between authors and their work is far from simple, even when the author is easily identifiable: the creator of a work may not be able to answer every question about it, either because it is a work of inexplicable inspiration or they have forgotten or wish to conceal something about it. The legitimate issue in postmodern criticism of the relationship between the author and the text may be one by which most dead authors, as well as some living ones, would be baffled. As discussed above, much of postmodern literary theory argues that the author should be conceived of as the site of clashing influences and forces rather than as the source of the literary work. Authors are products of outside forces, rather than independent subjects who have creative control over their writing. The work and the reader are more important than the author in determining meaning. In the same way it might be argued that the issue of the authorship of biblical texts is irrelevant to their interpretation. The origins of the writing of, for example, the Gospels are obscure and cannot be recovered with any certainty. Within the discipline of postmodern literary criticism there is justification for ignoring the process by which biblical texts were created, thus avoiding both the question of whether or not particular effects were intended by the author, and the issue of the freedom of redactors to change the traditions which were handed down to them. Writing from a postmodern perspective, Moore (1989: 40) criticizes biblical studies for being obsessed (as Ashton 1994 is[9]) with the notion of the viability and centrality of the recovery of an author's intention with which literary critics have been ill at ease for decades. Perhaps Barthes's analogy between God and the author has significance in the field of biblical studies, in which until recently the presence of God was often tacitly assumed although rarely stated. Reading the Bible as literature highlights important issues such as intention, which traditional biblical critics have tended to ignore, and offers a way to sever the link between the text, God and the author.

Within literary criticism there remain critics who continue to relate the meaning of texts to what is known about the author's life, intentions and experiences. Some share with many biblical scholars a refusal to consider the problematic relationship between authors' intentions and the texts they produce. Others are more aware of the problems caused by doing away with the author altogether. As Burke (1992: 154) comments, '[a] massive disjunction opens up between the theoretical statement of authorial disappearance and the project of reading without the author'. Authorial influence continues to be a factor to be considered and assessed. In the readings of Barthes, there is little attempt made to justify the notion of the death of the author on epistemological grounds. However, in the work of Derrida, the possibility that authorial intention may operate as a principle of uncertainty in the text, opening up new and elusive energies, rather than as a neutralizing or simplifying force, is considered and applied.[10] Within postmodern literary theory there is the potential for the author's troublesome presence to be recognized and discussed.

In his over-view of literary theory, Hawthorn (1993: 78) offers some generalized conclusions that have largely found favour within biblical studies. The conviction that a writer stands in a certain relationship to his or her words conditions our response to them. Conscious or unconscious elements in the author's mind may have a determining affect on the writing of a work of literature, and if these elements are known they may affect its reception. An author cannot intend all the implications or

---

9.   Ashton (1994: 192) argues that 'most texts will reflect the intentions of their authors, and in this sense it is legitimate to say that the meaning of texts is bestowed by their authors'.

10.   Derrida's discussions of the work of Rousseau and Lévi-Strauss (1976) make use of information about the lives of these authors, although this information is not given a privileged place in the interpretative process.

effects on a reader of his or her work, neither can he or she 'mean' in defiance of all linguistic and logical conventions. Hays (1989: 26-27) takes a similar standpoint in his investigation into the literary echoes in Paul's letters. His hermeneutical axiom is 'that there is an authentic analogy—though not a simple analogy—between what the text meant and what it means' (p. 27). Hay's reading of Paul's letters always takes place within a community of interpretation the hermeneutical conventions of which inform his reading: one of these conventions is that a proposed interpretation must be justified by the evidence provided both by the text's rhetorical structure and by what can be known through critical, historical investigation about the author and the original readers of the text. Hay's interpretative community holds to the conviction that a writer stands in a certain relationship to his or her words, and this conviction conditions our response to those words. Anything that can be found out about the background of a biblical text and its author may be considered to have had an effect on the work and is helpful for its interpretation, in turn changing the way the text is read. A biblical text may mean more to its readers than its author intended, but the linguistic conventions of the author's time are boundaries beyond which the author cannot have 'meant'. It is particularly important for biblical scholars to investigate the linguistic conventions within which the writers of the Bible were operating, as these conventions are generally so different from those of a twentieth-century writer.

Following this approach, then, involves accepting that the role of redactors and narrators in other first-century writing, in addition to the way Scripture was used intertextually, are as important as areas of research for literary critical scholars as for those with more traditional historical interests. Knowing as much as possible about the background of the text and its author is part of the hermeneutical process, affecting and potentially being affected by a literary reading. This approach will be taken in Part 1 of this book (Chapters 2 and 3). Here, the contexts in which the *Confessions* (Chapter 2) and Revelation (Chapter 3) were written will inform the readings offered. However, recognizing other branches of literary criticism which read new meanings in the text without arguing for indisputable or privileged authorial intention behind them, Part 2 (Chapters 4 and 5) will consider the two texts from this rather different postmodern literary perspective.

Two of the three components in the literary composition, the author and the text, have now been discussed in response to possible objections to a literary approach to the Bible. The third, the reader, is also a source of controversy. The importance of the role assigned to the reader in the creation of meaning is related inversely to the role assigned to the author. If the intention of the author is judged to be unknowable or irrelevant, the reader of the text has a vital role to play. Martin (1986: 157) notes the process that has led to recent renewed interest in the reader in all texts, including the Bible. In this century, eighteenth and nineteenth-century authors who addressed their readers directly have disappeared, and problematic or fragmentary narrators have taken their place. This has forced readers to participate in the production as well as the interpretation of texts. Once the skills necessary to construct meanings where none are specified are developed, the reader may return to texts of an earlier period. There readers may discover meanings which their former reading habits led them to overlook. This process can be seen in the work of biblical critics, such as Fowler (1991), whose work is considered below, who have adopted aspects of reader-response theory in their readings.

Booth (1961) offered a hermeneutical approach that recognized that fiction is a form of communication between writer and reader. He suggested a model in which the construct of the implied author presents information about characters and events to the reader. By suggesting that literary meaning was created in the relationship between this narrator and the reader, Booth offered new ways to understand what happens when we read. However, this model opened up many issues with which reader-orientated theories continue to grapple. For example, how circumscribed is meaning in this model, and how much space is opened for the reader's own involvement in the story? How far is the role of the reader controlled by the writer and the literary conventions of the text's genre and period? Do the writer and reader work together to create meaning in the text, or are the literary or cultural assumptions of the reader's interpretative community the real force behind this process? At the other end of the scale, is the meaning of all fictional narratives inherently unstable, dependent on the readings of each individual?

Iser (1974, 1978) is a leading exponent of reception theory, a reader-based approach that offers one set of answers to these questions. For Iser, reading is an interaction between the structure of the literary work and its reader. The text provides a pattern to guide the imagination of the reader, in the form of mutually agreed conventions. However, the pattern is incomplete and needs to be filled in by the reader. Meaning emerges in this process of interaction between the reader and the text: the reader is free to fill in the blanks, but is also constrained by the pattern of the text. Iser's implied reader, then, is both a construct of the text, and an empirical reality in the form of a real reader. Within the constructed reality of the text, each perspective offered, whether by a character or the narrator, changes the reader's understanding of past action in the narrative. Furthermore, the experience of reading a text may change the reader's own views, with the result that the reader may be a different person after finishing the text. As Martin comments, for Iser the reader is 'a transcendental possibility, that exists and changes only in the process of reading' (1986: 162).

Fowler (1991), applies what is essentially reception theory to a biblical text. Fowler claims that his area of interest is the world in front of the text, its reception rather than its production. The focus has shifted from the events told in the story of the Gospel narrative to the discourse of the narrative itself. The move is from the static and seemingly stable content of the story to the temporal ways in which the language of the narrative attempts to affect the reader. Fowler (1991: 3) asserts that '[n]o longer can the language of the Gospel be regarded as primarily referential or informative; it has become rhetorical, affective, and powerful'. Fowler's strategy is to identify those features in the Gospel whose purpose is to influence its reader. He suggests that the writer's chief concern is not the fate of Jesus or the disciples, but the reader himself or herself. One of the chief ways the writer seeks to influence the reader is by providing a 'reliable' narrator of events. The third-person, omniscient and unrestricted narrator is indistinguishable from the implied author of the Gospel. Fowler suggests this leads to a collapsing of the distance between the narratee and the implied narrator: the implied reader (narratee) is as close to Jesus as the narrator is to Jesus, and as distant from the other characters. It is an ironic distance that opens up between the narratee and the other characters such as the disciples, with the result that the reader is encouraged to adopt the narrator's and Jesus' point of view. An obvious example of this is the way in which the disciples are shown to be ignorant of the identity of Jesus until Mark 8, whereas the reader has known that Jesus is the Christ since the first sentence of the first chapter of the Gospel.

Fowler deals on two levels with the issue of the identity of the reader whose reading experience he seeks to follow. 'The reader' is both Fowler himself as a critical reader and a construct called the 'ideal' reader created out of an understanding both of Fowler's critical community and of the reader's identity implied in the text. In practice, however, the readers of Mark's Gospel in whom Fowler is particularly interested are the writers of the Gospels of Matthew and Luke. He assumes they have read Mark, and judges Mark's effectiveness by the ways in which Matthew and Luke rewrite his original text.

Ashton (1994: 190-99) rejects reader-response criticism on the grounds that it refuses to consider any extra-textual information about first-century readers, and that it assumes the implied reader is approaching the text for the first time, when in fact sacred texts were designed to be read often. On the more general role of the reader, Ashton argues that to allow any importance to the concerns and experiences of later-than-original readers takes away from the defining role of the author in bestowing meaning. All readings that allow a text an indefinite number of meanings reveal 'the polymorphous perversity of the human imagination' rather than the 'essential indeterminacy of texts' (1994: 193). Ashton argues for a separation between the understanding of a biblical text, based on an historical investigation into its original meaning, and the application of that text to the lives of modern readers. In doing so, he separates too readily the text as an independent entity with a recoverable history from the role of the reader as interpreter of the text. A reading of any commentary on John will reveal the extent to which its writer is influenced by his or her own beliefs or ideology. Ashton argues for a value-free reading: literary criticism, particularly in the last two decades, has shown that no text escapes the defining influence of its reader's prejudices, interests and beliefs.

Moore (1989: 71-107) offers cogent criticisms of both Fowler's work and reader-response theory in general, while allowing the reader a defining role in the creation of meanings. One of his first criticisms is that modern reader-response theory may be an anachronistic way to approach ancient texts: it may be a classical idea that a literary work is designed to sway its readers, but modern reader-response theory is more interested in the cognitive than in the affective effects of a text. The ancient narrator's intention may not connect with the focus of reader-response critics on a wholly cognitive role for reading, whereas any attempt to chart a reader's emotional responses to a text may be considered too subjective to be helpful. Moore also observes problems in the status of 'the reader' in biblical scholars' attempts to appropriate reader-response theories: the 'reader in the text' is understood to stand in a relationship to an actual audience, usually thought of as the original readers of the Gospels, although the contemporary Gospel audience may offer the modern critic a more vital reality. Critics have attempted to address this issue by suggesting either that the reader in the text is an unchanging property of the text, so that all audiences may be included equally in the interpretations of such critics; or that contemporary readers may be given a role in addition to the assumed original readers. However, can reader-oriented criticism adequately include the personal experience of a twentieth-century reader of the Gospels, who is also 'a child of the novel' (1989: 99)? In the ambiguity about the status of the reader already noted in Fowler's work, Moore finds contradictions. Theoretically Fowler's imagined readers can be recreated either socially, by the range of experiences that affect their interpretations, or structurally, by the demands of the text. In practice, however, the reader is always presented by Fowler as being in the firm grasp of the text, manipulated by the text as it is assumed the author intended it. The readings are not offered as one of a set of potential responses, but as normative interpretations. Epistemologically it may be no easier to define what is in the reader's experience than to define what is in the text. The fact that few if any contemporary readers of the Gospels experience the reactions reader-response critics put forward is ignored. Moore (1989: 106) comments that '[f]or biblical studies the moral is plain: criticism is an institution to which real readers need not apply'.

Moore's criticism of reader-response theory is part of his argument in favour of a postmodern literary critical approach. The challenge he lays down to biblical scholars demands full consideration, which will be given below. Other, less ideologically committed scholars have also found it appropriate to withdraw from the extensive emphasis placed on the reader by reader-response critics. Hays (1989: 26) notes that the reader implied rhetorically in the text and the actual, modern reader may both have a role to play in the hermeneutic task. But he also argues that what can be found out about the author and the original readers of the text, in addition to the role of the modern community of interpretation to which all readers belong,[11] are important components of that

---

11. Hays would, of course, reject Fish's (1980) understanding of the role of the interpretative community in the creation of meaning. For Fish, the reader's response *is* the meaning of the text. The act of recognizing literature proceeds from a collective decision about what counts as literature. This collective decision is taken within interpretative communities, the members of which have a shared experience of

task. The working method employed in his book *Echoes of Scripture in the Letters of Paul* is an attempt to hold all of these components together 'in creative tension' (1989: 27). This is also Hawthorn's (1993) approach to literary texts. Neither the reader nor the text nor the author has control over the meaning of the work. Literary works are suggestive rather than limited to one meaning alone: readers have a role to play in the creation of meaning, but the text and the author's intention also set limits within which meaning may legitimately reside. Some texts are more suggestive and open than others: most literary critics of the Bible would argue, with Auerbach (1953: 3-23), that many biblical texts are particularly suggestive and open to multiple interpretations. Again, both sides of this issue will be considered. Hays's 'creative tension' will be explored in the readings of the first two chapters; however, the short-comings of any attempt to recreate the role of the original reader will be highlighted in the following two chapters, and an alternative to this elusive reader will be suggested. In these chapters (Chapters 4 and 5), in place of the search for the original reader, the concerns and insights of a reader in the postmodern age will be offered.

Postmodernism and Biblical Criticism

It has been argued that it is not anachronistic to read the Bible as litera-ture, and that many of the apparent obstacles to reading the Bible as literature are not specific to the biblical text, and have been addressed by literary critics grappling with the same problems. However, although many of the ideas behind postmodern literary theory have been men-tioned, the full implications of postmodernism have not yet been faced.

In general terms, postmodernism as an aesthetic, literary and cultural movement challenges and disturbs much that traditional, liberal hermeneutics holds precious and self-evident, including the terms just used to describe it. The original form of a text, its author's intention and the context of its intended readers all lose their privileged position as guarantors of the text's meaning. Indeed, postmodernism questions any master narrative that claims or seeks a unified, totalitarian meaning in text, art or life itself.

---

internalized language rules. These interpretative communities produce meanings in texts and are responsible for the formal features of the text which they comment upon: '[i]nterpretation is not the art of construing but the art of constructing. Inter-preters do not decode poems, they make them' (1980: 327).

Postmodernism is not a master narrative or system that exists outwith that which it describes, as historical criticism attempts to operate. Rather, postmodernism highlights the inescapable processes of meaning-making in both the production and reception of art. Postmodernism explodes the myth that meaning exists in or behind the text, and locates it rather in the history of the discourse: the author-text relationship is replaced by the reader-text relationship. The unavoidable role of ideology in this relationship is acknowledged, and the politics of any reading is laid bare. Any reading that claims to be innocent or objective is deemed to be a falsification of the truth that we are all implicated in our own cultures and knowledge-systems. No text has a centre or a presence that is available to the suitably informed and equipped enquirer: there are only the multiple meanings of each reader, whose interpretation is inevitably conditioned by their experiences and all other texts they have encountered.

Postmodernism as a way of interpreting the world acknowledges the contingency and indeterminacy of all experiences, including those of art. Postmodernist art itself highlights the fictive, contingent world it creates. The traditional barriers between genres, author, reader and character are demolished or transgressed with ironic self-consciousness. Readers are confronted with their own role in the making of closure by the intrusion of the authorial voice addressing them directly. The narrative perspective shifts and changes throughout, stressing the subjectivity of all experience. The conventions of discourse are used and then abused: intertextual echoes and allusions are introduced, but with parodic irony. Another aspect of postmodern art is its refusal to acknowledge any traditional hierarchy of forms. Marginalized or 'ex-centric' voices within a culture are considered as valid as that which might have been categorized as high art, and form part of the intertextuality of other postmodern texts. Postmodernism, then, is an aesthetic attitude or mood that affects the reading of all texts, from any period. Postmodern art reflects this mood in its content and form.

Three terms, postmodernism, poststructuralism and deconstruction, are often discussed together and sometimes seem to be inter-changeable. In this book, their range of uses and meanings may be defined as follows. As has already been discussed, postmodernism is a general term that refers to changes and movements occurring in literature, art, architecture and philosophy in the last 40 or 50 years. Often understood as a reaction against modernism, features of postmodernism include anti-authoritarianism and anti-signification, relativism, eclecticism, parody and pastiche. Marxist, feminist, and psychoanalytic criticism are all aspects of postmodernism. Poststructuralism, which arose in the late 1960s, is another aspect of the same over-arching movement. Poststructuralism questions the assumptions of structuralism, and in particular concentrates on the essential instability of signification. It argues that the relationship between words (signifiers) and the concepts of reality to which they refer (signifieds) is not fixed as has been commonly assumed, but open to multiple interpretations. Whereas structuralism holds that an understanding of meaning is possible, if the codes of any text are analysed, poststructuralism holds that meaning is inherently unstable. This belief in the indeterminacy of language, based on the plurality of relationships between the signified and the signifier, is an important aspect of the practice of deconstruction. Deconstruction, for which Derrida is chiefly responsible, is the main poststructuralist theory used in literary criticism. As a way of reading and a mode of analytical enquiry, deconstruction focuses on the self-referential aspects of a text. Because of the lack of stable meaning, deconstruction argues that a text may be read as saying something quite different from what it appears to be saying. Furthermore, the meaning of a text cannot be construed or evaluated with reference to anything external to it. These three terms, postmodernism, poststructuralism and deconstruction, are central to this book. Further discussion of their various meanings will be given as they are used.

For Ashton (1994: 200-204), whereas literary criticism of the Bible in the form of narrative or reader-response criticism is simply a harmless waste of time, postmodernism in the form of deconstruction is destructive of everything that biblical scholarship should attempt to do:

> leap and cavort as they [deconstructive writers] will, taking off from the text in a fascinating variety of convoluted turns and twists, the value of their performance, in the last analysis, lies in its capacity to dazzle an admiring audience. What it cannot do without frustrating its own declared ends (and that would be deconstruction indeed) is to guide them into a fuller understanding of the text itself. Like a brilliant cadenza, it finds a starting-point in the text; but unlike any true cadenza it cannot lead us back into it (p. 203).

Instead of increasing understanding of the biblical text, deconstruction aims to frustrate indefinitely all attempts to assign it any stable meaning. However, Ashton rejects deconstruction without dealing with the claims of its philosophical foundation, on the grounds that such readings do not comply with what he perceives as the text's original purpose. Ashton misses the point of deconstruction, which is driven to its readings by the realization that the texts themselves demand such treatment. It is Ashton who ignores the implications of the deep fissures and inconsistencies in the text, and deconstruction that exposes them. By making a distinction between the understanding and application of a text, and by implicitly privileging understanding, Ashton (1994: 205-208) is also committed to accepting the text even when its message is, for example, misogynist. Caught up in the task of understanding the text, he can never judge it by the standards of today. By ignoring the claims of deconstruction, Ashton is committed to the search for a lost intention and an unrecoverable original meaning, and to the futile creation of a coherent reading of the text as he finds it.

Moore, one of the most ardently postmodern biblical critics, offers cogent arguments against such an approach. First, however, he argues with Ashton that much of the recent interest in literary theory in biblical studies has been based on the false idea of textual unity. The relative accessibility of literary theories such as narrative and reader-response criticism, which concentrate on plot, characters and readers has led to the adoption of these theories, or adaptations of them, by many biblical scholars. In Moore's view, the popularity of theories based on the unity of the text is 'often the incidental result of an inadequate grasp of the complexities of literary theory' (1989: xvii). Moore's criticisms of followers of reader-response theories, on the grounds that in practice they do not take into account the multiple readings that the theories themselves imply, have been noted above. His criticism of theories such as the narrative criticism defined in Powell (1993) centres on the belief of followers of these theories in the autonomous integrity of the Gospel writers' story worlds and in the primary, recoverable meaning of these texts that corresponds to the authors' intentions. For Moore, the concept of privileged authorial intention has been discredited by modern literary criticism and philosophy, as has the concept of a stable meaning 'in' or 'beyond' a text. In postmodern terms:

> A gospel's narrative discourse, instead of being conceived as dealing expressively with the essential elements of a prediscoursed narrative world…can now be conceived as dealing transformatively with a range of alternatively discoursed narrative worlds (1989: 67).

Most importantly, Moore argues that although poststructuralist readings can take in aspects of philosophy, history or psychoanalysis, they do not claim that any of these aspects are ultimate sources or expressions of truth.

Moore (1992) exclaims that for him, the text is 'an encrusted reading: an untotalizable sum of prior and potential readings, an unconscious reservoir' (1992: xviii). Building on and extending the basis of reader-response theory, postmodern literary theory rejects the idea that a text exists apart from its interpretation. Meaning no longer resides in the text, but in the consciousness of the one who reads: and that meaning will never be the same for two readers, or for the same reader twice. The text can no longer be considered the locus of revelation, example or inspiration, for it is a reader's own beliefs and experiences that generate the text. Any attempt to retrieve the original meanings of biblical texts is doomed to failure as the process can never be completed: there is no original meaning, only earlier readings that cannot be recovered untouched by the influence of a modern reader's interpretation. An uncontrollable excess of meaning exists within all texts, privileging no one reading of their semantic potential. Narrative and historical criticism block out the forces within a text which, in this melting pot of excess meaning, contradict and deny each other. Postmodern readings are alert to these forces and are free to read them without the need to harmonize them with explanation. Jasper (1989: 121) comments that through postmodern literary theories such as deconstruction:

> we come to recognize writing as a never-ending displacement and defer-
> ral, escaping the delusions of a stable and self-deceiving tradition. There
> are no answers, only extreme scepticism, and a continual evasion of the
> self-enclosed systematizing by which we long to find meaning.

In a postmodern world, two paradigm shifts impinge on biblical studies: the first is methodological, from diachronic to synchronic methods, from addressing history to addressing story; the second is epistemological, regarding the way we think about texts, words, the Word and the world. The first shift is in the process of being accepted by the guild of biblical scholars, although it is still under debate. The second is rarely addressed, and then, except by a small minority, often only to be rejected. One reason for this is the implication of postmodernism, and in particular of deconstruction, for biblical studies. Postmodern scepticism highlights the circularity of the argument that is grounded in accepting that Scripture is based on God's Word because the presence of God in Scripture is stated by Scripture. Although Derrida does not deal directly with the relationship between Jesus, the Son of God as the inscribed Word of God, and the Bible, the written Word of God,[12] he does include Christianity as a logocentric and therefore flawed philosophical movement. Derrida takes speech as a paradigm for presence and truth and argues that, because of this, Christianity privileges speech over writing (e.g. 2 Cor. 3.6; 2 Jn 12), despite its apparent emphasis on a written text, the Bible.[13] A deconstructive reading sets out to explode such logocentrism and to show the ways in which any stable, defining presence, such as God, truth or self, is ultimately a mirage. It is this loss of any stabilizing presence that many biblical critics find impossible to contemplate. Not all are wedded to the idea of the presence of God in the Bible guaranteeing meaning,[14] but many, such as Ashton (1994: 184-90, 204-208) are convinced that the methods of historical criticism will lead the careful scholar close to the (one) meaning of the text, which is its original meaning. Allied to this position, at least in Ashton's case, is the belief that the Bible is more than literature, and that to treat the text as a story is to misconstrue its intended purpose. Deconstruction argues that meaning is never fixed, and that 'original meaning' and intention are elusive and ultimately misguided points of reference. The Bible has only been considered as 'more' than story because of the unfounded logocentrism of the Christian religion. It has been accorded the presence of God to undergird its truth and meaning, although no such presence exists behind or under any text, speech or sign. This apparently problematic relationship between the claims of biblical

12. Derrida discusses the Bible in, among other essays, 'Edmond Jabès and the Question of the Book' (1978); 'Of an Apocalyptic Tone Recently Adopted in Philosophy' (1982); and in 'Des Tours de Babel' (1991). In his most recent work, *The Gift of Death* (1995), Derrida considers the theological issues of responsibility, life and death and includes a discussion of texts from the Gospel of Matthew.

13. Derrida (1976: 16-18) argues that the Bible, as God's Word, is understood as an example of the 'good' or 'natural' writing of the spirit, divinely inscribed on the heart, in contrast with writing 'in the common sense [which] is the dead letter...the carrier of death' (p. 17).

14. Ashton (1994: 204) fears the loss of this presence. He comments that few of the followers of deconstruction in biblical studies realize what deconstruction is 'really about': that it demands that 'the Word is displaced from the centre and God, along with his fellow-authors, is expelled from his pre-eminent place in the human cosmos'.

studies and those of postmodern literary theory cannot be ignored, and will be returned to in the course of the book.[15]

In this book, two texts are considered in detail from two postmodern literary critical perspectives: Revelation and Hogg's *The Private Memoirs and Confessions of a Justified Sinner* (1824). Neither of these texts could be defined as postmodern in any meaningful sense. However, it will be argued that both Revelation and Hogg's *Confessions* are particularly open to postmodern readings. Postmodern literary theory offers a sympathetic and illuminating context in which to consider these texts. In the following chapters, the arguments for this suggestion are considered, and the results of these readings are assessed.

Marginalization and Deconstruction

Lumsden (1992) argues that because Hogg and his work were, and continue to be, marginalized in many different ways, much postmodern literary theory is sympathetic to his formal and structural radicalism. Scottish literature in general lies on the margins of the canon of English Literature, and has failed to gain the recognition it deserves. In particular, Hogg's work has been neglected until comparatively recently. At another level, Hogg himself operated on the margins of the Edinburgh literary establishment of his time. Even when he was admitted into literary society both socially and in terms of his work, he was often a figure of ridicule and derision because of his background and education. Lumsden notes Hutcheon's argument (1988) that postmodernism opens up culturally 'ex-centric' voices for reconsideration. The validity and objectivity of the great literary tradition, including its preoccupation with the literary canon, is questioned, and its status as a totalizing narrative is rejected. Novels such as the *Confessions*, which have been largely excluded from the canon, are of particular interest. Furthermore, Hogg's own marginalized situation parallels postmodern literary critical

---

15. For further useful discussion of the implications of deconstruction for theology, see (Raschke 1982), particularly the essays by Raschke (pp. 1-33), Scharlemann (pp. 79-108) and Altizer (pp. 147-77). On the interaction between Derrida and theology, see Handelman (1982: 163-78) Detweiler 1982; Hart (1991: 281-340); and Moore (1994: 13-41). On the wider issue of poststructuralism and biblical studies, see Phillips (1990). Particularly valuable for drawing out the implications of poststructuralism on biblical studies are the contributions by Phillips (pp. 7-49) and Burnett (pp. 51-80) in this volume.

concerns. Just as a postmodern reading attempts to challenge any text's claim to a unified meaning, so Hogg challenges the fixed theories of his day, such as antinomianism or Enlightenment empiricism. Both Hogg and a postmodern author or critic offer decentred and decentering readings. However, argues Lumsden, Hogg's is not a self-consciously philosophical challenge to the totalizing structures around him. His work should not be considered 'postmodern' in the sense that a twentieth-century text might be. Postmodern literary theory offers a fruitful context in which to read Hogg, rather than a definition of his work. Its vocabulary and ideas provide a framework for discussing the *Confessions* which was previously unavailable, although the historical context in which Hogg wrote remains important. In Part 1 of the book (Chapters 2 and 3), the key theme will be the effect of the postmodern idea of marginalization on readings of both Hogg and Revelation. Lumsden's reading of Hogg will be discussed in Chapter 2, and the insights it offers into the interpretation of ex-centric texts will be applied to a reading of Revelation in Chapter 3.

The Bible and Culture Collective (1995) make a rather different case for applying postmodern literary theory to the text of the Bible. They go further than Lumsden in that their argument rests on the postmodern contention that the claims of traditional historical criticism are false. The emphasis on the quest for the original form of the biblical text and for the context of its intended readers has been accepted as valid without the critical assumptions of those involved in the quest ever being challenged. Postmodern literary theory offers such a challenge by self-consciously exposing the politics of reading a text. It seeks to make explicit whatever is hidden and repressed both in the interpretation of a text, and in the text itself. In its shift of emphasis towards the reader rather than the author, postmodern literary theory also brings the significance of the Bible into the culture of today, rather than of the past. When meaning is located in the relationship between the reader and the text, the biblical text is allowed to speak from within its present situation. Orthodoxy loses its control, but the text continues to reverberate in the context of each reader. In Pippin's (1992) essentially deconstructive reading of Revelation, the new context is that of a feminist reader who finds hidden in the text a savage denial of women's place in the sacred world, and a fear of their latent, threatening creative power. A historical critic might argue that such a reading is far from the intention of the author, but deconstruction nevertheless validates and celebrates such an approach. The postmodern, deconstructive ideas put forward by the Bible and Culture Collective and applied by Pippin are considered in Part 2, with reference to readings of the *Confessions* in Chapter 4 and of Revelation in Chapter 5.

The *Confessions* has been read by Lumsden within the framework of the postmodern notion of marginalization, which is deemed sympathetic because of the historical context of its author. Revelation has been considered by Pippin from a radically postmodern literary critical perspective, that of deconstruction, and judgments made upon the text on the basis of the reading of a twentieth-century woman. The aim of this book is to consider and expand these readings, but also to apply the approach of one reading to the other text. The postmodern literary critical insights of both marginalization and deconstruction will be applied independently. It will be argued that the *Confessions* may be read in a radically deconstructive way, and that Revelation may be considered as an 'ex-centric' text, the historical context of which makes a postmodern literary critical framework particularly sympathetic and illuminating. The implications of these readings will be considered, as will the apparent incompatibility of the two approaches. One focus of all of these readings will be each text's use of the Bible, in Revelation's case, of course, the Old Testament. Another will be postmodern literary critical responses to more traditional readings of both texts. In this way, the interaction between the texts and the reader, and the texts as offering readings of sacred texts, may be explored.

Part I
MARGINALIZATION

Chapter 2

HOGG'S READINGS OF THE BIBLE

> Writing from the self-deconstructing ground of Scottish experience,
> Scott, Hogg and Stevenson launch a challenge to all manifestations of
> 'grand narrative' deconstructing their boundaries. As a result, the post-
> modern context is one particularly sympathetic to their formal and
> structural radicalism (Lumsden 1992: ii).

The aim of this chapter is to assess and interpret from a postmodern literary critical perspective the nature of Hogg's readings of the Bible, as
exemplified in *The Private Memoirs and Confessions of a Justified Sinner* (1824, all quotations taken from the 1991 Canongate edition), 'The
Chaldee Manuscript' (1817) and *The Three Perils of Man* (1822, all
quotations taken from the 1989 Scottish Academic Press edition). Various interpretations have been offered in the past (Campbell 1972a and
b, 1988b) will be discussed below), but as yet none has highlighted the
subversive or decentred nature of Hogg's reading of the sacred text.
Hogg occupied an ambiguous position in the Edinburgh literary society
to which he sought to belong,[1] and his work, including the *Confessions*
and the 'Chaldee Manuscript' (1817), was often ridiculed, reviled or
treated with suspicion rather than praised. Lumsden (1992) has argued
that a characteristic feature of such marginalized literature is its use of
subversive strategies to challenge the dominant centre. In Hogg's
fiction the inadequacies of rigid epistemological systems such as those
of empiricism and of totalizing polarities such as antinomianism are
exposed. His complex and indeterminate work subverts the narrative

---

1.   Fielding (1996: 75) comments that '[a]s both a pastoral and actual shepherd
he seemed to embody both the idealized orality of the Romantic poet and the taint
of a class more commonly associated with illiteracy'. Hogg, the Ettrick Shepherd,
was both feted because of his natural, untutored genius and reviled because of his
rough manners. Mergenthal (1990) offers a full account of the ways in which the
persona of 'The Ettrick Shepherd' was created by Hogg and others.

totality of contemporary literature and philosophy. Because of its sensitivity towards the margins, postmodern literary criticism offers a sympathetic framework within which to explore Hogg's work. In Chapter 4, alternative readings of the *Confessions* will be considered, and aspects of Lumsden's own reading will be questioned. In this chapter, following a discussion of Lumsden's book, Hogg's reading of the Bible will be considered from the postmodern literary critical perspective she offers. Is Hogg, apparently so conservative towards the Bible, in fact offering a reading of scripture that challenges its centrality and presence?

Lumsden on Hogg: Reading for 'ex-centricity'

Lumsden highlights aspects of postmodern literary critical thought that make it a particularly fruitful context in which to read nineteenth-century Scottish fiction. The postmodern condition, she argues, is particularly sympathetic to the marginal, peripheral or 'ex-centric', in Hutcheon's terminology (1988: 12). Self-reflexively, it recognizes the impossibility of finding a point outside language from which language may be commented upon. Similarly, the search for knowledge itself is meaningless if no facts exist independently of our understanding and interpretation of them in language. We can know only interpretations, never facts. Acknowledging this, postmodern critical theories challenge any totalizing system, such as structuralism or binarism which assumes a point outside itself or beyond its context from which the structures within it may be commented upon with objectivity. Such structures themselves are falsifications that many critical theories attempt to undermine and expose.

In the past, Western thought has attempted to give total authority and presence to the text, and to silence any voices that have tried to disrupt it. Postmodern critical theories offer a critique of these attempts, and in particular of modernism's emphasis on empirical rationality and the idea of the unified subject. They seek to undermine such discourse by showing it to be founded on that which it excludes. Such critical theories reveal the dislocations, slippages and silences in all texts, and disturb their claims to be unified or totalizing. Lyotard (1984) demonstrates the cultural implication of these revelations, which challenge the old order and allow the development of a new world order based on structures that are flexible rather than rigid. For Lyotard postmodernism has social and political consequences. The postmodern condition perceives the dangers of fanaticism and totalitarianism and in particular their claims to embrace absolute values and truths. Because of this, Hutcheon (1988) has argued that postmodernism is a movement that is sympathetic to the marginalized, and that offers a context for cultural, political and social reassessment.

Lumsden takes Wittgenstein's approach as her model. Although he challenges totalizing structures and binary oppositions, Wittgenstein, unlike Derrida,[2] also provides a framework within which social and linguistic exchange may be carried out. While rejecting any notion of absolute meaning in language, Wittgenstein offers a way of exploring how, without it, communication continues. Meaning is regarded as an evolving of contexts within a set of grammatical relations.[3] The meaning of a word is to be found from its use in language, although its meaning on the level of deep structure cannot be demonstrated. Society is able to function without grand narratives because of the rules participants have worked out in each given context. New rules may be established at any time. Lumsden argues that postmodernism as a cultural and literary movement in reality follows Wittgenstein rather than Derrida: the writer and society itself must find a way to continue while facing the ontological uncertainties instigated by postmodernism. All must continue while acknowledging that there may be no final closure or centre.

If meaning evolves in socially agreed and flexible structures, reassessment and redefinition are openly allowed. In such a context, where the validity of previously-held systems is challenged, the de-centred becomes open to discussion, and marginalized groups, such as those that launch an attack on totality, are treated sympathetically. Nevertheless, new sets of rules and boundaries may need to be defined in order to discuss the new approach. Postmodern critical theory, then, offers the vocabulary and the context within which silenced and radical voices may be allowed to speak, and provides a sympathetic framework for the non-totalizing elements within such expression. However,

2.   For a discussion of the relationship between the work of Derrida and Wittgenstein, see Staten (1985).

3.   Wittgenstein asserts that '[e]ssence is expressed by grammar', and that "[f]or a *large* class of cases—though not for all—in which we employ the word "meaning" it can be defined thus: the meaning of a word is in its use in language' (1953: 116, 120, cit. Lumsden [1992: 11]).

Lumsden warns that she is not suggesting that writers such as Hogg be defined as 'postmodern', or that their challenge to the grand narratives of their day was as self-conscious as that of a twentieth-century writer may be:

> On the contrary, the challenge to absolutism and polarised frameworks which we meet in their works arises more often from the need to respond to the social, religious and political situation around them; from a need to write from their own context, itself often an ambiguous one (1992: 29).

Her purpose is to bring into the critical arena the formal and thematic strategies of Scottish writing that challenge totalizing narratives and demonstrate an awareness of the plural and ambiguous nature of life.

In her chapter on Hogg, Lumsden highlights the totalizing systems Hogg seeks to destabilize from his ex-centric position. She suggests that the way he challenges and explores absolute systems is particularly well understood in today's postmodern context. In the *Confessions*, antinomianism[4] is the absolute framework that is analysed and reacted against. Although the controversy had raged the century before, Hogg knew the issues of the debate, and would have been aware of the continued, incipient dangers of the doctrine. The work of Thomas Boston, a minister at Ettrick who had been accused of having antinomian sympathies, continued to be published and read, and will be considered below. Lumsden argues that antinomian beliefs are first introduced in the novel in the Editor's description of Mrs Colwan's faith: Mrs Colwan's conviction that the eternal fate of all is determined before they are born, and cannot be altered by any action of their own, is described by the Editor as a 'rigid' and 'deformed' (1824: 2) interpretation of the Gospel. Lumsden comments that few readers could disagree. This system upon which salvation and damnation depend is shown to be as fixed, unalterable and total in the beliefs of Mrs Colwan and, particularly, in Robert Wringhim junior and senior, as any challenged by postmodern critical theory. Lumsden affirms:

> Such models are, of course, recognised as dangerous by postmodernism also, for their desire to resist the dislocations, the slippages and gaps within their own rhetorics, for their silencing of the internal incongruities and alternative perspective 'in excess' of their apparent totality, leads

---

4.   Wain (1983) and Bligh (1984) offer similar readings of the role of antinomianism in the novel, although from a different theoretical position. Their work is discussed in Chapter 4.

them to deceptively convincing forms of 'reason' and discourse, and the need to negate all those aspects of experience which undermine their own position (1992: 96).

Lumsden finds evidence to suggest that Hogg had a similar distrust of any such system that offered a single, totalizing way to interpret the world. She argues that the *Confessions* offers a critique of such systems, while exploring their dangers. Although the narrative does not allow the reader to decide definitively about whether Gil-Martin is internal or external to Robert, Gil-Martin's appearance is closely linked to Robert's acceptance of the absolute system of salvation and damnation known by its opponents as antinomianism. Once the system is accepted, its evils progressively ensnare its victim. Robert is shown to be unable to avoid Gil-Martin, and his increasing despair leads to his suicide. Loss of personal self and free will are demonstrated in the *Confessions* to be the final consequence of accepting a totalizing system. However, it is this fixity that attracts Robert to the doctrine of his 'father' in the first place: antinomianism offers him freedom from the responsibility of a more flexible and ambiguous 'grammar' of morality based on experience. Belief in predestined election means freedom from the burden of moral responsibility, which Robert had found intolerable. However, it also results in a loss of choice and freedom.

Alternative and more flexible grammars of morality and human relationships are offered, according to Lumsden, in the preachings of Blanchard and in the attitude of George.[5] Blanchard preaches that morality should be understood as an evolving grammar adaptable to different contexts. This offers freedom from being possessed by a system, but also carries responsibility: salvation depends on each person's actions, rather than the whim of God. George is shown to follow such a flexible moral code. He is prepared to evolve new rules for relationships as the situation demands, and is willing to offer friendship to his brother on several occasions. Robert has such a flexible morality available to him, despite his upbringing, but always chooses the way of predestination. He hesitates before each murder, and is offered grace in the person of the White Lady on Arthur's Seat, but is always convinced by Gil-Martin's arguments. Such totalizing systems are shown to silence all opposition and deviance (Blanchard and George must be murdered), but they

5.   The work of critics such as Carey (1969) and Petrie (1992), which questions the apparently positive portrayal of these characters, will be discussed in Chapter 4.

are also ultimately self-destructive. When Robert realizes the consequences of his actions, he is unable to escape and the result is his own silencing death.

Such rigid codes also create a linguistic trap and contrive to silence all arguments against them. The *Confessions* demonstrate that once predestination is accepted, almost anything can be claimed in the name of its higher truth. Gil-Martin's logic is impeccable, once he has convinced Robert of the tenets of his doctrine, that nothing he can do on earth will alter the fate of his soul. The rigidity of Robert's beliefs leads him to accept even badly constructed arguments, such as Gil-Martin's explanation of the appearance of the White Lady as a warning about his loss of faith in his own salvation. All other arguments are silenced except those that seem to support Robert's understanding of what is absolutely true. As Lumsden comments, '[w]hen based on a belief in an essential epistemic "presence", language becomes totalising, silencing the gaps and slippages which subvert its total system' (1992: 107). The system Gil-Martin advocates and Robert believes is shown in the novel to rest on an inadequate polarization between the good and the evil, the damned and the saved. Its dangers are demonstrated and its logic deconstructed. Postmodernism, and in particular deconstruction, also discredits any understanding of language that proceeds by a system of oppositions rather than a process of slippage or 'différance' between terms. Such oppositional grammars are abandoned as inadequate ways of understanding the world, but it is recognized that these systems may be maintained by those at the apparent centre in order to retain their power. Accordingly, Robert's father constantly asserts the supremacy of the elect, and uses the doctrine of predestation to create systems of opposition in the most ridiculous situations.

Lumsden argues that there is evidence in Hogg's Lay Sermons[6] to suggest that he rejected such oppositional method of discourse, and any wrangling over spiritual matters. Certainly in the *Confessions*, such disputatiousness is shown to be both absurd and dangerous. The inevitable conclusion of a rigid, absolute and oppositionary system is monstrous. Hogg challenges the distorted view of the religion of the Wringhims by showing it is out of place in the world of experience. There is no place for absolute judgments in the temporal world: such totalizing categories belong in the spiritual world. In the Auchtermuchty Tale told by

6. Mergenthal (1991) offers a different perspective on the Lay Sermons.

Penpunt in the *Confessions* (1824: 162-66), the villagers' rigid righteousness is shown to be based on a false attempt to construct the self in
absolute terms, which opens the way for evil. They only discover a
healthy self-understanding when they learn to suspect the sublime and
absolute rhetoric that is at odds with their experience of life. Similarly
Hogg believed that judgment can apply only in the spiritual dimension.
Rather than a model of absolute good and evil, experience of the fallen
world demands a flexible, indeterminate framework. In postmodern
thought, totality is decentred: the all-encompassing way of life adopted
by Robert, which considers itself to be at the centre of a rigid system, is
shown to be of necessity a false construction.

Throughout his career, Hogg deals with ambiguous constructions of
experience and asserts different models to describe the world as it is
experienced. He rejects the absolute truth systems of religious certainty
such as antinomianism. In addition, however, he attacks the system
supported by contemporary empirical thought. In his fiction, reality and
identity are many-shaped: his own persona changes in his many contributions to the literary magazines of his time,[7] and disguise and doubling
are central features of his work.[8] In the *Confessions* the farcical trial of
Bell Calvert (1824: 53-57) suggests that the search for absolute truth
exemplified by empirical rationality is both impossible and deceptive.
The comic scene in which Mrs Logan's maid thwarts the prosecution

---

7.   Hughes (1983: 46) concludes that 'the influence exerted on Hogg's work by
the specific periodical for which he wrote could at times be considerable'. On
Hogg's different poetic and journalistic personae in general, see Murphy (1993).

8.   Many of the characters in the *Confessions* don disguises in order to hide
their true identity. At various times in the novel, Gil-Martin takes on the outward
appearance of George, Blanchard and Robert. Less dramatically, Mrs Calvert and
Mrs Logan dress up as 'country goodwives' (p. 66) in order to spy on Robert, and
Robert evades the mob approaching his house by putting on the clothes of Gil-Martin (p. 170). Characters who are doubles of others in the text play a similar role in
casting doubt upon the relationship between appearance and reality. George and
Robert, Robert and Gil-Martin, and Arabella Calvert and Arabella Logan could all
be described as doubles of each other in the *Confessions*, each representing one side
of the whole. Miller discusses the psychological role of doubles in the *Confessions*
(1985: 1-20). Jones (1988: 164-85) argues that Hogg was haunted by his literary
Doppelgänger in the *Noctes Ambrosianae* and that this is reflected in the multiplicity of doubles and doubling in the *Confessions*. The double is an emblem of a systematic duplicity that is demonstrated by the existence of evil in the world and the
unreliability of experience.

by finding legitimate ways to deny the obvious mocks the Editor's quest for the facts. Furthermore, Hogg implies that the introduction of the supernatural as, for example, in Penpunt's Auchtermuchty Tale (pp. 162-66), makes rational thought and dependence on the senses an unreliable way to proceed.

Hogg was in an ideal position to challenge the empirical rationality that gripped the Edinburgh society of his day. The ambiguity of his background and situation was discussed at the beginning of the chapter. Never truly fitting in to the literary world because of his perceived lack of education and his rustic manners, and at times badly treated by notable and influential figures such as John Wilson (otherwise 'Christopher North') and J.G. Lockhart,[9] Hogg's perspective was without doubt 'ex-centric'. The values of the Editor of the *Confessions* are those of such men of empirical and rational thought. His task is to explain the facts of the case and substantiate his theories with evidence. However, his work is a parody of Enlightenment principles. He silences or attempts to explain away any supernatural possibilities, and instead his own principles lead him to the ridiculous action of digging up old bones to discover the essential truth and confirm his own senses. Such a response is rejected by the figure of Hogg whom the Editor meets in the course of his investigations. Although Hogg had written to *Blackwood's* describing the traditions surrounding the body, he shows no interest in the physical remains, or in the values of the Editor which are shown in the novel to be a false search for knowledge. In the narrative, the Editor's certainty is undermined and the truth he presents is shown to be problematic. The damaged document he presents is given more authority than it deserves, and Robert's memoirs break free from the category of allegory or parable the Editor tries to apply to them.

In the narrative strategies he employs, Lumsden argues, Hogg challenges and unsettles ontological certainties. Stories are embedded within

9.   Alexander (1993) discusses some of the examples of mockery to which Hogg was subjected by the writers (Wilson and Lockhart) of the *Blackwood's* series *Noctes Ambrosianae*. Although Alexander argues that the portrayal of Hogg was basically accurate rather than wholly parodic, and emphasizes the fictitious nature of the essays, it appears that Hogg himself could be upset about the way in which he was depicted. Alexander (p. 42) cites Lockhart's letter to William Blackwood in which he comments that Hogg ('poor devil') is 'extremely sulky' about the *Noctes*, and suggests 'leaving Hogg out for a while' (letter of 20 February 1827, in NLS MS 4019, f.254r).

stories, narratives are framed in ways that undermine their claim to authority, and reflexive devices are used which call into question the status of the material presented. These strategies may be partially explained by Hogg's background in a fluid, oral tradition[10] far removed from Enlightenment rationality and linear narration. A rigid epistemic framework such as linear narrative cannot provide an accurate way to describe the ambiguities of the experiences of life. This recognition of life's indeterminacies is reflected in the lack of closure in Hogg's fiction. Lumsden concludes that 'narrative experimentation in Hogg's work...both in its disruption of linear progression and of closure, defeats the rigid search for essence and presence, revelling, rather, in the more evasive ontology of the text itself' (1992: 130).

In the *Confessions*, sophisticated narrative strategies result in postponed final meaning and avoided authority. The narratives of the Editor and of Robert frame and undermine each other, subverting and deferring meaning and centre. The claims of both narratives are denied and their ideologies revealed. The consequences for the reader are profound:

> Binary readings of the novel, which seek final conclusions in it, are arguably finally inadequate as methods for interpreting the material which we read, the structure and narrative material of the novel itself under-cutting secure interpretive structures suggesting that nothing in the world of lived experience—or within discourse—can be known with absolute certainty (Lumsden 1992: 133).

Lumsden's argument has been given in detail because her method is central to my approach in this chapter. A critique of certain of her readings, such as her judgments about the characters of George and Blanchard, will be offered in Chapter 4. Here, her method of reading Hogg's work in general within a particular postmodern literary critical context will be applied to a reading specifically of Hogg's approach to the Bible. Could Hogg's reading of the Bible be described as 'ex-centric', and, if so, what are the implications of this reading for an understanding of the *Confessions*?

Campbell has written extensively on the role of the Bible in Hogg's work.[11] For Campbell, Hogg's reading of the Bible, as exemplified in

---

10. The influence of oral tradition in Hogg's work is discussed in detail by Fielding (1996) with reference to *The Three Perils of Man* (pp. 74-98) and to various short stories (pp. 99-131).

11. See, for example, his articles (1972a) and (1972b), and his two contributions to Wright, (Campbell 1988a and b).

the *Confessions*, is orthodox rather than ex-centric. Hogg's use of the Bible in the text serves a didactic purpose: to enable the equally ortho-dox reader to recognize that Gil-Martin's message is of the devil. For Campbell, Lumsden's argument that the novel is simply Hogg's attack on the religious doctrine of antinomianism lacks credibility. The com-plexity of the novel's structure, the distancing of the authorial voice behind an ambivalent editor, a confused protagonist and the lack of direction pointing to 'good' and 'bad' characters, suggest a more subtle intention and purpose.[12] Campbell argues that it is not Hogg's dislike of antinomianism that informs and explains the novel, but more generally his understanding of the Bible and its message. This understanding is characterized by a belief in the Bible as a stable, sacred text.

Campbell defines the novel not simply as a satire of a particular doc-trine, but as 'a satire of human weakness, and the imperfections of a human intellect, especially one labouring under the sin of pride, when seeking to interpret scripture and doctrine' (1972b: 28). Robert is open to the influence of the devil because he has already subscribed to a doctrine of predestination that fosters his own spiritual pride and offers a warped biblical hermeneutic which is nevertheless favourable to him. The devil simply takes the logic of the doctrine to its logical extreme, and Robert is unable to recognize the dangers of the extremity. As Gil-Martin explains to him while persuading him to kill George:

> For a man who is not only dedicated to the King of Heaven, in the most solemn manner, soul, body and spirit, but also chosen of him from the beginning, justified, sanctified, and received into a communion that shall never be broken, and from which no act of his shall ever remove him,— the possession of such a man, I tell you, is worth kingdoms; because every deed that he performs, he does it with perfect safety to himself and honour to me (1824: 118).

Campbell (1988b: 102-103) suggests that Hogg uses the device of mis-applied language to control the reader's response to Gil-Martin. Characters such as Wringhim senior and Gil-Martin himself use biblical language and the tone of the pulpit in inappropriate ways: in the example above, formal, measured English replete with biblical and theological phrases is used to persuade Robert to murder his brother. The reader familiar with such language is at first confused and their

---

12. Some of these valid criticisms of Lumsden's work will be considered in detail in Chapter 4.

expectations are unfulfilled in the clash between Gil-Martin's register and his meaning. The use of this device of misapplied language throughout the novel blurs the ability of the reader to judge the plot and the novel as a whole, but it also transfers the task of decision-making from Hogg to the reader. The Wringhims do not hear Gil-Martin's parody of doctrine or the perversions of biblical meaning because he uses language with which they are familiar. For example, before encountering Gil-Martin, Robert assures himself in the following terms of his salvation despite his tendency to sin: 'I depended entirely on the bounty of free grace, holding all the righteousness of man as filthy rags, and believing in the momentous and magnificent truth, that the more heavily loaden with transgressions, the more welcome was the believer at the throne of grace' (1824: 92). The reader, however, is expected to recognize that the language of the devil is a perversion of the original, and to judge both him and the Wringhims for their deafness.

For Campbell, then, the novel's meaning is available and recoverable by the reader who shares Hogg's knowledge of the Bible and Christian doctrine. Campbell (1972a: 69-74) argues that Robert's strange and obscure vision of the golden weapons let down on a cloudy veil (1824: 129) assumes its meaning when it is read beside Acts 11. It is intended that the reader understand that Robert interprets the vision as an echo of the apostle Peter's dream which enables him to carry out the work of God among the Gentiles. Robert considers himself an apostle and is persuaded by Gil-Martin that the purpose of his vision is to encourage him to carry out the work of God by killing Blanchard. The reader and Gil-Martin realize that the vision is in fact offering Robert the chance to repent and turn the weapons on the Devil. In this scene, Robert is shown to be both puffed up with perverted spiritual pride and totally unable to read the signs sent him by God in the Bible and in the vision. Hogg controls the reader's reaction by his use of misapplied biblical allusions.

Campbell understands Hogg to have a clear belief in the possibility of an appropriate and proper use of the Bible. The effect Campbell suggests that Hogg strives for depends on there being, and the reader recognizing, a correct way to interpret and use the sacred text, which Gil-Martin deliberately avoids and Robert fails to notice. The argument of this chapter is that Hogg took a very different approach to the Bible. He occupied a marginalized position with regard to biblical hermeneutics, and, for this reason, Lumsden's postmodern literary critical approach to

Hogg's response to the rigid system of antinomianism is also applicable to an exploration of Hogg's readings of the Bible. A postmodern literary critical reading which is sensitive to a text's ex-centricities offers new insights which more conventional readings fail to notice.

The Role of the Bible in Hogg's Scotland

Before reading Hogg's work for its ex-centricities, it is necessary to consider the views which made up the 'centre' of biblical hermeneutics in Scotland in the early nineteenth century. In the Reformation in Scotland, beliefs about the role of the Bible occupied a central place. John Knox announced that 'faith hath both her beginning and continuance by the Word of God' (1855: 135) and the writers of the 1560 Scots Confession pledged to amend anything in their work that could be demonstrated to be 'repugnand' to scripture (Henderson 1937: 41). The more influential document, the Westminster Confession of 1640, allots a place to Scripture which is unique among the Protestant confessions of the period.[13] Ferguson (1982: 35) argues that in the mid-seventeenth century, the Bible's authority was being questioned by various forms of rationalism and mysticism, and there was a need to defend its status. Because of these outside pressures, he suggests, the divine authority of scripture was affirmed in the opening chapter of the Westminster Confession. The Confession explains that because natural knowledge of God and his nature was inadequate, God made a supernatural revelation of himself that was committed to writing in the form of the Old and New Testaments. In their original languages, these were directly inspired by God and are kept pure by his providence. Because they are divine, they are authoritative for individuals and the Church. However, it is only their author, the Holy Spirit, who brings their meaning to their hearers, and who is able to guide between different interpretations (Westminster Confession of Faith, chapter 1, paras. 8 and 10, summarized in Cheyne 1983: 5). Cheyne there comments that in fact sceptical Enlightenment ideas made little impact, and that 'the Divines, and as far as we can tell most Scottish believers between 1650 and 1800 were little inclined to question the infallibility of Scripture's pronouncements

---

13. Whereas the Westminster Confession opens with an affirmation of the divine authority of Scripture, Calvin's *Institutes* do not deal with Scripture until the sixth section of Book 1, and Knox's Scots Confession of 1560 discusses the matter only at Chapter 19.

or even the Almighty's personal responsibility for every syllable contained therein'.

The implications and extent of these beliefs may be tested by considering the preaching and writing of prominent Divines. What insights do the writing of Thomas Boston, Thomas Chalmers and Andrew Thomson offer into the way the Bible was read in the period before the *Confessions* was written?

The enduring popularity and influence of the minister and expository writer Thomas Boston is suggested by the 20 reprints by 1880 of his *Human Nature, in its Fourfold State*, a written version of sermons preached at Ettrick which was first published in 1720. Also indicative of his status is that although he was born nearly a century before Hogg, his presence is recorded in several of Hogg's works, and his *Fourfold State* is mentioned with approval. As Simpson (1962: 172) has pointed out, in Hogg's short sketch 'Odd Characters', which appeared in the Shepherd's Calendar series in *Blackwood's*, a dialogue between Boston and Daft Jock Amos is recorded in which Amos confounds the minister with a biblical text he did not know (1874c: 411), and in another section of the same sketch, Boston marries Willie Candlem and Meggie Coltard (p. 412). In a later story which appeared in *Blackwood's Magazine*, 'The Mysterious Bride', the old woman Lucky Black reads 'The four-fold state of man' (1874d: 457). In the poem 'The Pedlar', Boston is not named, but Hogg's editor Thomson confidently notes that 'The great and worthy Mr Boston was the person who was said to have laid this ghost' (1874f: 66). According to Hogg, the minister who performed the exorcism was 'a body o' skill,/ Nae feared for devil or spirit was he' (p. 66). Groves (1986: 142) notes a further reference to Boston in Hogg's essay 'Statistics of Selkirkshire' published in *Prize-Essays and Transactions of the Highland Society of Scotland* (1832: 303-304). Hogg compares the villages of Ettrick and Yarrow and finds the shepherds of the latter 'devout and decent, but [with] no desire for reading' (1832: 303) whereas the shepherds of Ettrick are 'intelligent and dogmatic, great readers, and fond of research in history and polemical divinity' (p. 303). The reason for this difference, he decides, is the influence of Thomas Boston:

> His memory lives embalmed in the veneration of the inhabitants, and
> justly so, for he impressed the hearts of their fathers with a love and a
> reverence for the doctrines of the cross, for which their children still
> retain a strong enthusiasm. It has been the fashion for a good while past,

with a certain class of professed Christians, both preachers and hearers, to sneer at the doctrines of Boston. I decidedly differ from them, and will venture to assert that there are no such fervour and strength of reasoning to be met with in any modern composition, as predominate in his. Let any person take up 'The Four-fold State of Man', and peruse [it] seriously and without prejudice... and he will join with me. There is even an originality of thought and expression in old Boston which are quite delightful and refreshing (1832: 303-304).

Boston is most famous for his involvement in the publication in 1718 and defence before the 1722 General Assembly of the Church of Scotland of Edward Fisher's *Marrow of Modern Divinity* (originally published in 1646). The *Marrow* is a discussion in the form of a dialogue about the relationship between law and grace in the salvation of humanity. The emphasis falls on the primacy of the free grace of God. Boston found a copy of the book in a parishioner's cottage while ministering in the border village of Simprin, and discovered in it an assurance of salvation for which he had longed. He brought the book to the attention of fellow-minister James Hog of Carnock (no relation to Hogg), who published a new edition of Part One. The antinomian tendencies of the book were pointed out by James Hadow of St Mary's, St Andrews, and the Assembly of 1720 forbade ministers to use or commend the book. In 1722 a representation in support of the *Marrow* consisting of 12 ministers, including Hog and Boston, was heard by the Assembly, but was unsuccessful in having the 1720 decision overturned. Nevertheless, in 1726 Boston published a new edition with his own explanatory notes.

Much of Boston's work is arranged under subject headings in *The Beauties of Boston: A Selection of his Writings* edited by M'Millan and first published in 1831 (reprinted in 1979). In the section 'The Manner of Discovering the True Sense of Holy Scripture', Boston writes that 'the sense of the scripture must be but one, and not manifold, that is, quite different and no wise subordinate to another, because of the unity of truth, and because of the perspicuity of the scripture' (1979: 7). He concedes that that one sense may have several parts, and that some of the parts will be subordinate to others, giving the example of prophecies regarding deliverance from Babylon that also spiritually refer to Christ and to heaven. Boston also understands that one event or character in Scripture may be a type of another. The 'literal' sense of Moses lifting up the serpent in the wilderness and healing all who look upon it is completed by the 'mystical' sense of Jesus being lifted up on the cross (p. 5). The 'true' sense of a difficult passage is to be discovered by searching the rest of Scripture, 'the scripture itself being the infallible rule of interpreting scripture' (p. 7). Like the biblical midrashists who will be considered in Chapter 3, Boston reads the Bible as a self-glossing book, each part interpreting and reflecting upon the rest. Everything in this organic whole must cohere, and therefore strategies of reading, such as the use of typology, are developed in order to make each part coherent. For Boston, the Bible is like no other book. It is directly inspired, it is to be revered in its entirety and it has salvific power to impart to its reader:

> It is the book of the Lord, dictated by unerring, infinite wisdom. There is no dross here with the gold, no chaff with the corn. Every word of God is pure. There is nothing for our salvation to be had in other books, but what is learned from this. They are but the rivulets that run from this fountain, and all shine with light borrowed from hence. And it has a blessing annexed to it, a glory and a majesty in it, an efficacy within it, that no other book has the like (1979: 22-23).

Boston's writings about biblical hermeneutics offer a picture of the 'high' view of the Bible in the Scottish church in the eighteenth century. What were later Scots preachers saying about the Bible? From 1815 until 1823, Thomas Chalmers was minister of Tron Parish in Glasgow, and from 1814 until 1831 Andrew Thomson was minister of St George's Church in Edinburgh. Both were renowned evangelicals whose sermons and beliefs were widely published. Chalmers believed that the preacher should ensure 'that the things which are written pass without change or injury from the Bible to the pulpit' (1849: 263). His hermeneutic was founded upon 'the integrity of the text and the interpretation of it' and involved a three-pronged methodology: 'the philological, the contextual, [and] the doctrinal' (1849: 282, 299). However, in practice, the search for the individual meanings of words, particularly with regard to their use in other scriptural texts, was subordinate to the quest for the doctrinal meaning of a passage. Enright comments that 'for Thomas Chalmers hermeneutics was the science of the doctrinal interpretation and utilization of scripture' (1968: 236), rather than a philological or historical pursuit. Doctrinally, atonement was more important than incarnation, and the purpose of a sermon was to awaken a need for salvation in the consciences of the hearers, and then to preach Christ crucified as a substitute for sinners. The emphasis was on Pauline texts rather than on the Gospels. Theological thinking about the death of Christ was more important than the details of his life.

Selectivity and an emphasis on the role of the Bible in elucidating doctrine, then, are the dominant features of Chalmers's approach to scripture.

The sermons of Andrew Thomson (whose 'bold energy' Hogg refers to in his poem 'The First Sermon' [1874b: 351]) display less of Chalmers's preoccupation with doctrine and carefully selected texts. In a series entitled 'Sermons on Hearing the Word Preached' (1825), Thomson considers some of the reasons why sermons on biblical topics do not have the desired effect upon their hearers. In the fourth sermon, Thomson considers those who hear 'with prejudice and partiality':

> Some of them will have nothing but doctrine, and privilege, and promise; and, in every allusion to good works, they descry a departure from saving truth, and must not incur the danger of being led away from the stronghold of faith and grace. Others would have us to insist upon nothing else than the precepts of the moral law, and shudder at the very mention of justification through the merits of a Redeemer, and of the sanctifying influences of the Spirit: and would have us to leave these for fanatics and hypocrites, and confine ourselves to what they are pleased to call intelligible and practical (1825: 65).

Thomson thus admits that there are many and conflicting ways of reading and interpreting the Bible and its message. Clearly, he implies that the extreme ways are wrong. The text is open to misinterpretation at the hands of those who read it with preconceived ideas about its meaning, particularly those who place particular emphasis on selected sections of the Bible. To avoid such preconceptions, Thomson advises the following approach:

> The Gospel consists of a variety of parts, but these parts are all in complete harmony; they are necessary to the beauty and perfection of the whole, and none of them are intended for separate exhibition, or capable of being detached from the rest, and yet answering their destined purpose, in forming the faith and the character of the Christian, and preparing him for heaven (1825: 69).

For Thomson as well as for Boston, the Bible is a self-glossing book in which each part is to be interpreted in the light of the rest. However, Thomson attempts to apply this idea in his preaching in a way that Boston did not do, by avoiding a concentration upon only a small number of texts interpreted in a narrow way. Addison (1936: 150) notes that from August 1721 until May 1722 Boston preached on the 'doctrinal theme' of 'The Covenant of Works', and for the following two years on

'The Covenant of Grace', in Addison's view 'the grand achievement of the preaching ministry'. Thomson's four-sermon series on 'Hearing the Word Preached' is very different, but is no less biblically based or mindful of the inspired nature of scripture. Unattributed biblical phrases abound in the text, contributing to the authority of the argument, but not forming the starting-point and basis of the debate Thomson enters into:

> We must preach the gospel as it is found in the inspired record—'the faith as it was once delivered to the saints'—'the whole counsel of God' as it is revealed by Christ and his prophets and apostles. Were we to do otherwise, we should be unfaithful to the trust committed to us; we should be 'handling the word of God deceitfully', and contributing, not to guide and to save, but to delude and to ruin the people who wait on our ministry (1825: 68).

The doctrinal hermeneutic of Chalmers is also avoided by this approach. As the first quotation from his sermon series suggests, Thomson shows an awareness of the dangers of allowing preconceived beliefs to cloud the interpretation of the gospel and the hearing of the word. Thomson may not have been able to agree with the Editor of the *Confessions* that it would have been better if certain parts of Scripture (such as Psalm 109, with its emphasis on revenge [Hogg 1824: 27]) had not been included in the canon. However, his approach is one that is aware of the possibility of multiple interpretations of the Bible. Nevertheless, Thomson is as certain as Boston or Chalmers that his reading is the correct one, and argues as strongly that his interpretation reflects the intended meaning of the biblical text, as a whole and in its parts.

Hogg and the Bible

What is the relationship between these orthodox readings and preachings of the Bible and Hogg's own approach, as exemplified in his work? It is well documented and much commented upon that Hogg from childhood was exposed to the Bible as a written text and as a book to be heard and sung in church and at home.[14] Along with the Catechism and the Paraphrases, the King James Bible was the text from which he began to learn to read and the source of a lively oral storytelling tradition. Strout (1946: 8-9) quotes from a letter from Hogg's brother, William, sent in 1818:

14. For example, Campbell discusses the issue of Hogg's childhood experience of the Bible (1988b: 94-109).

When he (James) learned to read he read much on the Bible; this was a book which our mother was well acquainted with, and was in it better qualified to detect him when he went wrong, than if he had been reading in any other book. And I can assure you, that in all my circle of acquaintances, either among old or young people, I was never conversant with anyone who had as much of the Bible by heart, especially of the Psalms, or could have told more readily where any passage was recorded than my brother James could have done. And, in my opinion, the beautiful descriptions of the nature and excellencies of the Divine Being, the sublime addresses to His grace and goodness that are interspersed through that invaluable work, more disposed his mind to utter his feelings in harmonies and poetic effusions than any native energy derived either from father or mother.

One way in which Hogg's early interest in the Bible developed was into a passionate belief in the appropriateness of the Scots language to translate the biblical text. In 1830 he entered a heated debate with James Tennant and others in the *Edinburgh Literary Journal* about the status of the Scottish metrical version of the Psalms.[15] Tennant rejected the Scottish Psalmody because he believed that Scots was inadequate to express the biblical text. The 'infelicities' he objects to, such as the 'scotticisms' in 'Froward thou kyth'st/ Unto the froward wight' (Ps. 18.26; compare the KJV, 'and with the froward thou wilt shew thyself froward', in Hebrew עם־גבר תמים תתמם), and 'Because he minded not' (Ps. 109.16; KJV, 'because he remembered not'), are a result of

the uncivilised state of our Scottish literature as compared with that of England, and to a want of familiarity with the models of good taste and elegant style which had already become acknowledged as standards in the capital, but which were little read, or not at all known, in that provincial degradation to which Scotland was then reduced' (Tennant 1830: 13).

Another objection relates to the attempt by the paraphrasers to retain a close correspondence with the original Hebrew of the Psalms. Tennant offers the example of Ps. 78.31 ('God's wrath upon them came, and slew/ The fattest of them all'),in which the Hebrew expression for 'fat' (במשמניהם, from מֹשֶׁן), meaning 'rich' or 'distinguished', has been translated literally. Another example is Ps. 18.29 ('And by my God assisting me,/ I overleap a wall'), in which the unembellished image of

---

15. Watson (1984) offers helpful background information about Tennant, and considerable linguistic detail about the debate.

remarkable, God-given strength is retained despite its oddity. Tennant prefers Sternhold's expanded translation: 'By thee I scale and overleap/ The strength of any wall'. For Tennant, the Scottish translations 'adhere with such Calvinistic inflexibility to the naked Hebrew expression, as to make the application of such words seem, to our conceptions, ridiculous, rather than strong or solemn, as they were surely designed to be' (1830: 14-15).

To address the new needs of Scottish worship, Tennant recommends a 'purification' (p. 36) of the Scottish Psalmody to be carried out by clergymen rather than poets, combining English 'taste and correctness with... Scottish fire and originality'. The language of the pulpit, the Bible and the Psalmody should be consistent rather than contradictory, and all should avoid the scotticisms of the past. The 'devotional feeling' of the 'politer congregations of our cities...is...interrupted or endangered where taste and sense of propriety are rudely assailed' (p. 34). Tennant's concern clearly demonstrates that Scots had lost its status and appropriateness as a language for all classes and all levels of formality. The reformers had asserted that the Old and New Testaments in their original languages were directly inspired by God. For Tennant, Scots no longer communicates the word of God to the people.

In contrast, Hogg's response is deeply conservative. He declares that '[t]hese Psalms have an old watchman guarding over them here, who has had them all by heart since he was ten years of age; and what he wants in education and ability, he has in zeal, to keep every innovation in due subordination' (1830: 27). The scotticisms to which Tennant objects are 'quite endearing qualities' (p. 26) to Hogg, evidence of the Psalms' 'simplicity and energy' which suit the form of worship for which they were written. The closeness of the translation to the Hebrew forms enhances Hogg's appreciation of the use of the paraphrases in worship. He even argues that the Scots translation enjoys a relationship with the original text which the English versions lack. He asks 'Is it not a glorious idea that we should be worshipping the same God, in the very same strains that were hymned to him by the chosen servants in the Tabernacle 3000 years ago?' (p. 29).

A concern for tradition, and for the needs of the lower, rural classes ('the most virtuous and most devout part of...[the] community' [1830: 32]), as well as a belief in the need to maintain the Scots language in its natural setting of worship seem to have motivated Hogg to participate in this debate. For Tennant, the language in which the Psalms are sung may be altered according to the dictates of good taste and fashion. Scripture is a fluid and adaptable concept that is open to manipulation whether for good or ill. Hogg argues against any alteration to the text he has known all his life, and even claims for it a connection with its original setting.

Although there is evidence that Hogg held deeply conservative views about the Bible, particularly when the sensibilities of the poor and the status of the Scots language were at stake, there is also evidence that his relationship with the text of the Bible is more complex than might have been expected. In the introduction to the short story 'George Dobson's Expedition to Hell', one of the series of short pieces published in 1827 in *Blackwood's Magazine* under the general title 'The Shepherd's Calendar', Hogg compares interpreting a dream with understanding the Bible. A philosopher cannot even discuss the nature of his own dreams:

> for the origin, the manner of continuance, and the time and mode of breaking up of the union between soul and body, are in reality undiscoverable by our natural faculties—are not patent, beyond the possibility of mistake: but whosoever can read his Bible, and solve a dream, can do either, without being subjected to any material error (1982b: 41).

Reading dreams and working out the meaning of biblical texts are equally subjective enterprises. Both dreams and the Bible are beyond the theories of the professional or scientific interpreter, although they may be experienced by anyone. There is something mysterious about both which resists being pinned down. Lacking solidity and certainty, they are open to many different interpretations, and no interpretation of them may claim to be correct because both are beyond the discovery of our 'natural faculties'. A similar subjectivity is suggested in the responses to the Bible portrayed by the characters in the *Confessions*: Wringhim senior believes his theology to be biblical, and Gil-Martin's use of biblical tenets convinces Robert. The message is that even the devil is able to use the Bible to his advantage. As Blanchard comments, '[t]here is not an error into which a man can fall, which he may not press Scripture into his service as proof of the probity of' (1824: 107).

In the light of Hogg's comments in the introduction to the short story 'George Dobson's Expedition to Hell', it may be argued that he took a decidedly ex-centric view of the Bible.[16] The reformers had asserted the

---

16. It is possible that Mrs Oliphant, writing at the end of the nineteenth century, recognised this ex-centricity in Hogg. With reference to the 'Chaldee Manuscript',

divine status of the biblical text, and leading preachers of Hogg's time were secure in the belief that the Bible had one meaning, of which they were guardians. Hogg seems to be more aware of the contingent nature of interpretations of the Bible. He argues for the maintenance of the metrical Psalms in their ancient form when social and national interests are at stake, but in the *Confessions* he offers no positive, stable or illuminating reading of the Bible. Even the apparently good Blanchard admits that the Bible lacks presence or centre. Just as modern readers of the *Confessions* have begun to appreciate its lack of closure and avoidance of authority, Hogg realizes the inadequacy of fixed interpretations of the Bible, and weaves that realization into his text. Lumsden had argued that the truth in the *Confessions* broke free from the ideologies of antinomianism and empiricism to which Robert and the Editor subscribed. In the *Confessions*, the Bible's truth also escapes from the doctrinal and homiletic framework of Hogg's time. Boston had had a remarkably similar experience with Fisher's text of the *Marrow* when he tried to annotate it into orthodoxy. Rather than accept the meanings and implications of the *Marrow*, Boston continued to attempt to struggle and contain the earlier text. In the preface to his 1728 new annotated edition, Boston writes that '[i]n the Notes, obsolete or ambiguous words, phrases, and things are explained; truth cleared, confirmed and vindicated; the annotator making no scruple of declaring his dissent from the author, where he saw just ground for it' (p. xv). In notes that frequently take up more of the page and in smaller type than the text, Boston struggles to make sense of Fisher's words within acceptable theological boundaries. In the text Fisher asserts:

> God cannot, by virtue of the covenant of works, either require of you any obedience, or punish you for any disobedience; no, he cannot, by virtue of that covenant, so much as threaten you, or give you an angry word, or show you an angry look; for indeed he can see no sin in you (1728: 143).

Boston anxiously and tortuously clarifies the text:

which will be considered below, she comments that although Hogg received very little formal education, he was 'no doubt steeped, like almost every other shepherd on the Scotch hills, in Biblical language, and also a little touched with that profane familiarity with sacred phraseology which is the reverse of that medal' (1897: 118). Her tone reflects the ambivalence with which Hogg was treated by the literary establishment, as was noted at the beginning of the chapter, but also that establishment's suspicion and unease about Hogg's use of the Bible.

And therefore since there is no covenant of works (or law of works, as it is called, Rom.iii.27) betwixt God and the believer, it is manifest there can be no transgressing of it, in their case. God requires obedience of believers, and not only threatens them, gives them angry words and looks, but brings heavy judgments on them for their disobedience; but the promise of strength, and penalty of fatherly wrath only, annexed to the commands requiring obedience of them, and the anger of God against them, purged of the curse, do evidently discover, that none of these come to them, in the channel of the covenant of works (p. 145 n. 9).

Boston self-consciously reinterprets the text, manipulating its meaning to suit his doctrinal position. He uses the words of the original to say something that is new, but he cannot control the ambiguities that remain. Here is Derrida's deferred meaning and endless supplementarity amply demonstrated in a text that is already profoundly unstable. Derrida highlights the two meanings of 'supplement': it is an optional feature that may or may not be required, but it is also that which is required to complete or fill up some existing lack. Derrida's 'logic of supplementarity' involves the reversal of values in which an apparently secondary or derivative thing takes on a crucial role in the determination of assumption.[17] This logic can clearly be seen at work in Boston's notes to the text. Do 'none of these come to them' (threats, angry words and looks and judgment) 'in the channel of the covenant of works', but do come to them in some other channel; or do 'none of these come to them' at all; or is it the less drastic judgment of 'fatherly wrath' and the 'anger of God...purged of the curse' which affects believers who sin? Boston cannot control the text he tries to interpret, but is unable to admit it. As a result, the text and its meaning(s) seep out around the edges of his clarifying commentary. Boston's text is in a constant state of unfulfilled meaning. In contrast, Hogg is well aware of the Bible's indeterminacies, and allows them free play in his novel. It is a postmodern literary critical reading that exposes the instabilities of all of these texts.

Boston may not have been a mainstream influence on biblical criticism in Hogg's time, but his version of the *Marrow* continued to have great popular appeal. As noted above, Hogg admits to having admired Boston for the originality and freshness of his thought. However, the character of the Boston found in Hogg's fiction is not entirely flattering.

---

17. Derrida considers the role of the supplement in the work of Rousseau (1976: 141-64). Norris (1987: 108-113), offers a helpful summary of the arguments.

In the section on Daft Jock Amos in 'Odd Characters' (1874c: 411), Boston is one of those who 'took on them to reprove [Amos's] eccentricities' and who is bettered by Amos's 'wicked wit and wavering uncertain intelligence'. The 'far-famed' Boston is made to look foolish by the fool, who challenges him with a biblical verse of which he has no knowledge. In the section on Willie Candlem (1827b: 412), Boston refuses entry to the 'motley crowd' who have arrived for the penny wedding, and allows only a 'few respectable witnesses' into the church. Boston's actions in 'The Pedlar' (1874f: 66) are undoubtedly brave, but the form of the poem gives him a pompous rather than an heroic air:

> He prayd an' he read, an he set them to bed,
> An' the Bible anunder his arm took he,
> An' round the mill-house he gade,
> To try if this terrible sight he could see.
>
> ...The minister opened the haly book,
> An' charged him by a' the Sacred Three,
> To tell why that ghastly figure he took,
> To terrify a' the hale countrye.

Boston is a stock ministerial character in Hogg's work, rather than a figure of respected theological prowess. The admiring tone of 'The Statistics of Selkirkshire' is not translated into the fiction in which Boston appears. As one of the 12 who had defended the *Marrow* at the 1722 General Assembly, Boston had been accused of antinomianism. He had denied this charge and, as has been seen, was at pains to rescue the *Marrow* from such misunderstanding. The *Confessions* is certainly a parody and repudiation of the dangers of rigid belief systems such as predestination. Boston's beliefs and writing are often introduced by critics as examples of the doctrine Hogg sought to parody and warn about (e.g. Brown 1976: 141; Groves 1988: 117-18). I suggest, however, that Hogg's portrayal of Boston throughout his fiction is a sign of his scepticism towards fixed readings of the biblical text, rather than a specific attack against a doctrine Boston denied that he held. From Hogg's perspective, Boston is a representative rather than a marginalized figure: a 'professional' reader of the Bible rather than a heretic.

The 'Chaldee Manuscript' offers an early example of Hogg's biblical ex-centricity. In Issue 7 (Vol. 2) of *Blackwood's Magazine*, which appeared in 1817, a translation from 'an Ancient Chaldee Manuscript' was published anonymously.[18] It was claimed that the Manuscript was held in the Library of Paris, and that 'Silvester de Sacy' was engaged in the publication of the original. The text is written in the apocalyptic tones of the biblical book of Revelation, and charts a similar confrontation between the forces of good and evil. The story of the confrontation is framed by a description of the visionary experience of the observer–narrator:

> And I saw in my dream, and behold one like the messenger of a King came toward me from the East, and he took me up and carried me into the midst of the great city that looketh toward the north and toward the east, and ruleth over every people, and kindred, and tongue, that handle the pen of the writer.
>
> And he said unto me, Take heed what thou seest, for great things shall come of it; the moving of a straw shall be as the whirlwind, and the shaking of a reed as the great tempest (1. 1-2 [The text is divided into chapter and verse headings]).

Comparisons with the opening chapters of Revelation are obvious:

> I was in the Spirit on the Lord's day, and heard behind me a great voice, as of a trumpet, Saying, I am Alpha and Omega, the first and the last: and, What thou seest, write in a book, and send [it] unto the seven churches which are in Asia; unto Ephesus, and unto Smyrna, and unto Pergamos, and unto Thyatira, and unto Sardis, and unto Philadelphia, and unto Laodicea (1.10-11).
>
> After this I looked, and, behold, a door [was] opened in heaven: and the first voice which I heard [was] as it were of a trumpet talking with me; which said, Come up hither, and I will shew thee things which must be hereafter. And immediately I was in the spirit: and, behold, a throne was set in heaven, and [one] sat on the throne (4.1-2).[19]

Also as in Revelation, events and characters are referred to in code-like, allusive language. The man 'clothed in plain apparel' whose struggle with perfidious writers forms the basis of the plot has both a name and a number that are visible to the narrator but that are hidden from the direct gaze of the reader:

---

18. Parsons's (1989) suggestion that the literary background of the text lies in Jacobean biblical parody is not particularly relevant to the present discussion.

19. All quotations from the Bible in this section are taken from the KJV, which would have been Hogg's Bible.

> I saw his name, and the number of his name; and his name was as it had
> been the colour of ebony and his number was the number of a maiden,
> when the days of the years of her virginity have expired (1.3).

The narrator of Revelation offers similar clues about the identity of 'the
beast' in ch. 13:

> Here is wisdom. Let him that hath understanding count the number of the
> beast: for it is the number of a man; and his number is six hundred three-
> score and six (13.18).

In both texts, mythical and supernatural figures intervene in the
events of the world: the 'aged man, whose hair was white as snow, and
in whose hand there was a mirror, wherein passed to and fro the images
of the ancient days' (1.39) offers advice to the plain man's opponent
(compare Rev. 1.13-16); and the help of 'the great magician who
dwelleth in the old fastness, hard by the river Jordan, which is by the
Border' (1.44) is sought by both sides but given only to the plain man.
A Moses–Jesus figure appears in ch. 2 who promises to bring about the
destruction of the 'two beasts' who had wronged the plain man. Like
Moses, he is veiled, carries a rod in his hand and hands down a tablet.
On the tablet are the names of characters the plain man is able to call on
for help: under the influence of the Moses-figure, now hidden in a
cloud, these people come without knowing why. The figure has the
appearance of Moses, but speaks the words of the Christ:

> he said, Arise, let not thine heart be discouraged, neither let it be afraid…
> Behold, if thou wilt listen unto me, I will deliver thee out of all thy dis-
> tresses, neither shall any be able to touch a hair of thy head (2.2, 4).

The clear echoes are of Jesus' teaching in Jn 14.27 and Lk. 21.18. The
veiled figure is bearer of salvation on a cosmic scale, encompassing the
promises of the Old and New Testaments. He corresponds to the conquering figure of the Lamb, who slays the beast and his followers in
Revelation 19.

In the *Blackwood's* article, the issue at stake is the future and ownership of a book. The two beasts promise the man in plain apparel that the
book they will produce for him 'shall astonish the children of the
people; and it shall be a light unto thy feet, and a lamp unto thy path'
(1.12). However, 'no words' are put into the book by the beasts, and the
man has to ask friends to contribute to it (1.14-15). The plain man's
opponent, the 'crafty man' who has a 'notable horn wherewith he ruled
the nations' (1.17) fears the power of this book. He warns:

> Lo! This Book shall become a devouring sword in the hand of mine
> adversary, and with it will be root up or loosed the horn that is in my
> forehead, and the hope of my gains shall perish from the face of the earth
> (1.20).

He wins the two beasts to his side, and promises to destroy the book
they had instigated. The remainder of the Manuscript describes the
efforts of the two factions to gather supporters and to prepare for the
final battle 'in the place of princes' (1.47).

In Revelation also, the written word plays a central role. In ch. 5
heaven and earth are searched in vain for someone able and worthy to
open the sealed book. However, only the Lamb who was slain is able to
open the seals and by doing so he sets in train the apocalyptic events
that form the basis of the rest of the text. Control of the book is shown
as central to the future of the world. In ch. 10, the angel brings the narrator a 'little book' and tells him to eat it. Sweet in his mouth, but bitter
in his stomach, the book nevertheless gives the narrator the ability (or
authority) to prophesy 'before many peoples, and nations, and tongues,
and kings' (10.11). Part of this role is presumably the creation of the
book he writes and the reader reads. Finally, in ch. 20, the judgment of
the dead is carried out on the basis of 'those things which were written
in the books, according to their works' (20.12). Even more stringently,
whoever is not found written in the opened book of life is 'cast into the
lake of fire' (20.15). Inclusion in a book determines one's eternal fate.
In both Revelation and the Manuscript, then, the function and control of
books, and the self-reflexive belief in the importance of the book being
written, are central themes.

The key difference between Revelation and the 'Chaldee Manuscript'
is of course that one is Scripture and the other is a joke text. Readers of
the *Blackwood* article who were aware of literary characters and dis-
putes in Edinburgh recognized that the publisher Blackwood was the
man in plain apparel, whose name 'was as it had been the colour of
ebony', and the number of whose office, 17 Princes Street, was 'the
number of a maiden, when the days of the years of her virginity have
expired' (1.3). His opponent is the publisher of the *Scots Magazine* and
the *Edinburgh Review*. The Book is *Blackwood's Magazine* itself. In
the original copy of volume 17 in the library of Edinburgh University, a
handwritten and anonymous key to the code of the text has been inter-
leaved, declaring the identities of the people and places referred to in
the text. However, the key is either ignorant of, or colluding in the pro-

tection of, the identity of the manuscript's author. Beside the reference in the text to 'the great wild boar from the forest of Lebanon [who]...roused up his spirit...and whett[ed] his dreadful tusks for the battle' (2.13), there is the note: 'James Hogg, the Ettrick Shepherd, the projector (*not* writer) of the Chaldee m.s.s.' In fact, Hogg wrote the piece which was then revised by Lockhart and Wilson.[20] The article caused great public outcry on account of its irreverence towards both the Bible and major literary figures, and involved *Blackwood's* in several lawsuits.[21] Most famously, the advocate John Graham Dalyell successfully sued the magazine in the Court of Session for its 'indecent, irreverent, and blasphemous application of Scriptural language' (Oliphant 1897: 131). In volume 18 the editor apparently innocently notes:

> that an Article in the First Edition of last Number, which was intended merely as a jeu d'esprit, has been construed so as to give offence to Individuals justly entitled to respect and regard; he has on that account withdrawn it in the Second Edition, and can only add, that if what has happened could have been anticipated, the article in question certainly never would have appeared (1817: iii).

In his short story 'Storms', published in two parts in *Blackwood's* in 1819, Hogg refers to the outrage caused by the publication of the Manuscript, and compares it with the disturbance caused by allegations that a group of shepherds had raised up the devil.[22] He suggests that

---

20. The authorship of the manuscript has caused some debate, details of which may be found in Royle (1980: 132-33). Royle's conclusion is that the first draft was written by Hogg, but that Lockhart and Wilson reworked the text.

21. Many documents relating to the 'Chaldee Manuscript' (most of them satirical), including a copy of the text with a 'key', letters about it by a figure called Calvinus addressed to Revd Thomas M'Crie and Revd Andrew Thomson, and some of the legal documents generated by its publication, are found bound together in the National Library of Scotland under the title of *Tracts on* Blackwood's Magazine (n.d.).

22. Mrs Oliphant, writing 60 years after the manuscript's publication, confirms its widespread effect: '[i]t seems scarcely necessary to explain what the Chaldee manuscript was, for never perhaps was there a satirical composition, certainly never one which concerned so small a circle, and was so purely local in its aim, which has had so much fame in the world, and become so universally known' (1897: 116). However, her assessment of the text as a harmless, extremely funny joke fails adequately to account for the ferocity of outrage expressed at the time of its publication. Royle's assessment of the text as 'a piece of literary dynamite...[which]

'[i]f the effects produced by the Chaldee Manuscript had not been fresh in the minds of the present generation, they could have no right conception of the rancour that prevailed against a number of individuals' (1982a: 17). The tone is of course ironic, but the comparison drawn is instructive.To parody the biblical text in the way the 'Chaldee Manuscript' does is devilish, shocking and dangerous to those who consider themselves at the centre and in control of the text.

In 'George Dobson's Expedition to Hell', Hogg compared reading and interpreting the Bible to understanding a dream. Here, in the 'Chaldee Manuscript', in a quasi-visionary dream, biblical language, themes and images are used for satirical and humorous effect. In doing so, the text deprecates itself, its rivals, but also, inevitably, the message and medium of Scripture. The reader is warned about the insignificance of what is to follow in the reported prophecy of 'the one like the messenger of the king': he warns that in the events to come, 'the moving of a straw shall be as the whirlwind, and the shaking of the reed as the great tempest' (1.2). The biblical language and cadence of the phrases obscure the self-deflating message, and the reader is carried along on its high-flown tone. In Revelation 5, the opening of the book, which can only be accomplished by the slain lamb, initiates the events of the end of the world. By placing the control of the book at the centre of the action, and following the apocalyptic tone of Revelation, the manuscript mocks those who claim importance for their literary power and influence. The future of the world hardly depends on the outcome of the battle begun in ch. 4 of the Manuscript. In Revelation 10 the narrator is authorized to prophesy by his eating of the small book. His implicit claim in 22.18-19 to be writing a sacred text (the emendation of which will bring about judgment by God) is validated by the inclusion of his book in the Bible, as the reader is aware. The authority of the narrator of the Manuscript is validated by his text's inclusion in the book at the centre of the power-struggle he describes (*Blackwood's Magazine*). Like the shorter version of Mark's Gospel, the text ends in fear and ignorance. In Mk 16.8 the women at the empty tomb 'fled from the sepulchre; for they trembled and were amazed: neither said they any thing to any man; for they were afraid'. In the 'Chaldee Manuscript' 4.41, as the battle-lines are drawn, the narrator is told by the messenger to 'Cry', but exclaims that he does not know what to cry. In the closing

changed the magazine overnight from its vapid torpor to a controversial, vibrant magazine of Olympian standards' (1980: 132) is probably more accurate.

verse he describes fleeing into an inner chamber to hide and not knowing what the great tumult was outside. Despite this uncertainty and lack
of resolution, the text appears in the book the survival of which it had
pictured in doubt. The continuation of the book, and the manuscript's
role in its success is equated with the survival and growth against resistance of the Gospel message. The interaction between the two aspects
of the equation deflates both sides: *Blackwood's Magazine*, like the
'Chaldee Manuscript', is not Scripture and has no claim to be a sacred
text. Scripture itself is deprivileged when it is used in a fraudulent document to make a satirical point.

Comparisons with a reference to another important book in Revelation are also significant in the 'Chaldee Manuscript'. As already noted,
a person's inclusion in the book of life in 20.15 is necessary to avoid
eternal damnation. Allusive mention of literary figures in the manuscript both judges and inflates. Well-known writers may have taken
exception to apparent references to them (correspondence rumbles on in
Blackwood's Magazine for some time), but their inclusion at least
granted their importance recognition. Furthermore, by boosting the
Magazine's sales, the manuscript's indirect naming of members of the
literati probably deliberately contributed to its survival. The manuscript
assumes the role of the book of life: recording the deeds of those it
names, making judgments but also bringing salvation to the contri-
butors who continued to have an outlet in *Blackwood's Magazine* for
their work. However, the future of a literary magazine is hardly comparable to the eternal fate of the soul. It is not surprising that the
Manuscript caused offence on the grounds that it was blasphemous,
particularly to those who believed that the Almighty had taken personal
responsibility for every syllable contained in the Bible.

The 'Chaldee Manuscript' dramatically and deliberately shocked the
sensibilities of the 'Establishment'. It openly parodied both individuals
and an over-reverent view of the Bible. In *The Three Perils of Man*
(1822), Hogg in a much more subtle way demonstrates a lack of orthodox respect for Scripture and its interpretation. The complexity of the
storyline of this novel almost defies summary.[23] The fourteenth-century
struggle between the Scots and English to take and hold Roxburgh
Castle is what might be called the backdrop of the novel. While the

23. In his introduction to the 1989 edition, Gifford comments that the '"plot" is
merely an excuse to delight with endless legends, characters and beliefs of the
Borders' (p. x).

exploits of the courtly figures of Princess Margaret, James, Earl of Douglas and Mar, and the English Musgrave family are returned to from time to time, it is the experiences of a group of followers of Sir Ringan Redhough, Warden of the Marches, which forms the central thread of the story. Wishing to know which side to support, Sir Ringan sends this group to Sir Michael Scott, the king of wizards, to find out what will be the outcome of the siege between the English and Scots at Roxburgh. Led by the brave but slow Charlie, the group includes a friar, who, it turns out, is Roger Bacon, the inventor of gunpowder, the Laird of the Peatstacknowe (teller of earthy tales), the Deil's Tam, known as the ugliest man in the Borders, a young poet and a young English girl called Delaney, both of whom are to be offered to Michael Scott to encourage him to use his magic powers to enlighten Sir Ringan. In the novel, writing, books and reading are central to the plot.[24] The Bible, its transmission, translation and reception are important aspects of these overall themes, and all are doctrinally ex-centric. The friar is reputed to be a renowned translator of the Bible whose work has led to his persecution and exile. He tells Delany his words resemble the language of his book, which he uses to enable his audience to 'hear and love them' (p. 131, all quotations from the 1989 edition). However, his speech echoes that of the sixteenth-century King James Authorised Version of the Bible, rather than any fourteenth-century translation. Indeed, the evidence of his translations offered to the reader are more often of a physical nature, 'translating' his victim Gourlay (the fearful guard of Scott's castle) from earth 'into the firmament with a tremendous flash of fire' (p. 187), than textual. It is knowledge of this translation that encourages the warlock Michael Scott to stay for the friar's prayers from the 'small psalter book' he keeps with him (p. 192). In the novel, the friar's Bible and Michael Scott's black book of magic are counterparts or doubles. Both are hugely powerful as material objects: sight of the words on a page of the black book might cause the seer to be 'changed into something unspeakable and monstrous' (p. 335); and the open book of the Gospels laid on the Master's heart by the friar is involved in the exorcism of the demon that has seized him. In the novel, the friar's 'book of wonders' (p. 131) is as mysterious and as powerful as any book of magic. Its contents seem to be less impor-

---

24. De Groot (1990) discusses the role of the reader, and Hogg's intention in writing *Perils of Man*. Fielding (1996: 74-98) considers the topic of storytelling in the text from the perspective of speech-act theory.

tant than the mere possession of it. In *Perils of Man*, distinctions between the spiritual and the material, the magical and the religious are collapsed into uncertainty.

In *Perils of Man*, as in the *Confessions*, the way the Bible is used and understood by each character is significant. As already mentioned, the friar speaks using biblical language, phrases and rhythms. The tale he tells to the others while they are incarcerated in Scott's castle is even divided into chapters and verses in the text (pp. 203-12), although its subject matter, the seduction, desertion and death of a young woman, and apparent murder of her child, does not make it an obvious story to be adapted into a biblical form. The friar is the embodiment of the vice of the people of Auchtermuchty in Penpunt's tale in the *Confessions*. In Auchtermuchty, '[t]he young men wooed their sweethearts out o' the Song o' Solomon, an' the girls returned answers in strings o' verses out o' the Psalms' (1824: 162). The Bible is used indiscriminately in incongruous contexts, and incites the 'deils in the farrest nooks o' hell' (p. 162) to action. The friar provokes a similarly confused, and at times hostile reaction. When the friar is overheard promising to tell Delany about the virtues of his book, the poet assumes he must be referring to a work of literature such as Sir Gawain, otherwise he is speaking 'absolute nonsense' (1824: 131). Tam Craik disagrees, and argues that it is a book of black art, gained in Oxford. They are so convinced the friar is seducing Delany, they interrupt him and provoke a fight (which the friar, with the help of his mule, wins). The reader is assured that the friar spoke 'in raptures of divine ecstasy' (p. 134), but his fervour appears inappropriate to the occasion. His language at the scene of the banquet offered by Michael Scott at Aikwood is similarly incongruous, and incites a passionate response. The friar's blessing on the 'beautiful smoking sirloin of beef' (p. 172) results in its transformation into 'a small insignificant thing resembling the joint of a frog's leg'. His response is to curse the steward:

> Cursed be thy malice, for it is great… Thou Nabal… Thou Judas, son of the Simon… Give unto me the precious morsel thou hast taken away, or lo! thou art in the jaws of destruction, and the pit openeth her mouth wide upon thee (p. 173).

Charlie's response to the friar's outburst deflates his rhetoric:

> Blethering gowk!… What signify a' thae strings o' gospel phrases at sic a time as this? Will they fill a hungry stamock, or mak the worthy senechal either better or waur than he is? (p. 173).

The friar eventually desists, but promises to visit the loss of the meat upon the steward's head, which he later does in a spectacular display of 'translation'. The friar's language makes him a figure of fun for the reader and the characters, but his application of biblical words and phrases in apparently inappropriate situations is not simply to be laughed at. As the others discover, the meal offered by the steward is deceptive and unfulfilling: the blessing had revealed its true nature. Neither the friar's words nor the food in front of them will fill their empty stomachs. In *Perils of Man* the Bible is like all other objects in the world: deceptive and deceiving, at times imbued with magic power, and resistant to a common sense approach. It is open to many different translations, just as there are several different sorts of translations, physical and textual, in the text of the novel. The Bible is not privileged above Michael Scott's black book: fixed readings of both are shown to be impossible to arrive at or to sustain.

The 'Chaldee Manuscript' and *Perils of Man* freely subvert the language, themes and content of the Bible, as it was read by the majority of Hogg's contemporaries, and certainly by those in the Church who claimed to interpret the Bible for others. The two early texts serve as an introduction to Hogg's extended and more sophisticated exploration of the same process in the *Confessions*.

The Ex-centric Role of the Bible in Hogg's Confessions

Campbell (1972b) argued that in the *Confessions* Hogg had set up a system in which right and wrong readings of the Bible were intended to be recognized by the alert, orthodox reader who shared Hogg's views on Scripture and its uses. However, a consideration of Hogg's earlier work has suggested that Hogg had a rather less orthodox view of the stability of the sacred text. Rather than the misapplication of biblical language, it is the acceptance of the polyvalence of scripture, and a realization of the dangers of a fixed interpretation that concern Hogg in the *Confessions*. In this text, more than any other, Hogg explores and extols his views about the Bible. The revelation of his ex-centricity has a point: to warn his readers against anyone who preaches the one meaning of the Bible. Gil-Martin and Wringhim senior follow the hermeneutical principles of Boston, Chalmers and Thomson. Their readings of the Bible are shown to be as possible as any other: such a text, particularly in the hands of professional preachers, cannot offer an adequate basis for life.

The doctrinal preoccupations of Chalmers and Thomson are clearly mirrored in the elder Wringhim's teaching. The theology of atonement is more important to Wringhim than the incarnation of Christ or any details of the life of Jesus. Pauline texts, rather than the Gospels, are central, and the exposition of doctrine rather than the recovery of a text's historical setting is the basis of each sermon. Specifically, the doctrine Wringhim takes as his hermeneutical lens is the eternal pre-destination of the elect. It is by this doctrine that all interpretations of scripture are judged. Because Robert can assure Wringhim that Gil-Martin adheres to the tenets of his religious teaching, Wringhim is convinced that 'he [Gil-Martin] was no agent of the wicked one with whom you held converse...for that is the doctrine that was made to overturn the principalities and powers, the might and dominion of the kingdom of darkness' (1824: 98). Compare the biblical passage to which Wringhim's words allude:

> Put on the whole armour of God, that ye may be able to stand against the wiles of the devil. For we wrestle not against flesh and blood, but against principalities, against powers, against the rulers of the darkness of this world, against spiritual wickedness in high places (Eph. 6.11-12).

In the context of Ephesians, the metaphor of the armour relates not to a belief in the doctrine of predestination, but to qualities such as 'truth', 'righteousness', 'the gospel of peace' and 'the word of God'. Wringhim has little regard for any of these, and the inadequacy of the doctrine on which he depends is clear: far from offering protection against 'the rulers of the darkness of this world', it seems to encourage their attack. The dangerous inflexibility of his blindly doctrinal approach is demonstrated by the fate reserved for Wringhim's and Gil-Martin's disciple. However, it is the text of the Bible that has offered Wringhim the vocabulary and themes he needs.

Gil-Martin also uses Scripture in a way that parallels the approach of the preachers Hogg heard each Sunday. The first example is taken from the period after Blanchard has been killed. Robert explains:

> My illustrious friend still continuing to sound in my ears the imperious duty to which I was called, of making away with my sinful relations, and quoting many parallel actions out of the Scriptures, and the writings of the holy Fathers, of the pleasure the lord took in such as executed his vengeance on the wicked, I was obliged to acquiesce in his measures, though with certain limitations. It was not easy to answer his arguments, and yet I was afraid that he soon perceived a leaning to his will on my

part. 'If the acts of Jehu, in rooting out the house of his master, were ordered and approved of by the Lord', said he, 'would it not have been more praiseworthy if one of Ahab's own sons had stood up for the cause of the God of Israel, and rooted out the sinners and their idols out of the land? "It would certainly", said I. "To our duty to God all other duties must yield." "Go thou then and do likewise", said he. "Thou art called to a high vocation; to cleanse the sanctuary of thy God in this thy native land by the shedding of blood; go thou forth then like a ruling energy, a master spirit of desolation in the dwellings of the wicked, and high shall be your reward both here and hereafter"' (1824: 121-21).

When Gil-Martin tries to persuade Robert to kill George, he uses the story of Jehu killing Ahab in 2 Kings 9–10 as scriptural warrant and tells Robert to 'Go then and do likewise' (p. 120). Jesus' words to his followers at the end of the parable of the good Samaritan, instructing them to care for their neighbour (Lk. 10.37), echo in Gil-Martin's speech, although Robert, finely attuned to Gil-Martin's gospel, hears only an exhortation to kill his brother. Biblical phrases also abound in Gil-Martin's speech of encouragement as Robert prepares to carry out the task:

I have been watching the steps and movements of the profligate one... and lo, I will take you straight to his presence. Let your heart be as the heart of the lion, and your arms as strong as the shekels of brass, and swift to avenge as the bolt that descendeth from Heaven, for the blood of the just and the good hath long flowed in Scotland. But already is the day of their avengement begun; the hero is at length arisen, who shall send all such who bear enmity to the true church, or trust in works of their own, to Tophet! (1824: 124).

The phrase 'Let your heart be as the heart of the lion' is taken from Hushai's advice to Absalom in 2 Sam. 17.10, but here the context is not one of encouragement to brave soldiers, but of warning that even the brave will not be able to stand against the forces of David: 'they shall utterly melt'. The reference to Robert's arms being as strong as 'the shekels of brass', echoes Job's poem about Behemoth, whose arms he describes as being like 'strong pieces of brass' (Job 40.18). To compare Robert either with brave but doomed soldiers, or with a mythic, monstrous being both deflates and ridicules him, although it also suggests the damage he might be led to do under the influence of these encouragements. Biblical phrases have been wrenched from their contexts and applied in ludicrous, contradictory or even dangerous ways. The reader may well be expected to recognize their incongruity in Gil-

Martin's speech, but the fact that Robert never does highlights the dangers of a biblical hermeneutic that looks for only one meaning in the text, and that understands the words themselves to be divine.

In other examples in the same passages, Gil-Martin appeals to a distorted biblical echo, using phrases that have a resoundingly biblical tone, but which do not appear in the Bible in the combination in which he uses them. The reference to Robert's 'high vocation' (p. 120) echoes Eph. 4.1-2 but there the vocation is to forbearance 'in love' towards one another, rather than to murder. Similarly, in the next phrase, Gil-Martin uses the words 'cleanse', 'land' and 'shedding of blood' in a way that seems plausibly biblical. However, these words are found together in completely different contexts in the Bible. In Genesis 9 God sets out the condition of his covenant, one of which is that fratricide will require the penalty of the murderer's blood. In Num. 35.33 the land is polluted by the shedding of blood, and cannot be cleansed except by the blood of the perpetrator. Both of these biblical examples point forward to signal Robert's fate. They speak the truth about the consequences of his actions, but he is not able to discern their possible implication. In the second passage Gil-Martin urges Robert to be as 'swift to avenge as the bolt that descendeth from heaven'. In the New Testament it is the spirit like a dove that descends on Christ at his baptism (Mk 1.10), rather than a bolt of vengeance, and in Romans 12, vengeance is described as an act of God alone rather than a task for the righteous on earth to carry out. These examples are all plausibly biblical because they take biblical words and phrases and reinvent their contexts, just as preachers such as Boston, Chalmers and Thomson did in their sermons. When responsibility for the interpretation of the Bible is given to others, its hearers lose their ability to distinguish alternative meanings for themselves. They are open to be manipulated or deceived.

In the final set of examples Gil-Martin refers to the Bible accurately but presents only one aspect of the biblical witness, ignoring other verses that refute or contradict the example given. In these examples, the subtlety and ambiguity in the biblical text is replaced with certainty and clarity. Gil-Martin's use of the example of Jehu stops before the point in 2 Kings in which Jehu is shown to have lost God's favour by continuing to allow idol-worship (10.29-32). Jehu's election is indeed dependent on his actions. The complicated issue of the timing of the punishment of the wicked is debated in Job and in the Psalms and elsewhere, but for Gil-Martin here there is only one answer: the righteous have a responsibility on earth to carry out God's punishment of desolation. Gil-Martin's confident reference to Tophet denies the ambivalence and confusion that surrounds the concept in the Bible. In some contexts the term seems to refer to the butchery or place of slaughter in Jerusalem, where a constant fire was kept for burning the carcasses. It is to this tradition that Isaiah seems to be referring when speaking of the defeat of the army of Sennacherib (Isa. 30.31-33). Another tradition, found in Jeremiah (7.31-32), speaks of Tophet as the place where child sacrifice was carried out, and where bodies which were refused burial were thrown. In Jeremiah Tophet is both a place that is under God's judgment (he abhors child sacrifice) and a place where judgment is carried out because Israel has participated in child slaughter. According to Gil-Martin, Tophet is simply the place where the damned are sent, and the element of judgment on the existence of Tophet is ignored. All hints of judgment on his and Robert's actions are avoided. Robert fails to read Gil-Martin correctly because he reads his Bible in the way in which preachers like Thomas Boston urged. He takes to heart Boston's belief that everything in the Bible is inspired and trustworthy, and he follows Boston in admitting only one, clear and discoverable meaning in the text, supported by selected readings from other passages. Once that meaning has been found in each case, the truth has been revealed for all time and is the sword with which to overcome all enemies and temptations. Robert has no strategy to deal with the devil's own use of Boston's hermeneutical principles.

Hogg's purpose, it has been suggested, is to highlight the dangers of dependence on a text, particularly one that has been granted a sacred status and that is interpreted by a small but influential group of people. Hogg offers the speech of Gil-Martin as a warning about the dangers of the kind of hermeneutical system that was prevalent in his time. As Blanchard comments, under the influence of Gil-Martin, Robert has carried his belief 'to an extent that overthrows all religion and revelation together; or, at least, jumbles them into a chaos out of which human capacity can never select what is good' (1824: 107). However, Hogg also fails to offer any positive or helpful readings or readers of the Bible to counteract this hermeneutical approach. Blanchard may recognize the dangers of the extremity, but he has only a limited, and weak, preaching voice in the text. Just as the Editor struggles to make sense of the written material he possesses, and the reader is left without the possibility of certainty about any of the events the Editor and

Robert describe, so the Bible remains in the *Confessions* a dangerously ambiguous book.

Lumsden argued that Hogg intended to demonstrate the dangers and inadequacies of relying on a rigid and inflexible system of beliefs, such as antinomianism or empirical rationality. Such systems cannot contain or describe the complexities and uncertainties of experience. In this chapter, Hogg's use of the Bible has been considered from this perspective. It has been suggested that the hermeneutical principles of influential preachers are criticized from a marginalized position which recognizes the difficulty of interpreting the Bible definitively. When the Bible loses its sacred status and escapes the control of the powerful religious interpreter, its unstable and ambiguous character may be recognized. Of course, many postmodern readers, particularly deconstructionists, would want to push the instability of the texts under consideration even further and argue that the Bible, Fisher's *Marrow*, Hogg's *Confessions* and the 'Chaldee Manuscript' are all endlessly ambiguous and resistant to closure. The intention of the author is unrecoverable and irrelevant and should not be used as a privileged interpretative tool. No discernible compact exists between the author and the ideal reader. The author is truly dead, and meaning is created by each reader of the text. In Chapter 4 the inadequacies of traditional readings of Hogg's *Confessions* will be highlighted from the perspective of deconstruction, and the attempts of critics such as Redekop (1985) and Petrie (1992) to use theories of deconstruction in their readings of the *Confessions* will be discussed. Then a new, deconstructive reading will be offered.

Chapter 3

REVELATION READING THE HEBREW BIBLE

Does postmodern literary theory offer a sympathetic way to understand Revelation? Following Lumsden's (1992) reading of Hogg's *Confessions*, is it illuminating to consider Revelation as a marginalized or 'ex-centric' text? Could it be argued that Revelation's reading of the Hebrew Bible demonstrates a postmodern scepticism towards the sacred text? In the following chapter, various attempts to apply the insights of postmodern literary theory to readings of biblical texts will be explored. Recent claims[1] that midrash is a proto-postmodern way of reading the Bible will be considered, and Hays's (1989) use of the theory of intertextuality will be discussed. Then, using Revelation 11's reading of Ezekiel 37 as an example, and a Qumran text's (4Q385 2) reading of the same text as a comparison, it will be argued that in its context Revelation is a marginalized text. It will be suggested that insights gained from postmodern literary criticism offer a sympathetic way and space in which to consider Revelation's ex-centricities.

Midrash and Postmodernism

No discussion of the influence of postmodern literary theory on readings of the Bible can ignore the claims of some biblical critics, such as Handelman (1982), that there are many and significant similarities between midrashic and postmodern readings. The on-going debate in literary studies about the unclosed and unclosable nature of texts such as the *Confessions* is alive also in the field of biblical studies. Twentieth-century readers are not only themselves deconstructing the Bible, they are also arguing that in the intertestamental period the Hebrew Bible was being read in what might be called today a postmodern way.

1. By, for example, Handelman 1982.

It is argued that midrashists read the Bible with no regard for its historical roots, and considered its verses in total isolation from their contexts.
For the midrashists, the Bible was a truly open text in the most postmodern sense. It is suggested that the parallels between the reading
strategies of the midrashists and of postmodern readers of texts such as
the *Confessions* are striking.

> Midrash...holds together two competing truths, first, the authority of
> Scripture, and second, that equally ineluctable freedom of interpretation
> implicit in the conviction that Scripture speaks now, not only then.
> (Neusner 1987b: 103)

The term 'midrash' is applied by various writers to many different
examples of interpretation. In rabbinic literature, midrash refers both to
a genre or method of biblical exegesis and to the compilations in which
these exegeses are to be found. In literary criticism the label 'midrash'
has been given to a descriptive and interpretative method associated
with the postmodern idea of intertextuality. In the following section the
exegetical needs out of which the principles of rabbinic midrash were
developed will be examined. There will then be a discussion about
whether or not these principles are paralleled in the readings of the
Hebrew Bible in the New Testament. Finally and crucially, should
midrash be classified as postmodern at all?

The earliest biblical occurrence of the verb דרשׁ[2] with the meaning
'to study God's word', is thought to be in Ezra 7.10, where the

---

2.   דרשׁ is notoriously difficult to translate. Its root, *drš*, is found in Aramaic,
Arabic, Ethiopic, Syriac and Mandean. The original meaning of the root is hard to
determine, although Wagner (1978: III, 294) suggests that the English translation
'seek', 'ask', 'inquire (of)' may be correct. In late Semitic languages, such as Middle Hebrew, Jewish Aramaic and Syriac, there seems to have been a change of
meaning in the use of the root, so that the word comes to mean not only 'interpret',
but also 'tread' and 'trample'. In Biblical Hebrew, *darash* generally means 'go to
see', or 'search for'. In addition to its literal (e.g. Prov. 31.13) and figurative (e.g.
Isa. 1.17) sense, it also has a legal sense of making investigation before a judicial
decision can be made (e.g. Deut. 13.15 [14]). More common than any general use in
the Old Testament is a specifically theological use of *darash*. When a person is the
subject, the object may be God (Amos 5.4-6), a place or text belonging to God
(1 Chron. 13.3), or an abstract idea such as justice connected with humanity's relationship with God (Isa. 1.17). When God is the subject of the verb, often juridical
ideas such as debt, revenge and contracts are involved, as in Gen. 9.4-6, Ezek. 33.6,
2 Chron. 24.22. The use of the verb in Ezra 7.10 is typical in that it implies doing
what one is seeking.

familiarly rabbinic ideas of teaching and applying the Law are also mentioned:

כי עזרא הכין לבבו לדרוש את־תורת יהוה
ולעשׂת וללמר בישׂראל חק ומשׁפט

For Ezra had set his heart to study the law of the LORD, and to do it, and to teach his statutes and ordinances in Israel.

The noun formed from the verb, מדרשׁ,[3] is found in the Bible only in 2 Chron. 13.22 and 24.27. In both contexts the noun might be taken to refer either to a book (LXX translates it βίβλιον) or, in the later sense of the word, to 'interpretative writing'. Although the word used by the Rabbis to describe their work is rarely found in the canon of Scripture itself, the interpretative procedure the Rabbis followed is already contained and discernible in their Bible. As several commentators (e.g. Bruns 1989: 625-28) point out, the Bible is a self-glossing book. In a hermeneutical progression, sacred accounts of God's acts in the past provided models for later accounts of his present and future activity.[4] When the writer of Isa. 51.3 speaks of a future act of God in terms of a new creation ('For the LORD will comfort Zion; he will comfort all her waste places, and will make her wilderness like Eden, her desert like the garden of the LORD'), he is placing that act in the same category as the first event of creation in canonical history and giving it a comparable poetic force. In the process defined by Fishbane (1986; 1988: 339-41) as 'inner exegesis', the Law is also subject to comment: in Jer. 17.21-22 the Law established in Deut. 5.12-14 is referred to as a reminder and a warning to the sons of the fathers to whom the Law was first granted. First and Second Chronicles are glosses on parts of Genesis, Samuel and Kings (compare, e.g., 1 Chron. 11.1-3 with 2 Sam. 5.1-3). They are rewritings that amplify the originals while saying something new themselves. The Bible as a whole may be studied by following the

---

3.   The derivative *midrash* is an Aramaic infinitive of the qal of the verb *darash*.

4.   Barr (1983: 6-10) may be right to argue that the development of Judaism as a scriptural religion, relying on authoritative written texts, is not evidenced until the Deuteronomic period (eighth to seventh centuries BCE). Only then is a verse such as Deut. 4.2 found in which a book is to be pondered and pored over, and kept in its original state. Barr also concedes, however, that cross-referencing between one Hebrew Bible source and another happened much earlier, and that some traditions were probably written down, although open to change and development and therefore not 'scripture' in the usual sense of a fixed and sacred text.

ways in which one part reveals new meanings in another. Any attempt to understand the Bible by working back to an original, uninterpreted intention is undermined by the redacted, self-interpreting nature of the text. The text itself encourages the view that revelation is an ongoing process, and gives rise to assumptions about the editorial and creative processes behind its creation. It seems likely that while the canon of Hebrew scripture remained open, the inspired revelations of individuals were granted the same status as tradition in times of crisis when a clarification or transformation of the tradition was needed. Barr (1983: 60-61) argues that until well into the first century CE, and beyond, the very idea of a 'canon' of the Hebrew Bible remained vague, fluid and a far less important and decisive factor in the religion of the Jews than it does to those who view the canon of Scripture through the eyes of Calvinism. Certainly tradition and revelation were regarded as 'interwoven and interdependent' (Fishbane 1986: 36). Once the official canon was finally closed and this process of rewriting within Scripture was prevented, there was a proliferation of modes of 'non-canonical' exegesis of the biblical text. Examples of this are to be found in the writings discovered at Qumran, in books of rewritten history such as *Jubilees*, and in the New Testament in the exegetical writing of Paul, such as Gal. 3.6-9 ('Thus Abraham "believed God, and it was reckoned to him as righteousness". So you see that it is men of faith who are the sons of Abraham. And the scripture, foreseeing that God would justify the Gentiles by faith, preached the gospel beforehand to Abraham, saying, "In you shall all the nations be blessed"'). The text of the Bible continued to be applied and adapted to new contexts.

The concept of an 'oral Torah' existing alongside the 'written Torah' is central to the interpretative method of rabbinic Judaism. The Rabbis believed that at Sinai God gave Moses both a written Law as recorded in the Bible and an oral Law 'by which alone the Bible can become fully applicable and the divine rule of life appropriate to a given situation' (Strack and Stemberger 1991: 36). This tradition allowed and demanded that a flexible, open-ended and authoritative interpretation was granted the same status as the eventually stable written text. Midrash as a technique and as a body of writing arose out of this tradition, and found its justification within this tradition. As Barr (1983: 61) comments, in rabbinic Judaism, 'the real and effective "canon" of authority is not the canon of scripture but a "canon" that is half within scripture and half outside of it: in rough terms, the Torah and the Talmud'. In common with other contemporary readers of the Bible, the Rabbis faced situations not addressed in the text, but also had to make sense of passages in the Bible that seemed to be deliberately allusive and ambiguous. Midrash met both needs in a creative, authoritative and apparently divinely-sanctioned way.

> And they read from the book, from the law of God, with interpretation [מפרש]; and they gave the sense, so that the people understood the reading (Neh. 8.8).

> Scripture engendered midrash, and midrash in its turn ensured that Scripture remained an active and living force in Israel (Vermes 1970: 220).

The biblical text self-consciously demands the interpretation of its readers. Nehemiah and Sternberg (1985: 58) agree that much of the Bible is 'difficult to read': terse narratives such as the story of Jacob wrestling at Peniel (Gen. 32) cannot be read with understanding without the reader filling in some of the gaps in meaning. Believing Scripture to be sacred, the Rabbis sought to show that the written text was self-consistent and internally coherent as a body of truth, containing no error of fact, and no redundancy. The indeterminate and contingent nature of many of the biblical narratives therefore demanded interpretation, and the notion of the oral Torah to explain and elaborate on the ambiguities of the written text allowed the text and its interpretation to be 'twin aspects of the same revelation' (Handelman 1982: 31). Vermes (1970: 203-20) calls this form of interpretation 'pure exegesis, developed to deal with scriptural passages that included words an interpreter did not understand, or which lacked detail, contradicted another biblical text, or offered an apparently unacceptable meaning.

Vermes distinguishes 'pure exegesis' from 'applied exegesis': in applied contexts, midrash was employed by interpreters who sought to connect contemporary customs and beliefs with Scripture and so justify them. The result was a body of systematic exegesis determining social and individual life. Two principles of interpretation underpinned this approach: 'there is no chronological sequence in Scripture' (*b. Pes.* 6b [Handelman 1982: 37]); and 'a scripture passage has several meanings' (*b. Sanh.* 34a [Strack and Stemberger 1991: 260]). The Bible was not considered to be in chronological order, with the result that the past, present and future were understood to be contained in the narratives simultaneously. This facilitated the second principle, that multiple meanings were inherent in every event described. It was therefore entirely valid to interpret Scripture in the light of present circumstances, and to relate interpretations to events not addressed in biblical texts. Having developed out of the same exegetical background as rabbinic Judaism, this example from the Pesher on *Hab*. 1.5 from Qumran (1QpHab 1.16–2.10) highlights the specific while at the same time polyvalent nature of midrashic interpretation:

> Column 1
>
> 16. [...LOOK, O TRAITORS, AND] S[EE;]
> 17. [WONDER AND BE AMAZED, FOR I AM DOING A DEED IN YOUR DAYS THAT YOU WOULD NOT BELIEVE IF]
>
> Column 2
>
> 1. IT WERE TOLD. [The interpretation of the passage concerns] the traitors together with the Man of
> 2. the Lie, for [they did] not [believe the words of] the Teacher of Righteousness (which were) from the mouth of
> 3. God. And it concerns the trai[tors to] the new [covenant,] for they were not
> 4. faithful to the covenant of God, [but they profaned] his holy name.
> 5. likewise, the interpretation of the passage [concerns the trai]tors at the end of
> 6. days. They are the ruthless [ones of the coven]ant who will not believe
> 7. when they hear all that is going to co[me up]on the last generation from the mouth of
> 8. the priest into [whose heart] God put [understandi]ng to interpret all
> 9. the words of his servants the prophets by [whose] hand God enumerated
> 10. all that is going to come upon his people and up[on his congregation.]
>
> (trans. Horgan 1979: 12-13)

The lives of specific characters presumably known to the original readers are offered as valid interpretations of the ancient biblical text. Three interpretations of the identity of the 'traitors' are given: those who did not believe the Teacher of Righteousness; those who profaned God's name; and the 'ruthless ones' who refused to accept the priest's teaching about the last days. The role of the priest (elsewhere identified with the Teacher of Righteousness) is also significant: he has been given the ability to interpret definitively the words of the prophets for the present generation. It is strongly suggested here that Scripture as it applies to present experience is incomplete without further, authoritative interpretation.

For the Qumran sectarians there could be more than one valid interpretation of a biblical text, but only the interpretations of those within the Community were authoritative. One of the debates about the wider nature of midrash centres around whether the Rabbis who practised it were entirely free in their interpretations, or whether limits were placed on their thinking. Following his comment that the Bible is difficult to read, Sternberg (1985: 57) suggests that it is also 'easy to...overread and even misread'. Would the idea of overreading or misreading a biblical text have had any meaning for rabbinic midrashists? The techniques used in midrash, which included elaborating the meanings of words from their contextual use in other books and filling in lacunae in elliptical texts, are open to very wide application. The relationship of the interpretation to the text may have been one of contiguity, juxtaposition and association, but a glance at a page of the Talmud leads a reader to wonder whether midrash is anything other than a spontaneous overflow of random thoughts springing from an idea or phrase in the biblical text before the interpreter (Handelman comments that 'the style is often freely associative and laconic' [1982: 49]). Rules were drawn up by Rabbis such as R. Ishmael, for example that the provision of one law may also apply to another on the basis of an identity of expression, but these rules are bound up more with the application and justification of certain principles in specific situations than with limiting the scope of midrashic interpretations in general.

At this point it will be useful to consider an example of rabbinic midrash. *Genesis Rabbah* is an exegetical midrash on parts of the book of Genesis. It offers verse-by-verse analysis in the form of explanations of words and sentences, and amplifications and interpretations of the narrative often in the form of parables and sayings. The text is commonly accepted to have dated from the first half of the fifth century CE (see Strack and Stemberger 1991: 303-305). The voices both of the authors of the paragraphs and of the editor of the collection may be heard in the text and there is some debate about whether the editor has a variety of written texts in front of him from which he is free to quote or whether he has access to earlier versions of the extant text or to a common oral tradition. This unresolved debate need not impinge upon the proposed discussion of the evidence of the text itself. The translation in Appendix 1 is found in Neusner (1987a: 77-79), and is based upon Neusner's expansion of Theodor and Aleck (1893–1936: Vols. I–III).

Passage 19.9 tells its story by means of a montage of quotations applied and reapplied. The technique of speaking about one thing (the Exile) in terms of another (the Fall) is representative of the Rabbis, as is the repointing of the consonants of a word (the word translated as 'Where are you?') in the key text to mean something completely different ('How has this happened to you?') in order to develop an argument. In this passage it is God's emotional reaction to Adam's sin which is central: the questions raised by God's apparent ignorance of Adam and Eve's hiding-place are avoided by a transformation of his question into an expression of lament. God is a tragic figure who has twice been forced to put away creatures whom he has cared for and who have let him down. Hosea's reference to Israel being 'like a man' (6.7) enables a retelling of the story of the Exile as the story of the Fall, using isolated proof-texts as validation. The task of the midrashist seems to be to read the Bible as an integrated whole, each word and sentence affecting the overall story of God's dealing with his people. Israel is potentially the counterpoint and completion of the creation story, brought into a land of plenty and into the sphere of God's care, but allowed the opportunity to rebel. The consequences of her rebellion are judgment, exile and God's own sense of grief. The rhetorical force of the midrash to an original reader may have been an exhortation to obey the commands of God in order to open up the possibility of a new creation, and to comfort a grieving God. The Fall, the Exile and the present experience of a Jewish reader are collapsed into the world of the story.

The next passage, 19.10, exemplifies a second midrashic technique: the telling of a homely parable to illuminate the unstated motives of the biblical characters. As in the previous passage, the ignorance of God about the actions of his creatures is understated. Here, instead, the central themes are the loving concern motivating God's seemingly random command about the fruit of the tree, and the potential destruction caused by the raising of unfounded suspicions about the motives of others. The Eve–wife figure is shown to be dim-witted and easily led. The motive of the serpent–neighbour seems to be as simple as the desire to disrupt and make trouble where there is apparent harmony. The commands of the God–husband figure are shown to be based on sensible care for the welfare of the woman, rather than on pettiness or duplicity. The unstated inference is that the pain that is the consequence of the wife's action is deserved and fair. The passage carries both a theological and a moral message: God is vindicated from the charge that he enforces capricious rules and hands out harsh punishment; and a warning is given regarding the everyday temptation to listen to poisonous suggestions about the motives behind sensible rules.

The past of the Bible's narrative is made to speak to the reader's present experience.

As well as offering examples of representative midrashic techniques, passages 19.9.10 reveal the ways in which the practice of midrash was restrained. Midrash was interpretation with a purpose and with a rhetorical aim: as Bruns argues, it was 'a way of keeping the Bible open to the histories of those who answer its claims' (1989: 629). The Rabbis' task was to appropriate the text in order to understand it reciprocally and reflexively. Midrash was the 'radical interpretation' (p. 637) of a text restated in an alien conceptual framework where a literal interpretation would be incomprehensible. Its purpose was to mediate God's Word to the world and its methods were conformed to that end, rather than playfully free and wild. The imaginative powers of the interpreters were encouraged but it is not implausible to suggest that interpretations that did not bring the biblical text into the lives of its readers were unacceptable (although proving this is difficult, of course). The boundaries of midrash were formed from within the dialogue between the biblical text and its demands as a sacred text, the imagination of the interpreters and the needs of their readers. Midrash arose in a culture that believed in the concept of the oral Torah and that, because of this, granted interpretation a comparable status to Scripture. The existence of the Targums is evidence that translation and interpretation could become absorbed into a sacred text. In this culture, it is likely to have been unacceptable for a midrashist to allow his own imagination to take over his exegetical responsibility.

Clearly the New Testament's use of Old Testament texts and themes has an exegetical purpose. The New Testament writers sought to bring the Old Testament into the context of their and their readers' experience of Christ. It is asserted (e.g. Bruns 1989: 634-36) that the New Testament is to be read as a kind of midrash upon the Old Testament. Bruns comments (p. 635) that New Testament interpretation is continuous with midrash in being 'rooted in the figure of Jesus as the sectarian midrashist who appropriates the sacred text, seeing its meaning in its application to himself'. For the people of the New Testament, the Hebrew Bible, although authoritative, is no longer a sufficient communicator of salvation, particularly to the Gentiles. Only the (oral) preaching of the crucified and risen Christ communicates Christian salvation. As Barr (1983: 14-16) notes, Jesus' attitude to the Hebrew Bible, as depicted in the Gospels, is independent and at times critical, as, for example, in Mt. 5.21. Jesus claimed authority for his own teaching, just as the midrashists claimed authority for theirs. Perhaps following the example of the teaching of Jesus, implicit reinterpretative renderings of the Hebrew Bible are found throughout the New Testament. Just as *Genesis Rabbah* speaks of the Exile in terms of the Fall, Luke speaking through Mary transposes Hannah's song in 1 Sam. 2.1-10 to refer to the birth of Jesus (1.46-55). In 1 Cor. 2.9 a particular, christological application of a conflation of Isa. 64.4 and 65.7 is offered. Explicitly midrashic use of Scripture is also found both in the mouth of Jesus (or in the pen of the evangelist) and in the writing of Paul. In Mt. 12.1-8 Jesus clusters together individual citations from several different biblical sources (Deuteronomy, 1 Samuel, Leviticus, Numbers and Hosea) and offers his own interpretation of them in a manner very similar to the writer of the Qumran Pesharim. Stegner (1984: 37-52) argues that in Rom. 9.6-29 Paul is consciously writing a midrash: he cites as evidence Paul's use of key catchwords (such as 'mercy', vv. 15, 16, 18, 23) to draw in new Old Testament texts; his use of parallel texts to supplement each other (for example the two quotations from Hosea in vv. 25 and 26); and the correspondence between the opening and closing parts of the midrash (vv. 6 and 29). Rabbinic midrash, however, cannot offer a strictly historical background against which the thought of the writers of the New Testament may be understood, because of the late date of the rabbinic sources available to us (the earliest have been dated to the fourth century CE). Hays (1989: 10-14) rejects any appeal to midrash as an explanatory device for understanding Pauline exegesis for this reason and on the grounds that midrash was only one of several exegetical methods that were developing in parallel during the period of the writing of the New Testament. It has been suggested here, however, that these different methods, including the biblically-based writing of the Qumran Community, belong to the same milieu of exegetical understanding and practice itself begun within the text of Scripture. The later written midrash of the Rabbis and the New Testament are aspects of the same Judaic understanding of Scripture as direct address to its readers. For Hays, if the claim that Paul's exegesis is midrash means simply that Paul wrote as a Jew seeking to interpret Scripture in such a way as to make it applicable to his own time, such a claim is true but trivial. I have sought to show that it is far from trivial to claim that Paul shared with the midrashists an understanding of Scripture as alive, open and demanding interpretation. It is significant rather than vacuous to suggest that the writers of the New Testament as Bible interpreters were rooted in and remained in continuity with the traditions of the Jewish community, and that these traditions were motivated by the same exegetical concerns that were later exemplified in rabbinic midrash. The earlier antecedents of these traditions affected the way in which the writers of the New Testament expected their texts to be read and interpreted.

The exegetical purpose of the writers of the New Testament, of course, was very different from that of their Jewish contemporaries: as noted above, their interpretations were orientated and focused around the person, life, death and resurrection of Jesus Christ. For the writers of the New Testament, interpretation became the revelation of how the Hebrew Scriptures point to and are fulfilled by the Word of flesh. For Handelman (1982: 60) this marks an end to the possibility of midrash in a Christian context. The Old Testament narratives were considered by the New Testament writers to be figures, types and shadows of the truer realities now revealed:

μὴ οὖν τις ὑμᾶς κρινέτω ἐν βρώσει καὶ ἐν πόσει ἢ ἐν μέρει ἑορτῆς ἢ νεομηνίας ἢ σαββάτων· ἅ ἐστιν σκιὰ τῶν μελλόντων, τὸ δὲ σῶμα τοῦ Χριστοῦ.

Therefore let no one pass judgment on you in questions of food and drink or with regard to a festival or a new moon or a sabbath. These are only a shadow of what is to come; but the substance belongs to Christ. (Col. 2.16, 17)

The rabbinic understanding of multiple levels of meaning in narratives which have lost their chronological reference was changed into an understanding of events occurring in a sequential time-line culminating in the life of Jesus. For Handelman, then, the New Testament should be seen as a tightly controlled midrash on the Old Testament, offering the one true reading of the older texts. Subsequent Christian interpretations of Old Testament texts by their presuppositions cannot allow the multiplicity of meanings inherent in rabbinic midrash.

However, Handelman neglects the fact that different readings and interpretations of the New Testament have continued to be suggested since the New Testament first came into being, from the time of writers such as Tertullian and Irenaeus to the present day. Like the rabbinic midrashists, these writers have often had an exegetical and rhetorical purpose in the creation of their interpretations. Unlike the midrashists however, who apparently accepted multiple readings of the same text, many of the Christian writers did believe that their reading was the only correct one,[5] although more recently the polyvalent nature of Scripture has become a more accepted concept, particularly by poets and novelists who have found inspiration in Scripture in many different ways. Coleridge, for example, attempts to preserve the tradition of a multi-layered approach to the Bible by taking biblical symbolic language as 'the living educts of the imagination' (quoted in Prickett and Barnes 1991: 97). For Coleridge the importance of the Bible is not secured by divine right but is something to be discovered by the practical and imaginative experience of the reader. The work of Coleridge and many others suggests that the figure of Christ as the fulfilment of the Old Testament prophecies need not inhibit further interpretations of the New Testament. The status of these later interpretations may not have been as significant as that of rabbinic midrash, but the creative process behind them seems very similar. As Davis has commented, the way religious people have traditionally interpreted the Bible may be closer to deconstructive criticism than 'the anxious search to determine a single, original meaning, which has dominated modern biblical scholarship' (1982: 282). Texts gave rise, and continue to give rise, to multiple and contradictory meanings. Modern attempts to halt the play of significations by appealing to historical facts outside the text, or by determining the one, original intended meaning of the author are the expression of 'an illusory desire for security, for a reassurance that overcomes anxiety' (1982: 282). Before the rise of 'historical anxiety' (p. 283) in the eighteenth century, reading of the Bible was characterized by a flexibility of interpretation which shares features both with midrash and deconstruction.

In the context of postmodern literary criticism there has been a tendency to take the implications of these shared features of midrash and deconstruction further. Handelman (1982) has noted that the Rabbis viewed Scripture as non-representational and self-referential; they recognized the elasticity and polyvalence of language and indulged in the playful association of different texts; they accepted that there was no one 'correct' reading and they allowed their interpretations to become part of the text. The followers of deconstruction make many of the same claims for literature in general and for their own interpretation of

---

5.   Thomas Boston, whose work was discussed in the previous chapter, is a perfect example of such a writer on the Bible and doctrine.

it. There is an important difference between midrash and deconstruction, however: midrash is rooted in a text that is viewed as both sacred and demanding purposeful interpretation.[6] Midrash is created out of the imagination of the interpreter in dialogue with the biblical text and the exegetical needs of the reader. Deconstructive interpretation does not work within these constraints and so for many literary and biblical scholars, it cannot be considered convincingly analogous with midrash. Derrida himself affirms the distinction between the work of the creative writer and the professional, religious interpreter. Derrida (1978: 67) defines the rabbinical interpretation of interpretation as a seeking of final truth: for the Rabbi, interpretation is seen as an unfortunate necessity leading back to a possible origin. In contrast, poetical interpretation of interpretation affirms the play of interpretation over the search for truth or origin:

> The necessity of commentary, like poetic necessity, is the very form of exiled speech. In the beginning is hermeneutics. But the *shared* necessity of exegesis, the interpretive imperative, is interpreted differently by the rabbi and the poet. The difference between the horizon of the original text and exegetical writing makes the difference between the rabbi and the poet irreducible. Forever unable to unite with one another, yet so close to one another, how could they ever regain the *realm*? The original opening of interpretation essentially signifies that there will always be rabbis and poets. And two interpretations of interpretation (1978: 67).

Derrida (1966: 292-93) reaffirms the distinction, and suggests that although the two interpretations of interpretation are irreconcilable, they 'together share the field which we call, in such a problematic fashion, the social sciences'. He calls for a reconsideration of 'the *différance* of this irreducible difference' (p. 293), and a facing of its 'terrifying form of monstrosity' (p. 293). Today the two interpretations of interpretation share the field of biblical studies. One of the aims of this book is such a reconsideration of the relationship between the interpretations of the poet and the religious commentator; another, in Chapter 5, is the facing of the 'terrible monster' created by deconstruction.

6.   Even Barr, who is sceptical about the role a written scripture played in this period, argues that the midrashists operated under constraints: 'What controlled midrashic exegesis was not the canon, but the religion' (1983: 81).

Intertextuality and the New Testament

Although the identification of midrash with deconstruction is unconvincing, midrash does offer a way to begin to consider the role of postmodern intertextuality in biblical criticism. Hays cannot accept that Pauline texts are midrash, but he reads both the letters of Paul and midrash as 'paradigmatic instances of intertextual discourse, both wrestling with the same great precursor' (1989: 14). When Fisch affirms that '[t]he novel is rooted in exegesis' (1986: 213) he is making the same claim for the novel and midrash. The novel interprets other texts, such as the Bible, and it in turn demands the interpretation of the reader. By talking about the novel and midrash as aspects of the one category we may say something about the way in which stories and hints of stories are generated by the art of interpretation; and about the way in which the new is created while the transmitted past remains in evidence. As Fisch (1986: 229) comments, '[w]e never escape the magic web of intertextuality. That is the peculiar characteristic of the novel; it is also the way midrash works'. For Fisch, reading the Bible, midrash and the novel for intertextual echo involves understanding the poetic effect and larger meanings produced by the writer's use of a precursor text. It demands an historical knowledge of the tradition to which the echo points, of the way the allusion was understood in the writer's culture and of the contemporary experience with which the writer links the tradition. Fisch warns his reader that midrash and the novel are not entirely comparable in that, as noted above, midrash is rooted in and constrained by the text of Scripture. The intertextuality of the novel moves freely within the corpus of all literature. However, reading nineteenth-century fiction for echoes of the Bible, and taking into account the historical role of biblical hermeneutics in the writers' use of biblical intertexts may be a process very similar to reading midrash (and to reading the New Testament for the echoes of the Old). The writers of the New Testament, and of rabbinic midrash, and of many examples of nineteenth-century fiction believed that the revelation of the Bible was not bound to one time or place. For them the Bible was to be understood as 'the continuous and ongoing self-referential debate over the nature of man and God, good and evil, words and the Word' (Prickett and Barnes 1991: 138). Writers through the ages have found creativity in the Bible's referential strength and in its multi-layered meaning. The study of the Bible undertaken by midrashists and novelists may be read as paradigmatic of humanity's search for meaning about itself.

The theory of intertextuality has offered several biblical and literary critics a way to understand the Bible within a postmodern context. Intertextuality is not a well-defined or unified literary theory, and is used differently by each critic. Kristeva (1986) was the first to coin the term, but the idea of intertextuality did not originate with the publication of her article. Worton and Still (1990: 2-7) find similar ideas in the work of Plato and other classical writers: their conclusion is that theories about intertextual relationships, that is, the ways in which texts are read and rewritten in later works, have existed from the time that texts have been discussed. Intertextuality as defined by Kristeva insists that a text cannot exist as a self-sufficient whole and cannot function as a closed system. This is because all writers are readers of texts before they are creators of texts, and their work is inevitably shot through with references and influences; and because a text is available only through some process of reading and that which is produced at the moment of reading is due to the interaction of the text with all the texts of which the reader has memory. Later literary critics have disagreed about the extent to which readers' and writers' cultures influence their approach to texts, and about the range of possible intertextual readings of any one text. Both of these issues impinge upon the application of any theory of intertextuality to biblical texts.

In New Testament studies, intertextuality has been associated with the more traditional source or redaction criticism. Both deal with the relationship between texts and their precursor texts. Source criticism, however, is writer-oriented and works with an idea of a text as the completed form of a process of influence: it compares the final, closed text to its intertexts primarily with regard to the intention of the author of the later text. Such comparative studies of the New Testament start from the assumption that the earlier text has influenced the later text. In contrast, intertextuality assumes that the later text assimilates and adapts the earlier, which only achieves significance through what the later text makes of it. The writer is viewed not as a completely autonomous authority, nor as a reproducer of older texts, but as a 'reader, digester and rearranger of texts and experiences' (van Wolde 1989: 46). For most New Testament scholars who seek to read intertextually, that which may be known about the culture of the New Testament writers is useful for the interpretation of New Testament texts: these writers are understood to be part of the intertextual world of their own time and to have been constrained by its codes and conventions. As Freyne (1989: 84) comments, '[w]e can scarcely ignore the discursive practices of a particular culture as these are known to us, especially in dealing with strange or unusual texts'. Boyarin concurs, 'Reality is always represented through texts that refer to other texts through language that is a construction of the historical, ideological and social system of people' (1990: 14). The text's genre, its rhetorical strategy and the situations it addresses are areas of interest for most of those who study the intertextuality of the New Testament, such as Hays (1989) and Boyarin (1990).

A second issue about the theory of intertextuality that is debated by literary critics is the extent of the possible range of intertextual readings. Are there as many intertextual echoes of Old Testament texts in a New Testament text as a twentieth-century reader can find? Referring to literary works, Riffaterre defines an intertext as, 'one or more texts which the reader must know in order to understand a work of literature in terms of its overall significance (as opposed to the discrete meanings of its successive words, phrases and sentences)' (1990: 56). For Riffaterre, intertextuality is in effect constrained by the intention, whether conscious or subconscious, of the author. The intertextual drive operates only when the intertext is obvious and compulsory to understand the (one) meaning of the text. For other critics, such as Kristeva (1986) and Bakhtin (see Worton and Still 1990: 12-13), intertextual play is potentially infinite and is restricted in practice only by the imagination of the reader.

Intertextuality as an interpretative perspective has been defined as ideally suited to the readings of Scripture which the Qumran texts and the New Testament offer. Midrash and intertextuality are closely related, as noted above, and both speak to the nature of the biblical text itself. Boyarin (1990: 15) comments that 'the very fractured and unsystematic surface of the biblical text is an encoding of its own intertextuality, and it is precisely this which the midrash interprets'. The writers of the New Testament and of the Qumran scrolls, working within the tradition out of which rabbinic midrash developed, knew that scriptural intertextual echoes establish continuity with the past but also renew these later texts for the future. Like all texts, these texts absorb and transform earlier texts, in a process of rejection and preservation of the past. It is argued that reading these texts for intertextual echoes of the Old Testament sharpens our understanding both of the nature of the biblical texts, and of the exegetical perspective of their first-century readers.

Hays is a biblical critic who has applied the theory of intertextuality to New Testament texts. In his book *Echoes of Scripture in the Letters of Paul* (1989) and then in 'Paul and the Scriptures of Israel' (1993), Hays's stated aim is to retrace Paul's readings of Scripture and to follow the hermeneutical path along which he leads his readers. For Hays, Pauline epistles, like literary texts such as those in the canon of English literature, are intertextual. Hays briefly outlines the classic theories of intertextuality defined by Kristeva, Barthes and Bloom, acknowledges their contribution to the philosophical debate about the nature of texts, but chooses instead the approach of John Hollander (1981). Hollander focuses neither on the workings of the poet's inner self nor on the historical presuppositions behind poetic allusions, but on the rhetorical and semantic effects of those allusions. The critic's task is to point out the presence of echoes of and allusions to other texts, and to give an explanation of the distortions and new configurations they generate. Hollander draws particular attention to the role of metalepsis or transumption: when a literary echo or allusion links a text to an earlier text, its figurative effect may lie in the unstated, suppressed or 'transumed' points of resonance between the two texts. The critic's task is to recover the unstated material, those aspects of intertextual meaning beyond the explicit allusions to and echoes of the earlier text. A text places a reader in 'a field of whispered or unstated correspondences' (Hollander 1981: 65), and expects the reader to attune his or her ears to the internal resonances. For Hays, Hollander's insights are particularly applicable to Pauline epistles. Paul is enveloped in what Hollander calls 'a cave of resonant signification', which Hays defines as scripture. Hollander's literary critical approach is justified when applied to Pauline letters because the Pauline texts are analogous to literary works (they are poetic, polyvalent and tend to use language and symbols from Scripture to apprehend present experiences), and because it helps modern readers to recover the idea of Paul as in Hays's words 'a thinker within scripture' (1980: 20).

Quite apart from disagreements about specific readings of texts, Hays has been criticized for what Green calls his 'minimalist notion of intertextuality' (1993: 59): he lacks grounding in the classic literary theory. However, Hays claims to be very conscious both of the philosophical framework in which Kristeva and others work (as he makes clear (1989) and in his rejoinder to Green [1993: 70-96]) and of the hermeneutical issues his notion of echo raises. He offers answers to two of the perennial questions raised by the theory of intertextuality. The first of these questions involves the origin of the intertextual relationship. Does the intertextual fusion that generates meaning occur in the mind of the writer, or of the original reader? Is intertextual meaning a property of the text itself; or does it occur in my act of reading, or in my or another community of interpretation? Hays seeks to hold all five possible answers to this first question 'in creative tension': he aims to produce twentieth-century readings of Paul informed by intelligent historical understanding. Hays's hermeneutical axiom is 'that there is an authentic analogy—though not a simple identity—between what the text meant and what it means' (p. 27). The act of intertextual comprehension occurs in Hays's reading of the text, which takes place within a community of interpretation, one of whose hermeneutical conventions is that the proposed interpretation be justified both by the text's structure and by a historical understanding of the author and the text's original readers. The related and second question asks, How should these readings be tested? In answer, Hays offers seven criteria for testing claims about the presence and meaning of scriptural echoes in Paul: the availability of the earlier text; its volume and prominence in the Pauline text and in Scripture; its recurrence in Paul; the degree of thematic coherence the alleged echo brings to the argument of the later text; the historical plausibility of Paul's intended use of the text, and of his readers understanding it; the acceptance of the presence of the echo by other readers; and the level of satisfaction the alleged echo brings to a reader in terms of making sense of the text. As Hays points out, not all of these tests will be applicable in every case. He is also keen to allow the generation of meanings by texts that transcend the conscious intention of the author.

Hays seems over-anxious to defend every possibility, and I suggest that his tests might be simplified (as they are in effect in Hays's readings of Pauline texts) to those of historical plausibility and reader satisfaction. Hollander himself does not in an extended way address the issue of where intertextual meaning occurs, although at one point he comments that he does wonder whether many of the echoes he discusses are a result of his invention. He offers no guidelines to test the validity of his findings, although he assumes Hays's test of historical plausibility, and in his comparison between echoes and dreams, he suggests that the creation of some intertextual resonances is unconscious and does not depend on the assumed recognition of the reader. For Hollander, the moment of creation of an echo is less important than the experience of reading and appreciating it, and he is clear that this depends on the reader's 'access to an earlier voice, and to its cave of resonant signification, analogous to that of the author of the later text' (1981: 65).

Several commentators have considered the use of the Hebrew Bible in Revelation (e.g. Vanhoye 1962; Vogelgesang 1985), but few have taken a literary critical approach comparable to Hays's reading of Pauline texts. However, Moyise (1995) offers a reading of Revelation's use of the Hebrew Bible from the perspective of intertextuality taken by Hays. Rather than concentrating on an understanding of John's purpose in using an allusion or echo from the Hebrew Bible, Moyise attempts to assess the effect of such an allusion on a reading of the text. Using the theory of intertextuality, he considers the relationship or dialogue inevitably set up between the text read and the text and its context that is alluded to. This relationship is outwith the control of the writer, and will vary from reader to reader. The commentator's task, Moyise argues, is 'to give an account of how these two contexts affect one another' (1995: 135), or, as Hays puts it, 'the distortions and new figuration that they generate [1989: 19]'. In this intertextual relationship, readings of Revelation affect readings of precursor texts such as Ezekiel, just as a knowledge of Ezekiel affects the way in which Revelation is read. It is a dynamic relationship, in which meaning resides in the tension between an allusion's former context and its new setting. Such a reader-centred approach, Moyise argues, does not impose on the text, but does justice to its complexity, given its habit of avoiding explicit quotation and of forcing the reader to make their own judgment about the presence and significance of allusions.

Moyise's work is an important and ground-breaking contribution to literary studies of Revelation, but, like the work of Hays, it fails fully to grasp the challenge of postmodern literary theory. The implications of the tension between the two texts is not fully explored, and the potentially subversive nature of Revelation's readings of the Hebrew Bible is given little consideration. For Moyise, John the writer of Revelation continues to read the Hebrew Bible as a stable, privileged text. Ezekiel functions in John's text largely to comfort and encourage those facing persecution and future difficulty, in the same way that it functioned in its own context. The intertextual process is one of transformation and reconfiguration rather than subversion.

Revelation as a Marginalized Text

Moyise's reading of the context of Revelation is now questioned in a way that suggests that Lumsden's approach towards Hogg's *Confessions* may also be illuminating if applied to the biblical text. The key issue is the relationship between Revelation and the context in which it was written, and the effect of this relationship on Revelation's reading of the Hebrew Bible. Traditional commentators, such as Beasley-Murray (1974), assume that the writer and original audience of Revelation are in a situation of crisis. John used traditional language and imagery, such as the sea monster in ch. 7 or the beasts of ch. 13, in such a way that his first readers would recognize the intended caricature and approve of the implied judgment on the nature of the tyrannical Roman Empire of their day. Following the tradition supported by Irenaeus,[7] Beasley-Murray sets Revelation at the end of the terrible reign of Domitian. John has been banished to the island of Patmos as a result of active hostility by the state which had not been shown towards the church prior to the later years of Domitian's reign. The situation of danger and doom that is reflected is caused by the extension of the cult of the emperor which developed at this time. John's purpose in writing is to prepare his readers for the further persecutions that await them, and to encourage them, with promises of future reward for them and of the destruction of the forces of evil, to resist the temptation to compromise with the state.

Even commentators who take a less traditional hermeneutical approach make the same assumptions about the text's context. Fiorenza (1985) argues that Revelation has a socio-theological function that is best approached with an integration of literary-aesthetic analysis and traditional historical research. John's use of the letter form for his prophetic address to the people of the revelation of Jesus Christ performs a similar function to Paul's letters. From the evidence of verses

---

7. Irenaeus, who came from Asia Minor and knew Polycarp, the Bishop of Smyrna (who died c. 155 CE), states that the visions described in Revelation were experienced 'no very long time since', but 'almost in our day, towards the end of Domitian's reign' (*Against Heresies* 5.30.3).

such as 13.10, 14.12 and the letters to the churches in chs. 2–3, John's purpose is to encourage, strengthen and correct Christians in Asia Minor who were facing persecution by the State, and who must expect further suffering and harassment. The central issue for John is political power. Fiorenza (1985: 24) argues that 'Revelation demands unfaltering resistance to the imperial cult because honoring the emperor would mean ratifying Rome's dominion over all people and denying the eschatological life-giving power of Christ'. Paul had presented the alternative for Christians: choose between the lordship of Christ and the lordship of cosmic powers. For John, Christians must choose between the lordship of Christ and of the Roman Empire. As John makes clear, the consequence of choosing Christ may be exclusion from economic and social life, and the very real threat of captivity and death. Those who have capitulated to the state, such as the Nicolaitans and others condemned in the letters and in the central section of the text by the code-words 'idolatry' and 'immorality', are promised judgment when the power of God and Christ prevails.

Fiorenza stresses John's continuity with Paul in the form, function and content of his work. They share christological beliefs, concentrating on the death and resurrection of Jesus rather than his life, and both use the image of Christ as the lamb (e.g. 1 Cor. 5.7). By using the letter form, John indirectly claims the authority of Paul for his message, and deliberately entitles his work 'The Revelation of Jesus Christ' to characterize his own experience as a Christian prophet in terms similar to the call-experience of Paul as detailed in Galatians. Fiorenza also points out the apocalyptic elements of Paul's writing, often found in the opening and final greetings of his letters. Both faced a similar dilemma over the amount of contact Christians should have with the world expressed in terms of eating food offered to idols. Fiorenza compares Paul's teaching in 1 Corinthians 8–10 with that of John in Revelation 2, and argues that both deal with the issue with reference to the apocalyptic question about who has lordship over the world: both stress that Christ has overcome, but that Christians may still fall victim to the opposing powers (cosmic forces for Paul, the Empire for John). Only in bodily obedience to Christ does the church prove itself to be a new creation and realize the lordship of Christ in the world. For both John and Paul, idols still have the demonic power of Satan behind them.

For Fiorenza, Revelation is a poetic and rhetorical work. It seeks to persuade and motivate its readers by constructing a 'symbolic universe'

which invites imaginative participation by virtue of the evocative power
of its symbols. Its vision of an alternative world is offered to encourage
Christians facing persecution. This is the historical situation which the
poetic-rhetorical construction of Revelation 'fits'. Eating food
sacrificed to idols, as some were suggesting, brought political, economic and professional advantage to the Christian (such meat would be
on offer at meetings of trade guilds, business associations and private
and public functions); but it also signified compromise with the imperial cult. John argues that such compromise, which some may have
attempted to justify with reference to Rom. 13.7 'Pay all of them their
dues, taxes to whom taxes are due, revenue to whom revenue is due,
respect to whom respect is due, honor to whom honor is due' or 1 Tim.
2.2 ('[pray] for kings and all who are in high positions, that we may
lead a quiet and peaceable life, godly and respectful in every way'),
denied the reality of the lordship of Christ. John's language to construct
the heavenly and future world, often using images from the Hebrew
Bible and the cult of Israel, alienates his audience from the imperial
cult, but also projects a stable, coherent picture of eternal bliss. This
picture is designed to enable his audience to overcome their experienced alienation.

In terms of the approach introduced by Lumsden's reading of Hogg,
the traditional view of the context of Revelation could offer interesting
possibilities. John, his first readers and the text exist in a marginalized
position to the rest of society. Revelation could be read (and is read by
commentators such as Fiorenza) as a destabilizing critique of the dominant culture of its day. Its purpose is to discredit the certainties of its
world, and to offer new possibilities for existence (Fiorenza's alternative symbolic universe, perhaps). However, such a reading fails to do
justice to the complexities and contradictions in the text. Fiorenza's
symbolic universe is more stable than the text allows. Just as the indeterminacies and ambiguities of Hogg's *Confessions* respond to the
insights and space offered by postmodern literary critical thought, so it
is these aspects of Revelation that are opened up by the application of
elements of postmodern literary theory. However, first, an alternative
and opposing view of the historical situation of Revelation offers a new
perspective on the text's ex-centricities.

In contrast to the traditional view, Thompson (1990) argues that at
the time Revelation was written, during the reign of Domitian,
Christians lived quiet, largely undisturbed lives at peace with their

neighbours. This was not a time of economic or political unrest; Domitian was not a mad, ferocious leader demanding greater obeisance from his subjects than his predecessors; and the threat of widespread imperial persecution did not hang heavily over followers of Christ. John's rhetoric did not 'fit' a historical situation, operating within the theological tradition of Paul: instead it attempted to create an awareness of crisis within its audience, and argued against the teaching of Paul. Revelation is marginal to the rest of Christianity, as well as to its culture.

Thompson argues that Revelation's classification as apocalyptic has been instrumental in the assessment of its context as one of crisis. Apocalypse is generally viewed as a function of its social setting. Rapid social change, particularly with cross-cultural contact, exacerbates disorder, disorganization, conflict, and a sense of deprivation, and sets the stage for apocalyptic. As a response to such crisis, a group may embrace apocalypticism as a perspective from which to construct an alternative universe of meaning. This alternative view affirms that God is about to intervene on behalf of his endangered people. Apocalypses such as Revelation are produced by such apocalyptic movements, and reflect that group's alienation from its society. However, in opposition to this deterministic understanding of the basis of apocalypses, and in response to the suggestion that it cannot be proved that all apocalypses were written in crisis situations, the notion of 'perceived crisis' has arisen. The author of an apocalypse considers a situation to be a crisis, but the crisis dimensions of the situation are evident only through his perspective. Prior to the knowledge revealed in an apocalypse, there need be no crisis. Readers only discover the crisis dimensions of their situation by reading an apocalypse, which brings comfort and assurance and enables people to perceive themselves as needing such functions. The reader is encouraged to take the perspective of the author, and to see the human situation in terms of transcendental reality. Thompson argues that the notion of 'perceived crisis' may add to our understanding of the way in which an apocalypse functions within a social setting, but it adds little to our understanding of the social occasion out of which the apocalypse was written, since any social setting may be perceived by someone as one of crisis. Commentators must find other sources to justify their reconstructions of the social setting of an apocalypse.

Having discussed the relationship between apocalypse and social setting, Thompson then assesses the standard portrait of Domitian. He notes that the picture of the emperor generally accepted is drawn from the evidence of a group of writers working a few years after Domitian's death, such as Pliny the Younger, Tacitus and Suetonius; and from the work of Dio Cassius who wrote his history a century later. All paint Domitian as evil, and several describe him as becoming more cruel as his reign progressed.[8] According to these accounts, his life is characterized by savageness, unbridled passion, madness and the pursuit of revenge on all who oppose him.[9] During his reign, political disorder, economic disarray and military dissatisfaction and dissension create general chaos throughout the empire.[10] His megaolomaniacal tendencies result in an expansion of the imperial cult, and an increased threat to those who refused to participate.[11]

Thompson points out that none of these portraits is painted by a neutral observer. All emphasize the evil, attribute malicious intentions to good deeds and omit the favourable aspects of Domitian's character and reign. In fact, the standard description is not supported by the evidence of the time. For example, writers such as Quintilian, Statius and Martial, Domitian's contemporaries, praise his military successes.[12] There is nothing to suggest that Domitian extended the imperial cult,

---

8.   Suetonius comments that Domitian's reign began with 'leniency and self-restraint', but that these attributes 'were not destined to continue long, although he turned to cruelty somewhat more speedily than to avarice' (*Lives of the Caesars: Domitian* 10.11).

9.   According to Pliny, the palace under Domitian was a 'place where…that fearful monster built his defences with untold terrors, where lurking in his den he licked up the blood of his murdered relatives or emerged to plot the massacre and destruction of his most distinguished subjects. Menaces and horror were the sentinels at his doors…always he sought darkness and mystery, and only emerged from the desert of his solitude to create another' (*Panegyricus* 48.3-5).

10.   Pliny refers to his experience of the army in Syria during Domitian's reign, when 'merit was under suspicion and apathy an asset, when officers lacked influence and soldiers respect, when there was neither authority nor obedience and the whole system was slack, disorganised and chaotic, better forgotten than remembered' (*Letters* 8.14.7).

11.   For example, Suetonius writes that Domitian loved 'to hear the people in the amphitheatre shout on his feast day: "Good Fortune attend our Lord and Mistress" ' (*Lives of the Caesars: Domitian* 13.1). He comments that Domitian sent letters in the name of 'Our Lord and God' and that 'the custom arose of henceforth addressing him in no other way even in writing or in conversation' (13.2).

12.   Quintilian writes 'Who could sing of war better than he who wages it with such skill?' (*Institutes* 10.1.91).

which had been established several generations before. No evidence from the time suggests he used or sought the title 'Our Lord and God'.[13] Nor is there any suggestion that he was particularly power-hungry or attempted to silence opposition with the excessive use of informers.[14] Thompson suggests that the commonly-accepted view of Domitian developed from the desire of one of his successors, Trajan, to disseminate the idea of a new era dawning with his reign. By slurring the reputation of Domitian, men of letters such as Pliny and Tacitus rhetorically highlighted the best qualities of Trajan, and in the process advanced their own careers.[15] As a result, the history of Domitian's character and reign was distorted for all future generations.

Such a reassessment of Domitian's reign calls for another look at the evidence of the social status of Christians in Asia at the time of Revelation. The main source of such evidence comes from the Christian writings themselves. Thompson argues that given the evidence of the church in Asia offered in Acts and in the Pastoral epistles, it is only the writer of Revelation who was hostile towards urban culture and opposed to Christian accommodation towards it. In contrast to Fiorenza, Thompson convincingly argues that Paul's views on the acceptability of eating meat offered to idols are very different from

13. As Thompson (1990) observes, no coins, inscriptions or medallions from the time of Domitian's reign refer to Domitian as 'Lord and God'. Moreover, Statius, a poet commissioned by Domitian, writes that when Domitian was acclaimed *dominus* at a Saturnalia, 'this liberty alone did Caesar forbid them' (*Silvae* 1.6.84). In his biography of Domitian, Jones (1992: 109) concludes that from the evidence available Domitian 'obviously knew that he was not a God, but whilst he did not ask or demand to be addressed as one, he did not actively discourage the few flatterers who did'.

14. Even Suetonius (although he is writing about the first part of Domitian's reign), comments that Domitian 'checked false accusations designed for the profit of the privy purse and inflicted severe penalties on offenders; and a saying of his was current that an emperor who does not punish informers hounds them on' (*Lives of the Caesars: Domitian* 9.3).

15. Thompson argues that 'a retrospective presentation of Domitian and his reign serves as a foil in the present praise of Trajan... The opposing of Trajan and Domitian in a binary set serves overtly in Trajan's ideology of a new age as well as covertly in his praise' (1990: 115). As Pliny recognizes, 'eulogy is best expressed through comparison, and, moreover, the first duty of grateful subjects towards a perfect emperor is to attack those who are least like him: for no-one can properly appreciate a good prince who does not sufficiently hate a bad one' (*Panegyricus* 53).

those of John. In 1 Corinthians 8–10, Paul allows the eating of such meat at private functions, and only objects to participation on public occasions if there is a fellow Christian present whose conscience might be troubled. In contrast, John rejects any Christian participation in professional and civic life. It seems that Paul, the 'strong' at Corinth and the Nicolaitans, who may all have been of a social class for whom participation in public meals was important, share a similar attitude to public life, which was very different to John's.

Although there is evidence that Christians could be treated with suspicion at a local level, there is little evidence of a widespread attack on them during this period. From Pliny's letter to Trajan (*Letters* 10.96-97), it seems that Christians were not sought out by the Romans, although when locals brought those suspected of being believers to Pliny, he dealt with those who would not recant by executing them.[16] Local difficulties may have arisen because of Christians' refusal to recognize the divine object of any worship other than Christ: they rejected all forms of sacrifice on the grounds that Christ was the one final sacrifice. Thompson suggests that sacrifice to the emperor often took place at local shrines, and that the sacrifice to local gods on behalf of the emperor was part of the social life of a town. Christians would have met with hostility for refusing to participate in these local events. Nevertheless, the evidence of 1 Pet. 2.12 ('Maintain good conduct among the Gentiles, so that in case they speak against you as wrongdoers, they may see your good deeds and glorify God on the day of visitation') and 1 Tim. 2.1-2 suggests that overt conflict between Christians and their neighbours was rare. In view of this, Revelation should be regarded as a minority report on the relationship between Christians and the Roman Empire.

Thompson concludes that Revelation urges its readers to see conflict in their urban setting where there was very little, and to think of the

16. Pliny writes that 'the method I have observed towards those who have been denounced to me as Christians is this: I interrogated them whether they were Christians; if they confessed it I repeated the question twice again adding the threat of capital punishment; if they still persevered, I ordered them to be executed... Those who denied they were, or had ever been Christians, who repeated after me an invocation to the Gods, and offered adoration with wine and frankincense to your image, which I had ordered to be brought for that purpose, together with those of the Gods, and who finally cursed Christ—none of which acts it is said those who are really Christian can be forced into performing—these I thought proper to discharge' (*Letters* 10.96.5-6).

Roman Empire as the enemy, without great justification. In the text of
Revelation, there is an expectation of tribulation from the outside world
in the near future (e.g. Rev. 2.10-11) and a description of visions which
refer to the judgment to befall the political and social institutions of the
Roman Empire (4.1–22.5), but little reference to present social stress.
The conflict between the Christian community and the social order in
Revelation belongs in John's perspective, not in social reality. In this
way, Revelation fits the genre to which it belongs. Like other apocalypses, it offers a constructed reality in which readers may see their situation as one in need of the comfort and hope it provides.

John's Revelation proclaims divinely-revealed information in opposition to the accepted public discourse. His style of writing in peculiar
Greek protests against the higher forces of Greek culture.[17] The fluidity
of his language endangers public order by blurring the categories
essential to stability. Thompson suggests that only the image of a
stream, rather than sets of oppositions with victorious hope on one side
and despairing oppression on the other, begins to capture the linguistic
unity of Revelation: 'the seer's language flows into and out of images,
figures, reiterations, recursions, contracts, and accumulations as whorls,
vortices, and eddies in a stream' (1990: 52). His playful puns, riddles
and jokes[18] manipulate reality: that which appears publicly contrasts
with what really is. Those who appear wealthy are really the poor;[19] the
glories of the Roman Empire are masks for satanic forces about to be
defeated. In the language of private dream rather than public discourse,
the Roman order is labelled as demonic by the anonymous casting of it
as mythic beasts, such as the devouring dragon in ch. 12. Thompson
comments that '[t]he language of the Seer subverts and offers an alternative order' (1990: 184). For Thompson, this subverted order is a
stable and consistent vision of the world, in which the deep structures

17. Bousset (1906: 159 cited in Kümmel 1975: 465) comments that 'throughout
the entire book are found grammatical and stylistic difficulties of a special kind and
in such quantity as is evident only in Revelation: mainly, grammatical incongruities
which lend to the linguistic character of Revelation its particular mould'. He offers
Rev. 1.5-6 (τῷ ἀγαπῶντι...καὶ ἐποίησεν...αὐτῷ ἡ δόξα) as an example of such
an irregular construction.

18. For example, the speaker tells the Ephesians that 'I know your works...how
you cannot bear [βαστάσαι] evil men...[and are] bearing up [ἐβάστασας] for my
name's sake' (2.2-3).

19. The believers at Smyrna are poor but rich (2.9), whereas the Laodiceans are
rich but poor (3.17).

of binary oppositions and boundaries are clearly established. In this world, insiders are distinguished from outsiders, and true knowledge from deceptive lies. In opposition to the deceptions of public knowledge, the divinely-revealed world given to John is the only path to true knowledge.

Thompson's work has been criticized by other Revelation scholars for taking a position that is too extreme. For example, Collins (1991: 749) comments that the portrayal of Domitian by Pliny and Suetonius may have been a caricature, in order to highlight Trajan's qualities, but it is unlikely to have had no basis in fact. The subject of caricatures must be recognizable for the satirical depiction to work. Moreover, Collins argues, although there was no sustained attack on Christians at the time that Revelation was written, Christians had good reason to view the Roman Empire with antagonism, as the future was to prove. Thompson may indeed have overstated his case, as Collins has argued, but he has highlighted the dissonance between contemporary writing about Domitian, and the view of his reign and character offered by later writers such as Pliny, who had much to gain from the new emperor, Trajan, and whose opinions have generally been accepted without question by modern scholars. However, in his biography of Domitian, the classical scholar Jones supports the picture of Domitian's reign painted by Thompson. Jones (1992: 117) argues that 'no convincing evidence exists for a Domitianic persecution of the Christians'. He notes that 'no pagan writer accused Domitian of persecuting Christians', and that the legend of such persecution developed long after Domitian's death (p. 114).[20] For Jones (p. 198), Domitian's character

---

20. Jones (1992: 115-16) notes that the first precise reference to Domitian attacking the church comes from Eusebius's citation of comments by Melito, Bishop of Sardis in around 170 CE, to the effect that Nero and Domitian were persuaded by evil advisors to slander Christian teaching (*Hist. Eccles.* 4.26). At the end of the second century Eusebius quotes Tertullian as claiming that Domitian 'almost equalled Nero in cruelty; but—I suppose because he had some commonsense—he very soon stopped, even recalling those he had banished' (*Hist. Eccles.* 3.20). Eusebius's own account is very different from this comparatively mild picture: Jones argues that this is evidence of an ongoing blackening of the situation really faced by Christians under Domitian, culminating in the work of Cardinal Caesar Baronius, written between 1588 and 1607, in which the death of Flavius Clemens (hailed by Syncellus in the eighth century as a Christian, without any contemporary evidence), is linked to a general persecution of the church and Domitian is accused not only of exiling John to Patmos but also of killing Cletus, the second bishop of Rome.

'remains an enigma' because, as Thompson has argued, 'assessing Domitian's character and that of his reign is bedevilled by two separate factors, the bias of the literary sources[21] and the judgmental standards adopted by the aristocracy' (Jones 1992: 196). Furthermore, Thompson has avoided the pitfall of reading the later history of the Church into the text and context of Revelation: John and his readers could not have predicted the persecution that was to follow. The evidence of earlier texts such as Rom. 13.7 and 1 Tim. 2.2-3 paints a very different picture of the lives of Christians under the Roman Empire from that offered in Revelation. Thompson's book may not be so extreme after all.

Certainly Thompson's reading of Revelation shares similarities with Lumsden's interpretation of Hogg's *Confessions*. Thompson makes the following telling comment:

> the book of Revelation has been a literary vehicle for providing a 'cognitive distance' from the public, social order and thereby providing space for critiques of the public order, for creating a satisfying dissonance in human activity (a bulwark against boredom) between public and revealed knowledge (1990: 197).

Revelation, like the *Confessions*, offers a critique of its society by operating at society's margins and subverting society's claims to certainty. In the *Confessions*, the fixed systems of antinomianism and of Enlightenment empiricism are presented and then shown to be inadequate ways to interpret the complexities of reality. Its own indeterminacies and resistance to closure has provoked many attempts to define its meaning, but, as Lumsden argues, the *Confessions* is best understood when these features are accepted rather than explained away. The novel reflects life and human relationships that are ambiguous and complex: each situation encountered needs to be assessed separately and on the basis of past experience, rather than by applying an unchanging rule. Revelation, as interpreted by Thompson, offers a similarly ex-centric view of its society, both in terms of the state and of the community of the church. Revelation subverts society's and the church's claims to possess the truth, and offers a different way to interpret reality. To do this, it creates an alternative world in which the language and symbols

---

21. Jones (1992: 196) offers the work of Martial as an example of this bias: writing under Domitian, Martial praises the new palace as surpassing the pyramids (*Epigrams* 8.36.1), but once Domitian has died, he dismisses the palace as the 'whims and oppressive luxuries of a haughty monarch' (*Epigrams* 12.15.4-5).

of society and the faith are used and reused in deceptive and beguiling ways. The text forces the reader to see that things are not as they seem. The discourses of society and the church are inadequate to describe the present situation. In Chapter 5 it will be considered whether or not Thompson's view about the stability of the alternative world offered is sustainable. Here, his book about Revelation's critique of the church's language and construction of reality will be assessed. How ex-centric is Revelation's reading of the Hebrew Bible, and what are the implications of these readings? In the following section, a comparison will be made between the readings of Revelation and those of another crucially marginalized group, the Qumran Community.

Readings of Ezekiel 37 in Revelation 11 and 4Q385.2

והנבאתי כאשר צוני ותבוא בהם הרוח ויחיו ויעמדו
על־רגליהם חיל גדול מאד־מאד

So I prophesied as he commanded me, and the breath came into them, and they stood upon their feet, an exceedingly great host (Ezek. 37.10).

ויאמר שוב אנבא על ארבע רוחות השמים ויפחו רוחותע
השמים בהם ויחיוע ויעמד עם רב אנשים ויברכו את יהוה
צבאות אש]ר חים[

And he said again: 'Prophesy concerning the four winds of heaven and let the win[ds of heaven] blow [upon them and they shall revive,] and a great crowd of people shall stand up, and they shall bless Yahweh Sabaoth wh[o has given them life again.'] 4Q385.2.7-8[22]

καὶ μετὰ τὰς τρεῖς ἡμέρας καὶ ἥμισυ πνεῦμα ζωῆς ἐκ τοῦ θεοῦ εἰσῆλθεν ἐν αὐτοῖς, καὶ ἔστησαν ἐπὶ τοὺς πόδας αὐτῶν, καὶ φόβος μέγας ἐπέπεσεν ἐπὶ τοὺς θεωροῦντας αὐτούς.

But after the three and a half days a breath of life from God entered them (the two witnesses), and they stood upon their feet, and great fear fell on those who saw them (Rev. 11.11).

Ezekiel 37, the Qumran text 4Q385 fragment 2 of what is commonly called 'Second Ezekiel' (see Appendix 2 for a reconstruction and translation of this text) and Revelation 11 are all linked. All share the text of Gen. 2.7; and 4Q385 and Revelation may be taken as readings of

---

22. Trans. Strugnell and Dimant (1988: 49). All references to 4Q 385.2 are taken from this translation.

the Ezekiel text. The intertextual relationship is signalled by the reference in each text to the revitalizing power of breath or spirit. The Qumran text and Revelation 11 belong on different rungs of the rhetorical hierarchy of allusive modes: 4Q385 is a curious blend of quotation of and allusion to Ezekiel 37, whereas Revelation 11 echoes rather than alludes to the scriptural text. However, in both, a relationship with the past and a message for the future are implied in the reconfiguration of the earlier text. In both, the earlier text is absorbed and transformed in a process of rejection and preservation of the past. Before considering the two readings of Ezekiel in detail and assessing the level of their ex-centricity, Ezekiel's context will be discussed briefly, and the contents and setting of the Qumran text will be considered in greater detail.

The actual setting of the book of Ezekiel has been debated by modern scholars, but is not important to the present discussion. In this chapter I follow the majority view that the book of Ezekiel embodies a response to the events of the beginning of the sixth century BCE. The text of Ezekiel places itself in exile in Babylon, at a crisis point of the nation of Israel. Judah's sister kingdom, Northern Israel, had faced a similar experience a century and a half earlier, and had not survived. Ezekiel seeks answers to questions about the survival of the nation and the existence of the presence of God among the exiled people. The question is voiced in 9.8:

אהה אדני יהוה המשחית אתה את כל־שארית ישראל
בשפכך את־חמתך על־ירושלם

> Ah Lord God! Wilt thou destroy all that remains of Israel in the outpouring of thy wrath upon Jerusalem?

In answer, the text begins with an extravagant assertion that visions of God are possible even in exile (chs. 1–2), and ends with the fantastic promise of the detailed restoration of the temple (chs. 40–48). The role of Ezekiel the prophet (3.4) and priest (1.3) is to help his fellow Israelites to face up to their situation, with a message of judgment on Judah and Jerusalem in chs. 3–24, and then to encourage them to look beyond it, beginning with oracles against foreign nations in chs. 25–32. Even after the second fall of Jerusalem the tone of the latter part of the book is optimistic. The dominant theme of chs. 33–48 is hope in the promise of the restoration of the people to their land. Chapter 37, the vision of the valley of dry bones, is an example of this optimistic hope.

Several copies of the biblical text of Ezekiel have been found in the caves at Qumran.[23] However, six copies of parts of a text that has come to be known as Second Ezekiel have also been found in the Qumran caves: 4Q385 to 390.[24] Most extensively preserved is 4Q385, which is written in a late Hasmonaean or early Herodian hand and contains 48 mostly very short fragments. Three of these fragments are preserved to the width of one whole column, and it is one of these (Fragment 2) which is a version of Ezekiel 37. The same text is found in even more fragmentary forms in 4Q386 1.1 and 4Q388.8. The other particularly significant and well-preserved fragment (Fragment 4) is a retelling of the Merkabah vision in Ezekiel 1.

Strugnell and Dimant (1988 and 1990) were the first commentators to publish and discuss these manuscripts, although since then, 4Q385.2 has provoked only limited scholarly discussion. Eisenman and Wise (1992: 59-64) have published the text with a brief commentary, and it also appears in the translations of García Martínez (1994: 286-87) and of Vermes (1995: 327-28). Brooke (1992: 317-37) offers a brief discussion of the text and the views of its commentators. More detailed work on the text, and some re-evaluations of initial interpretations are to be found in Dimant (1992b: 405-448), and Kister and Qimron (1992: 595-602). Bauckham (1991: 437-46) has suggested the presence of a quotation from 4Q385.2 in the Apocalypse of Peter: the opening command to prophesy and the phrase 'bone to/with bone' are common to both the Apocalypse of Pet. 4.7-8 and 4Q385.2.5.

In their 1988 article Strugnell and Dimant establish the general features of the preserved fragments (pp. 47-48). Second Ezekiel is written

---

23. Copies of the Masoretic Text of Ezekiel found at Qumran are: 1QEzek, 3QEzek, 4QEzek[a,b,c], 11QEzek.

24. Strugnell and Dimant (1988: 46) suggested that at least five copies of this work had been found at Qumran, namely 4Q385-390. However, in her contribution to the 1991 Madrid Qumran Conference, Dimant (1992b: 409) reconsiders the original classification of all of these manuscripts as copies of Second Ezekiel. Maintaining that there are five copies of the text, she nevertheless suggests that only fragments 1, 2, 3, 4, 5, 6 + 24,12 of 4Q385; 4Q386; fragments 5, 7, 8 of 4Q387; fragment 8 and possibly fragments 5 and 7 of 4Q388; and (perhaps) most of the fragments of 4Q391 should be assigned to Second Ezekiel. Other fragments from 4Q385-389 belong to two distinct literary units, which she designates as Pseudo-Moses and Apocryphon of Jeremiah.

Brooke (1992: 322) considers 'there may only be three, or possibly, four copies of this work', and comments on the difficulty of assigning fragments to particular texts (p. 321).

pseudepigraphically by the prophet Ezekiel himself, and takes the form of divine discourses. God is the main speaker in dialogues with an individual identified explicitly in several passages as Ezekiel (as for example in 4Q385.3.4, 24.1). Some of the fragments preserve dialogues in which Ezekiel asks questions about what he has been told or shown. In 4Q385.2 the answer is given in a dialogue about the meaning of the vision of the dry bones. Strugnell and Dimant (1988: 46) speculate that the number of manuscripts of Second Ezekiel found at Qumran indicates that the text was much read, and perhaps copied there. As the text contains expressions and ideas similar to those found in the sectarian literature (such as קרי̇א̇י שם, 'summoned there', 4Q385.42 and 14.3), it may be that the work belongs to the corpus of the sect's own compositions. However, Strugnell and Dimant also note that the form and style of the text is different from the other sectarian writings, and that the text contains several locutions not found elsewhere. In subject matter, style and vocabulary the fragments are a combination both of the prophecies of the biblical Ezekiel, and of the historical apocalypses such as Daniel, *4 Ezra* and *2 Baruch*, which combine prophecy and admonition. Where the text follows the biblical account, it does so with striking adherence to the Masoretic Text of Ezekiel. In biblical sections such as 4Q385.2.5-8, the editor's hand is evident primarily in the omissions he makes, which will be discussed in detail below. In the explanatory or dialogue sections of the text, such as 4Q385.2.2-4 and 9-10, the language, style and content is closer to that of contemporary Jewish apocalypses such as *4 Ezra* and *2 Baruch*.[25] The vision of the dry bones, for example, is interpreted as predicting historical or eschatological events in the symbolic way in which similar visions are interpreted in these apocalyptic writings. The dominant themes in these texts, as in 4QSecond Ezekiel, are the history of Israel, the problem of retribution and recompense, and the question of the resurrection.

To sum up this introduction to the text of Second Ezekiel, it would be fair to say that the text was important to members of the Qumran community, and may have been written by them. The text combines close adherence in places to the biblical Ezekiel with new elements that are more familiar in contemporary apocalyptic writings. The sectarian and the traditional exist side by side. It is at least plausible that the text arose in the kind of community which produced the Community Rule,

25. For further discussion about the similarities between Second Ezekiel and *4 Ezra* and *2 Bar.*, see Strugnell and Dimant (1988: 56-57).

the Temple Scroll and the Habakkuk Pesher: a community that saw itself as continuing a life of pure devotion and service to God in the face of opposition from outsiders, and as possessing special insight into the meaning of Scripture as it applied to the imminent future. In other words, Second Ezekiel may have arisen out of this thoroughly marginalized context. The purpose of the community was to:

> be converted from all evil...to separate themselves from the congrega-
> tion of perverse men...under the authority of the sons of Zadok, the
> priests who keep the covenant, and under the authority of the majority of
> the members of the community (1QS 5 [trans. Collins 1992: 87]).

The Teacher of Righteousness was the one 'to whom God made known all the mysteries of the words of his servants the prophets' (1QpHab. 7 4-5, trans. Horgan 1979: 16). Much of this interpretative gift involved reading out of the biblical texts the life and downfall of the Wicked Priest who pursued the Community, and the Community's reward for its faithfulness:

> 8. ON ACCOUNT OF HUMAN BLOODSHED AND VIOLENCE DONE
>   TO THE LAND, THE CITY AND ALL ITS INHABITANTS.
> 9. The interpretation of it concerns the [W]icked Priest, whom—because of
>   wrong done to the Teacher of
> 10. Righteousness and his partisans—God gave into the hands of his
>   enemies to humble him
> 11. with disease for annihilation in despair, beca[u]se he had acted
> 12. wickedly against his chosen ones.
>
> (1QpHab. 9.8-12)
>
> 17. [THE RIGHTEOUS MAN WILL LIVE BY HIS FAITHFULNESS.]
> 1. The interpretation of it concerns all those who observe the Law in the
>   House of Judah, whom
> 2. God will save from the house of judgment on account of their tribulation
>   and their fidelity
> 3. to the Teacher of Righteousness.
>
> (1QpHab. 7.17–8.3, trans. Horgan 1979: 18, 17)

In 4Q385.2 neither the Teacher of Righteousness nor the Wicked Priest is mentioned, but the righteous indignation of a group believing themselves to be right despite appearances to the contrary and awaiting vindication by God is evident in the almost petulant:

> [And I said: 'Yahweh,] I have seen many men from Israel who have
> loved Thy name and have walked in the ways of [righteousness; and
> th]ese things, when will they be, and how will they be recompensed for
> their loyalty?' (4Q385.2.2-3).

This rewriting of the biblical Ezekiel sits squarely within the ex-centric experience of the Qumran Community itself.

The members of the Qumran Community had chosen a life on the margins of their society, in response to, as they saw it, the hopeless corruption of the temple and its priesthood. They had faced persecution, and were sustained by the hope that those in power would be punished and they would receive the reward they deserved. Following Thompson's (1990) assessment of the context in which Revelation was written, John attempts to instil a similar self-understanding among his readers. His aim is to enable his readers to see that things are not as they seem: the Roman Empire masks the work of the devil and will soon be judged; following Christ demands no compromise with the State, and will lead to persecution; reward for the suffering of the faithful will come in the imminent future. The Qumran Community apparently had this self-understanding. From a comparison of the two texts, 4Q385.2 and Revelation 11, what strategies did each employ either to reinforce or create this self-understanding in their readers?

Second Ezekiel is written pseudepigraphically by the prophet Ezekiel himself. The fragmentary state of the manuscripts makes it difficult to establish the sequence and structure of the work, but Fragment 2 of 4Q385 is well enough preserved to offer an indication of its own internal structure and thematic development. The passage divides into four units, marked by the spaces left by the scribe at the end of lines 1 and 4 and at the beginning of line 9. The first unit (1.1) is the end of a divine discourse in which God refers to 'my people' (עמי) and asserts that he redeems them and will give them the covenant. In the second unit (ll. 2-4), Ezekiel questions the specific meaning of the vision of dry bones he was presumably shown in the previous column. His question indicates that the vision refers to a future situation that has been revealed to him. God answers briefly with a word of assurance that Israel will be given the knowledge that Ezekiel himself now has. In lines 5-8, following and condensing the biblical text, the prophet is told to prophesy over the bones, and his prophecy takes place. In the final unit of the fragment (ll. 9-10), Ezekiel again asks about the timing of the future event revealed in the vision, and God begins to answer.

The immediate context of Revelation 11 is available to the reader and may be illuminating for the present study. Revelation 10.8-11 alludes to the commissioning of Ezekiel found in Ezek. 2.8–3.33: while these passages are not under discussion here, the fact that an allusion to Ezekiel is clearly found in the vicinity of ch. 11 may reinforce the likelihood that an echo of Ezekiel will be heard in that chapter. Indeed, ch. 11 opens with another scene that alludes to Ezekiel: the narrator is told to measure the temple of God, just as Ezekiel in ch. 40 participates in a measuring of the heavenly temple. A prophecy is made that 'the nations' will wage war on the 'holy city' (ἐδόθη τοῖς ἔθνεσιν, καὶ τὴν πόλιν τὴν ἁγίαν πατήσουσιν [v. 2]), and that 'two witnesses' will be given power to prophesy (καὶ δώσω τοῖς δυσὶν μάρτυσίν μου καὶ προφητεύσουσιν ἡμέρας χιλίας διακοσίας ἑξήκοντα [v.3]). While carrying out their task these witnesses are able to defend themselves and to carry out prophetically significant signs such as the closing up of the sky and the bringing of plagues upon the earth (vv. 5-6). Once their task is completed, 'the beast' ascends to kill them (τὸ θηρίον τὸ ἀναβαῖνον ἐκ τῆς ἀβύσσου [v. 7]). They lie unburied for a period of three and a half days while those they had tormented with their message rejoice (vv. 7-10). Then 'the breath of life from God' enters them, to the fearful astonishment of onlookers they arise and at the command of a heavenly voice they ascend into the sky (vv. 11-12). A tenth of the inhabitants of the city die in an ensuing earthquake, but the response of the rest is to give glory to God (καὶ ἐν ἐκείνῃ τῇ ὥρᾳ ἐγένετο σεισμὸς μέγας καὶ τὸ δέκατον τῆς πόλεως ἔπεσεν καὶ ἀπεκτάνθησαν ἐν τῷ σεισμῷ ὀνόματα ἀνθρώπων χιλιάδες ἑπτὰ καὶ οἱ λοιποὶ ἔμφοβοι ἐγένοντο καὶ ἔδωκαν δόξαν τῷ θεῷ τοῦ οὐρανοῦ. [v. 13]).

Court (1979: 82) refers to ch. 11 as an 'interlude' of independent themes within the structure of the plague sequences, heightening tension by creating a delay between the opening of the sixth and the seventh seal. The interlude consists of a flashback to the time of the fall of Jerusalem and to the witness and martyrdom of Peter and Paul in Rome. The purpose of the passage is to reassure readers facing persecution of the reality of God. According to Bauckham (1993a: 83-84), ch. 11 is the revelation in parable form of the content of the scroll in ch. 10, placed here to indicate the way in which the church's witness to the nations intervenes before the final judgment, the seventh trumpet. The section introduces in brief the major themes of the following chapters: the great city (11.8), the beast waging war against the saints (11.7) and the symbolic time period of conflict (11.1-3). For Farrer (1964: 137), 11.1-13 is an allegory about the destinies of the church and the ministry of the Gospel in the form of a story about Moses and Elijah returning to prophesy in Jerusalem. Thompson (1990: 51) argues that the story of the two witnesses depends upon the messianic vision of Zechariah 4, and that the two are prophets with the power of Moses and Elijah. However, having established these allusions to the Old Testament, John then subordinates them to the Christian proclamation. The Moses/Elijah figures become reiterations of the pattern of Jesus, who is their Lord (11.8): they are killed, brought back to life and ascend to heaven. Thompson argues that this adaptation of the Old Testament to the Christian message is a consistent feature of the writing of the Seer. The significance of the passage is debated, then, but there seems to have been little scholarly interest in the function of the echo of Ezekiel's vision of dry bones beyond noting that the language of v. 11 seems to have been drawn from Ezek. 37.10.[26]

One of the areas of difference between the readings of Revelation 11 and 4Q385.2 of Ezekiel 37 is in their understanding of the role of the prophet. In Ezekiel 37 the prophet has a role to play in the revivification of the bones: to prophesy as 'commanded' (צוני [v. 10]). Although the Lord asks and answers his own question, and tells Ezekiel what to do and say, in vv. 7 and 10 it is Ezekiel's actions that are seen to bring about the miracle. In Second Ezekiel the role of the prophet is initially expanded. In the dialogue it is the prophet who actively asks the questions about the meaning and timing of the vision (ll. 2-3, 9). However, in the central section (ll. 5-8) when the prophecy is delivered and the revivification begins it is the Lord alone who acts: commanding Ezekiel to prophesy; in line 5 telling him what to say; and in line 8 predicting the unseen outcome. The role of the prophet is hidden from the reader by the narrative, for example in ll. 5-6:

---

26. Charles (1920: 290) suggests that Rev. 11.11 looks like an independent translation of Ezek. 37.10. Beckwith (1967: 603) notes that the language of Rev. 11.11-12 follows Ezek. 37.10 closely, and suggests that the ultimate origin of the representation of the revivification of the two corpses is probably Ezekiel's vision rather than the resurrection of Jesus. According to Kiddle (1940: 202-203), Rev. 11.11 is more than a literary recollection of the Ezekiel vision: John has taken Ezekiel's prophecy literally as a promise that the followers of Christ would be martyred and then restored to their own land, which is heaven. Ford (1975: 181) argues that the Revelation text is 'obviously influenced by Ezekiel 37, especially 37.10', and suggests that Ezekiel's allegorical symbolization of the expected restoration of Israel supports his argument that the two witnesses are collective figures representing the Christian community. None of these commentators develops the function of the Ezekiel intertext any further.

[And He said:] 'Son of man, prophesy over the bones, and say: be ye joined bone to its bone and joint [to its joint'. And it wa]s so.

In this section it is the Lord who is centre-stage, and there is a strong intertextual echo from Genesis 1. Indeed, in the second of the three commands to prophesy, the jussive forms ויעלו 'let come upon' and ויקרמו 'let be covered' (1.6), and the plausibly reconstructed [ויה] כ' 'and it was so'[27] completely change the Ezekiel precursor, in which the Genesis story had been only faintly recalled. In this section, the later writer's hand is clearly to be seen. The picture metaleptically invoked is of a new creation in which no intermediary is necessary: the prophet's role is to frame the scene with questions that specify its relevance to his readers. The fulfilment of his final task of prophecy, implicit in the Lord's command, is never described. Instead, the recreation of those who 'have loved...(the Lord's)...name and have walked in the ways of [righteousness]' (ll. 2-3) is pictured as a future act of God alone comparable to the first creation. The work being done among them in this isolated community is the creative work of God: the old creation is finished, and the addressees of the text are assured that they will be participants in the new order that is to come.

The form of Revelation 11 is different from that of Second Ezekiel. The passage is a vision of a prophet in which two further witnesses to God, the μαρτύρες, are killed, and their exposed bodies are revived by God after three and a half days. The prophet recounting the vision has been commissioned by the eating of an open scroll which is sweet in the mouth but bitter in the stomach to 'prophesy about many people and nations and tongues and kings' (προφητεῦσαι ἐπὶ λαοῖς καὶ ἔθνεσιν καὶ γλώσσαις καὶ βασιλεῦσιν πολλοῖς [10.11]). Ezekiel is commissioned in the same way, but his mission is solely to 'the house of Israel' (אל-בית ישראל, Ezek. 3.1, 4) and the reader is told only that his scroll was sweet in his mouth (בפי כדבש למתוק [3.3]). In the text of Revelation the role of the prophet is reconfigured and the risks are different. In this Revelation passage, prophets are defined as the mysterious 'slain' (הרוגים) of Ezek. 37.9, and as those who hope for new life. The Ezekiel–John narrator figure in Revelation, by describing his calling,

---

27. The verbal form ויה in ll. 5 and 7 is enclosed in square brackets, indicating a reconstructed text, in both Strugnell and Dimant's, and Kister's translations. However, I note that in García Martínez's translation (1994: 236) there are no square brackets around 'And so it happened' in either line. From the manuscript evidence, the text is unclear at this point.

identifies himself with the mysterious witnesses/prophets, fears death at the hands of those to whom he prophesies, but hopes too for resurrection. His purpose in the telling of the story of the two witnesses is to create a world in which the need for encouragement, and encouragement itself, is presented to his readers. The vivid, surreal story makes his point. There is very little in the story that is not created out of ideas already formed in the Old Testament. Many commentators (e.g. Court 1979: 82-105; Beasley-Murray 1974: 176-84) have noted the use of the stories of Moses and Elijah in the description of the two witnesses: for example, in 11.7, the story of Elijah stopping the rain (1 Kgs 17.1) and of Moses turning the water of the Nile into blood (Exod. 7.17) are incorporated into John's vision. The witnesses are portrayed both as eye-witnesses of God's work in the world and as representative bearers of God's word to the people, just as John himself proclaims to his readers the vividly sensuous revelation he has received from God. Of course, Jesus was also witness and prophet, as well as martyr in the later, technical sense. The allusion to the story of Jesus in the description of the witnesses' resurrection and ascension (vv. 11, 12) offers the story of Jesus as an example for believers to hope in, and also places Jesus within the category of prophets such as Moses, Elijah, Ezekiel and John. The idea of recreation which is strong both in the Ezekiel and the Qumran text is less important here than the portrayal of a continuing and authoritative prophetic tradition stretching from the time of Moses through Ezekiel to the time of the narrator. This section of ch. 11 is the verification of John's task and calling. He has eaten the scroll, and is able to interpret God's spoken command, his Scripture and his purpose in Christ. His message is made authoritative through its invocation of the prophetic tradition, and its presentation of the death and resurrection of Christ as normative for its readers. John destabilizes the message of hope offered in Ezekiel's vision by identifying the two witnesses, the slain in Ezekiel's text, with all faithful Christians following the example of the martyr-Christ. He thus disturbs the peace of those living in comparative ease who see no need to seek martyrdom. Having demonstrated the need for encouragement, he then offers this encouragement in the resurrection scene that follows the martyrdom.

The words chosen in each text to refer to the agent that brings life to the corpses supports these readings. In Ezekiel 37 רוח is used throughout, and is translated by the RSV as 'breath' in vv. 5 and 8-10 when referring to the life-giving agent, as 'winds' in v. 9 when referring to the place from which the 'breath' is to come, and as 'my Spirit' in v. 14 to describe the gift God promises to give to Israel in order that they might live. In the LXX πνεῦμα, commonly translated 'spirit', consistently replaces רוה in this chapter. The only variation occurs in 37.5 where the prophecy of a πνεῦμα ζωῆς is made over the bones: in the Hebrew two phrases are used for the same idea, מביא בכם רוח וחייתם 'I will cause breath to go into you, and you will live'. In Second Ezekiel it is the ארבע רוחות השמים, the four winds of heaven, which, it is promised, will revive the corpses. In Rev. 11.11, as in the LXX version of Ezek. 37.5, it is a πνεῦμα ζωῆς which comes from God into the two witnesses. In what might be called the precursor text of them all, Gen. 2.7, the 'breath of life' which enters Adam is in Hebrew נשמת חיים and in Greek πνοὴν ζωῆς. Although the word translated in English as 'breath' in this verse is different in both the Hebrew and the Greek from the words used in Ezekiel, Second Ezekiel and Revelation, it is still plausible to suggest an intertextual relationship between Genesis and these later texts. The mundane and narrow idea of breath which makes Adam live, distinguishing him from a corpse, is widened and deepened by the transformation of נשמת into the elusive and almost magical רוח, and of πνοή into πνεῦμα (although BAGD notes that πνοή can mean either 'wind' or 'breath', and that in the Papyri Graecae Magicae 12, 331 and 333 it 'passes over to the meaning πνεῦμα': however, πνεῦμα retains its widely known polyvalence, whereas the distribution of πνοή remains more limited). Both רוח and πνεῦμα are elastic, highly charged words.[28] Only πνεῦμα is an adequately supple translation of the polyvalent רוח. Both words share both the natural, physical idea of life-giving breath, and the spiritual, divinely ordained aspect of revivification that the context of the stories demands. The use of רוח in the text of

28. According to Koehler and Baumgartner (1990: 1117-21), among the meanings of רוח are breath (Isa. 42.5); air for breathing (Jer. 14.6); breath in the sense of that which is transitory or empty ('flüchtiger Hauch' [p. 1118]) (Jer. 5.13); wind (Ps. 1.4); the natural life-bearing spirit of humanity ('Lebensträger' [p. 1118]) (Zech. 12.1) or its disposition or mood ('Gesinnung/ Mut' [p. 1119]) (Deut. 2.30, 1 Kgs 21.5); that which is not flesh (the opposite of בשר) (Isa. 31.3); or specifically the spirit of God (1 Sam. 10.6) or his holy spirit (Isa. 63.10). According to Bauer (1979: 674-78), πνεῦμα can mean, amongst other things, physical breath (2 Thess. 2.8) or wind (Jn 3.8a); the spirit or soul that gives life to the body (Lk. 8.55); or, in contrast to the 'flesh', the immaterial part of a personality (2 Cor. 7.1); God himself (Jn 4.24a); the spirit of God (1 Cor. 2.11b) or of Christ (Acts 16.7) in the sense of the active bearer of divine will; or, more specifically, the Holy Spirit (Mt. 12.32).

Ezekiel 37 and πνεῦμα in Revelation 11 add a new dimension or 'surplus' meaning to the Genesis text (2.7) in which Adam is brought to life. This new dimension is an emphasis on the ideas both of God's role in creation, and of the prophet's commissioned task as the proclaimer of God's word. It is the רוח אלהים (LXX πνεῦμα θεοῦ) which was 'moving over the face of the waters' (Gen. 1.2) in preparation for the creation of the world. The same phrases are used in 1 Sam. 10.10 to describe the power that enables Samuel to prophesy. In 2 Kgs 2.9 it is a double share of Elijah's רוח which Elisha asks to inherit; and after Elijah is taken up into heaven and Elisha puts on his mantle, the sons of the prophets at Jericho come to honour him saying 'The spirit (רוח) of Elijah rests on Elisha' (2 Kgs 2.15). The significance of the use of רוח/ πνεῦμα in Ezekiel/Revelation lies in the reference each includes to the creative power of God and to the ongoing prophetic tradition,[29] which the more straightforward נשמה and πνοή lack.

The discussion of the two dominant ideas of recreation and prophetic tradition may be continued in a reading of the echo of 'standing up' (עמד/ ἵστημι) which occurs in Ezekiel 37, Second Ezekiel 4Q385.2 and Revelation 11. The sharing of the phrase also focuses attention on the reconfiguration in Second Ezekiel and Revelation of ambiguities in Ezekiel about who the 'slain' were and what happened to them after they were brought to life. In Ezekiel itself, a specific, explanatory interpretation of the vision is offered (37.11-14), which grounds the vision in the life of its implied readers. The picture of the bodies standing up is interpreted as the exiles being rescued from the place of their captivity and being brought to their own land. The place of the dry bones is read as the 'grave' of the exiles in the sense of their existence away from their homeland. The 'standing up' image is re-read in terms of God giving the exiles a new, Spirit-filled life in their own land. Most commentators (for example, Zimmerli 1983: 263; Eichrodt 1970: 509; and Wevers 1969: 367) agree that it is not literal, physical resurrection from the dead which is implied in this section, but political reinstatement. However, the use of terms such as being raised from graves (vv. 12, 13), having God's Spirit put in one and being promised life (v. 14) leave the meaning at least ambiguous. In Revelation the ambiguity is resolved, and physical resurrection is the offered meaning, following

29. In their definition of רוח as 'heiliger Geist', Koehler and Baumgartner note that it is 'a) Kraft der prophetischen Inspiration und b) Kraft der Belebung, Lebensgeist/ Lebenshauch' (1990: 1120).

the example of Christ. I suggest that the same meaning is to be found in Second Ezekiel in its reconfiguration of the allusion to Ezekiel's 'standing up' corpses.

In 4Q385.2 the promised revivification of the corpses is said but not shown to have been fulfilled in the description of the vision. The phrase that signals the occurrence of events such as the covering with skin, 'And it was so' (l.5), is absent in l.8. If it is correct that, as has been suggested above, the bones in the vision are metaphorically understood to be those of faithful Israelites for whom a recompense is sought, the idea of physical resurrection makes most sense in the context. The resurrection is something to be hoped for in the future, and is therefore plausibly promised but not shown as the culmination of the vision. The reaction of the 'great crowd', which is not given in Ezekiel, will be to bless Yahweh Sabaoth for giving them life again (l.8): an acceptable response from those who have been raised from the dead. Indeed, Kister and Qimron (1992: 597) cite a parallel description to be found in the *b. Sanh.* 92b: 'The dead resurrected by Ezekiel stood on their feet and sang [in honour of God] and died.' Ezekiel's question in the final unit ('O Yahweh, when shall these things be?', l.9) suggests a belief in the vision as something that is actually going to happen, rather than as a parable offering a nebulous hope for the future. The story is a call and a warning for its readers to 'see' and to 'know' (l.4) that it is the true followers of righteousness who are promised the reward of life after death. This concept of resurrection is not totally without precedent in the Qumran texts: in the so-called resurrection fragment, 4Q521, Isa. 61.1 is alluded to and a reference to resurrection added in column 2, l. 12: 'He will heal the wounded and revive the dead (ומתים יחיה) and bring good news to the poor.'[30] There is nothing definitely sectarian in this fragment, so it does not offer conclusive evidence for the Community's own view of life after death. As with the Second Ezekiel text, the most we can say with certainty is that a text seeming to refer to resurrection is found in the Qumran library. In both cases, a biblical text promising hope in the future to the people has been reconfigured to involve a reference to the resurrection of individuals. The ambiguities and hints have been resolved into a picture that offers most hope to those who have made the choice to separate themselves from society and whose self-understanding involves a belief in their own righteous-

30. Translated in Vermes (1992: 303), and also in Vermes (1995: 244-45). Puech discusses this text in detail (1992: 475-519).

ness. Their prospects of reward on earth are slim, but this is compensated for by a belief in heavenly glory. A vision of national salvation is domesticated and diminished into a promise of individual salvation for the marginalized few.

In Revelation 11 the scarce details about the corpses given in Ezekiel are echoed in a self-contained story. The two witnesses are both the subject of the prophecy itself and, within the structure of the story, bearers of God's word. Picking up details that are left unexplained in Ezekiel, they are indeed 'slain' (Ezek. 37.9 and Rev. 11.7), the place where they lie dead is specified in Rev. 11.8 as 'the great city which is spiritually called Sodom and Egypt' (ἥτις καλεῖται πνευματικῶς Σόδομα καὶ Αἴγυπτος) (compare the 'plain' הבקעה of Ezek. 37.1: both are places of spiritual wasteland), and the reason why the corpses are left unburied is explained in terms of the cruelty and relief of those the witnesses had 'tormented' with their prophecies (vv. 9-10). Unstated but obvious references to the parallel story of Christ's resurrection and ascension (in addition to the echoes of Ezekiel) serve as the prophetic voice that brings about the witnesses' own resurrection and ascension. Their prophetic role is shown to continue even beyond their death and ascension: echoing the crucifixion picture in Mt. 27.54, an earthquake occurs and brings about the conversion of the survivors (v. 13). The narrator of Revelation identifies himself both with the prophet Ezekiel as the teller of his recreated story, and, as a fellow-prophet, with the two witnesses and with Christ whose life, proclamation, death and promised resurrection are all part of their prophetic calling and function. Despite appearances, and his self-deprecating claims, John presents himself as the representative of the Christ, in the prophetic tradition of Ezekiel, and offers himself as martyr to his cause. Ezekiel's visionary detachment is lost: John's self-importance as prophet bleeds into the text.

An incidental aspect of the proposed reading of a creation theme in 4Q385.2 is the enlightenment it brings to the meaning of 1.10 of the fragment.[31] Several commentators, including Kister (1990), Philonenko (1993–94) and Puech (1994), have puzzled over the meaning of this line without coming to agreement. I suggest that the creation motif offers a new way to read and understand this enigmatic line.

---

31. A version of the following section of the book appears in the Autumn 1996 edition of the *Journal of Jewish Studies*, and is used here with the editors' permission.

Line 10 of *4Q385* 2 reads:

[   ] ﬠﬧﬢﬨ ﬠﬗ ﬡﬗגּ[ﬢ]ﬠ[   ]

...and a tree shall bend and shall stand erect...

(following Strugnell and Dimant's vocalisation of the two verbs: since both verbs seem to refer to the tree, it makes sense to vocalise ﬠﬗ[ﬢ] in the qal and ﬨגּﬢﬗﬢﬢ in the niph'al [1988: 54])

The statement is the Lord's answer to the prophet's question: 'When shall these (things?) be?.' 'These (things)' presumably refer to the fulfilment of the vision of resurrection which in turn is the Lord's answer to the prophet's question about the reward of the righteous. The Lord's answer refers to an eschatological sign involving a tree (or trees: ﬠﬗ has both a singular and a collective meaning) bending and then standing upright. Strugnell and Dimant (1988: 54) go no further than commenting that the meaning of this line is 'mysterious'. Dimant concludes that 'the reference to a tree which will bend down and straighten itself up remains enigmatic' (1992a: 18).

This particular eschatological sign has no obvious precedent in the literature of the period. Kister's aim is to clarify the meaning of the apparent parallel in *Barn.* 12.1, which reads:

Similarly, again, He [the Lord?] describes the Cross in another prophet, who says: 'And when shall all these things be accomplished?' The Lord says: 'When a tree shall bend and stand upright (ὅταν ξύλον κλιθῇ καὶ ἀναστῇ), and when blood shall flow from a tree' (trans. Kister 1990: 64).

Kister notes previous attempts to interpret this verse either, in a Jewish context, as a reference to a miraculous sign of the end of time, the rising up of trees which have fallen (1990: 65 n. 7), or, in a Christian context, as a reference to the cross and resurrection of Jesus (1990: 65 n. 8). However, the discovery of the fragment from Second Ezekiel proves the non-Christian origin of the prophecy quoted in the *Epistle of Barnabas*, and eliminates some of the interpretations of the Greek text previously suggested. Kister admits, however, that 4Q385.2 'does not offer an easy solution to the riddle of the original meaning of this phrase' (1990: 66). In a footnote, he comments that the image of a tree bending and rising up must refer to a miraculous sign that the eschatological age was about to begin, but 'it is difficult to tell what this sign was, and why it was chosen' (p. 66 n. 10). The aim of Kister's article is to suggest the origin of this sign in the *Epistle of Barnabas*, rather than to interpret its meaning in its original context. In a later article, Kister and Qimron (1992) suggest that a clue to the meaning of the phrase may be found in Suetonius's *Life of Vespasian* 5. In this text, a cypress tree is described as having been inexplicably torn up by its roots and thrown down, only to have risen again the next day stronger and more luxuriant. This is interpreted as an omen for Vespasian's future rule. Kister and Qimron note the possibility that a similar omen was chosen as a sign that God's rule was about to begin, and suggest that 'our text used a wide-spread omen putting it within the framework of Jewish eschatology' (1992: 602). However, they offer no evidence to support their argument that this sign was 'wide-spread'. Indeed, there are far more likely and meaningful allusions to trees to be found in the Hebrew Bible, as Philonenko suggests. He argues that the tree in this fragment represents the tree of life, and further that '[p]our le Pseudo-Ézéchiel l'arbre de vie est le symbole de la résurrection' ('[f]or Pseudo-Ezekiel, the tree of life is a symbol of the resurrection'; 1993–94: 482). He asserts that the themes of resurrection from the dead and the tree of life were traditionally associated, as in *4 Macc.* 18.16-17, and argues that the writer at Qumran gave a new interpretation to the symbol of tree of life, adding the idea of it bending and rising, by relating it to the vision of the dry bones coming back to life. The collocation of the two verbs in the so-called 'Resurrection Fragment' 4Q521, in the form of a meditation on Ps. 146.8, attests that the metaphor of bending and rising could be understood as a prophecy of resurrection.

Responding to Philonenko, Puech (1994) rejects any interpretation of the tree in Second Ezekiel as either the tree of life or a symbol of resurrection. Puech argues that Philonenko's conclusions go beyond the textual evidence: the reference in *4 Macc.* is not necessarily to the future or to *the* tree of life; there is no necessary relationship between resurrection and the verbs of bending and rising in 4Q521; and, most importantly, Philonenko offers no evidence of a symbolic tree of life bending and rising up. Puech asserts that ll. 9 and 10 of the fragment answer the question about *when* the righteous will be rewarded, and suggests that interpreting the tree as a symbol of the tree of life only answers the question about *how* this will happen. Puech argues that the tree refers to the eschatological picture of the kingdom of God given in Ezek. 17.22-24, rather than to the creation story in Genesis 2. The righteous will be rewarded when, after their humiliation, they inherit the earth in the messianic epoch.

There is no reference to a tree bending and standing up as an eschatological sign in Ezekiel, but there is no doubt that 4Q385.2 is a rewriting of the dry bones episode in Ezekiel 37. It was argued in the above section on the role of the prophet that the echo of the creation story in Genesis 1 is strong in this Second Ezekiel text. Indeed, the emphasis on the creative power of God is one way in which Ezekiel and Second Ezekiel differ here. However, is it likely that the use of עץ both in l. 10 of this text and in Gen. 2.16-17 and 3.1-6 is significant? In contrast, Strugnell and Dimant (1988: 54) suggest that there may be a comparison between the use of עץ in this text and in Ezek. 37.16-20. However the meaning of עץ in that Ezekiel passage is itself less than clear. Zimmerli (1983: 273) comments that the word is 'remarkably undefined'. The LXX translates the word as ῥάβδος, which can mean rod, staff, stick or more specifically the ruler's staff or sceptre as it does in Heb. 1.8. The latter is Zimmerli's preferred translation in Ezekiel 37: he comments that the kingdom has already been represented by the shoot of a tree in Ezek. 19.11-12, and suggests that here the idea of states becoming one about which the image speaks is best represented by two sceptres bound together and displayed to the people. In Second Ezekiel, however, the context of the passage and the verbs to which the tree is linked do not encourage a reading about uniting states. If *Barn.* 12.1 is indeed a quotation of 4Q385.2.10, then the fact that עץ is translated as ξύλον rather than as ῥάβδος may suggest that Ezek. 37.16-20 is not (or certainly was not considered to be) the defining idea behind this line.

It may be that the verbs and the context of the text rather than the noun provide a clue to the meaning of the line. As Philonenko (1993–94: 402) noted, the verbs כפף and זקף are found together in two Psalms (145 and 146) which speak of the kindness and justice of God particularly towards those who are righteous but persecuted:

סומך יהוה לכל־הנפלים וזוקף לכל־הכפופים:

The LORD upholds all who are falling, and raises up all who are bowed down (Ps. 145.14).

יהוה פקח עורים יהוה זקף כפופים יהוה אהב צדיקים:

The LORD opens the eyes of the blind. The LORD lifts up those who are bowed down; the LORD loves the righteous (Ps. 146.8).

These verses of Psalm 145 and 146 offer praise to a God who keeps his promises and rewards the faithful. Their context echoes in the Second Ezekiel text. Line 10 of 4Q385.2 is God's answer to the prophet's question about when the reward of the righteous will occur, as Puech stressed (1994: 436): part of God's answer is that those of Israel now bowed down by some kind of persecution will in the end be lifted up by God as he has promised in the Psalms and in the vision he has just given the prophet. The issue for the implied reader is the just compensation of those who have loved God's name, implicitly in the face of difficulty, rather than the reunion of the nation.

A further Qumran text in which the same two verbs are found may provide a clue to the particular significance of the tree as a sign of the end-times. It has been argued in this chapter that, unlike in Ezekiel 37, the vision in 4Q385.2 refers to the physical resurrection of the righteous.[32] In this fragment, as was noted above, the promised revivification of the corpses is referred to but not shown to have been fulfilled in the description of the vision. The phrase that signals the occurrence of events such as the covering with skin, 'And it was so' (1. 5), is absent in 1. 8.[33] The resurrection of the faithful, suffering group of Israelites is plausibly promised but not referred to in the vision. The reaction of the 'great crowd' is an expected way of responding to God's act of resurrection. This concept of resurrection is not without precedent in the Qumran texts, as was noted above. In 4Q521, Isa. 61.1 is alluded to and a reference to resurrection added in column 2, 1. 12: 'He will heal the wounded and revive the dead (ומתים יחיה) and bring good news to the poor.' Significantly for 1. 10 of the Second Ezekiel fragment, 4Q521 also alludes to Ps. 146.8, as Philonenko had noted (1993–94: 402):

---

32. This view is supported by Strugnell. With reference to 1. 3, Dimant comments 'Selon J Strugnell nous aurions ici la plus ancienne allusion à la résurrection comme récompense (comparer par ex. *Daniel* 11)' (1992a:18).

33. Kister and Qimron (1992: 597)) restore and translate ll. 7–8 in a quite different way. Strugnell and Dimant took everything from ויאמר שוב up to the end of 1. 8 as representing God's command. The outcome of the prophecy is not described and there is no need for the tag which signals the outcome in ll. 6–7: כן ויהי. Instead, Kister and Qimron offer the reading and restoration 'WYPHW RWH [BM WYHYW WYHYKN] WY'MD' and suggest that the passage which follows [WYHY KN] should be translated: 'And a great crowd of people stood up and blessed YHWH Sabaoth who had given them life again' (p. 597). This reading, if correct, undermines one element of my argument, but it does not rule out the likelihood that the writer envisaged physical resurrection as the reward promised to the righteous by God. Kister and Qimron believe this to be the case, and comment that 'the author indicates, in the words that he ascribes to God, that the vision of the Dry Bones (Ezra 37.4-10) was His way of demonstrating to the Children of Israel that the righteous would be rewarded by being resurrected' (p. 596).

and he will glorify the pious on the throne of the eternal kingdom, he who liberates the captives, restores sight to the blind, straightens the bent (קף כפופים) (ll. 7-8).

The two verbs are surprisingly rare in the Hebrew Bible and in the Qumran texts. Here we have the same cluster of ideas, resurrection and restoration from crookedness in an eschatological context, in both Second Ezekiel and 4Q521. Apparently the writer of *Barn.* 12.1 drew on the same cluster of ideas and related the tree to the cross. Is it possible to argue that in the Jewish text 4Q385.2 a bent and lifted up tree might be understood as a renewed tree of life signalling a reversal of the Fall? Certainly this would make sense in the general context of the echoes of Genesis 1 already proposed. It is interesting to note that Puech includes creation as a theme in the document 4Q521:

> Les diverses allusions au Jour de YHWH de la finale *Malachi* 3, 18-24, aux faits glorieux qui n'ont pas encore eu lieu (*Isaïe* et *Daniel* 12) s'inscrivant dans une sorte de midrash du *Ps* 146, hymne au Dieu secourable, qui a fourni quelques thèmes centraux, Dieu créateur et sauveur, distinction entre justes et impies (1992: 514-15).

> The various allusions to the Day of YHWH at the end of Malachi 3.18-24, to the glorious deeds which have not yet taken place (Isaiah and Daniel 12) are written in a kind of midrash of Psalm 146, a hymn to a benevolent God, which has supplied some central themes: God the creator and saviour; the distinction between the just and the impious.

There are many references in contemporary literature to the more general idea of the restoration of paradise in the future age. In his article on the Sibylline Oracles, O'Neill (1991: 94) offers a list of references attesting to the idea of the restoration of paradise. Of these references, several are particularly relevant to 4Q385.2.10. There is little doubt that the renewal of creation and the participation in it of the righteous was a powerful and widespread eschatological belief, attested in, for example, *4 Ezra* 7.75 and *T. Levi* 18.10-11. The presence of the tree of life and the availability of its fruit is specifically mentioned in *4 Ezra* 7.123, 8.52, and 1 En. 24.2–25.7. In Isa. 65.22 (LXX) the length of the life of the people of God is equated with length of the life of the tree of life in God's new creation:

> τὰς ἡμέρας τοῦ ξύλου τῆς ζωῆς ἔσονται αἱ ἡμέραι τοῦ λαοῦ μου

> the days of the tree of life will be as the days of my people.

Also of significance, as Philonenko (1993–94: 401-402) suggested, is *4 Macc.* 18.16. Here the mother of the martyred brothers extols the teaching of their father, who, she says, recounted to them the proverb 'There is a tree of life for those who do his will'. This is a modification of Prov. 3.18 which highlights the righteousness of the recipient of the tree of life. In opposition to Puech (1994: 432 n. 21), I suggest that the most natural way (and certainly a possible way) to read the proverb is as a reference to the tree of life in Genesis 2. Finally, in Rev. 22.1-5, the tree of life, restored and abundant with fruit, is an important symbol of the New Jerusalem. Although, as Puech (1994: 432-36) argues, no references have been found that include both the symbol of the tree of life and the idea of it bending and rising up, the notion of the recovery or restoration of Paradise, including the tree of life, is well attested. As Philonenko (1993–94: 402) suggests, the combination of the symbol and the symbolic action may have been the writer's own, in response to the story he had told of the prophesied standing-up of the corpses. Even in Puech's preferred precursor, Ezek. 17.22-24, although there is reference to movement up and down (v. 24), the verbs used are not the same as the verbs of movement in 4Q385.2.10.

In what ways might these references be clues to understanding the meaning of the picture in 4Q385.2.10 of a tree bending and standing erect? The statement is the partial answer to the question of when the righteous will be rewarded with the promise of resurrection. Taking the tree mentioned in the text as a reference to the tree of life makes sense both in the context of the understanding of the end-times we have discovered in other intertestamental texts and in the context of this fragment of Second Ezekiel. The picture of the tree bent over, as if crippled, suggests the present and future denial or destruction of both the tree of life and of Paradise, which the righteous people of God are apparently experiencing in their persecution and rejection. The issue of when the reward will come to those who have 'walked in the way of righteousness' (4Q385.2.2-3) is particularly acute for those who are suffering because of their 'loyalty' (1.3). The restoration of creation and Paradise, and the promise that the righteous will participate in it (*4 Ezra* 8.52; 1 En. 24.4–25.7 and so on) is aptly signalled by the lifting up (זקף) of the tree of life. That creation is a powerful theme in this fragment has already been suggested in the echoes of the creation story in Genesis 1 noted above. Line 10 of this Qumran text weaves together the promises of God to restore the righteous in Psalms 145 and 146 with the hope of creation renewed in the sign of the re-establishment of the tree of life. It is a picture that would speak to those who deemed themselves persecuted for their faith but hopeful of reward, in the form of resurrection, at the imminent inauguration of the end-time. The emphasis I have suggested on the theme of creation throughout the fragment does not exclude the possibility that Ezek. 17.22-24 was also an important precursor text for the writer of Second Ezekiel. In these verses too there are strong echoes of the creation theme and in particular of the perfection of the original Paradise restored. It is for this time that Second Ezekiel longs. Even if Puech's argument is accepted and resurrection is not the reward in view, I suggest that a dominant theme in 4Q385 is the renewal of creation and that the tree of life is the most obvious interpretation of the symbol of the tree in l. 10.

In conclusion, it has been suggested in this chapter that the idea of God's recreation of the righteous is dominant in Second Ezekiel, whereas the theme of an unbroken prophetic tradition beginning with Moses and continuing through Ezekiel, Jesus and John the narrator is uppermost in Revelation 11. In the context of Second Ezekiel, Ezekiel's message of encouragement about the restoration of the land to the exiled is radically transformed into a promise to a suffering, excluded and righteous people that their resurrection will be part of a completely new creation. The old order will be judged and then abandoned. In Revelation, an alternative world is created out of the text of Ezekiel, in which persecution, death and resurrection are the expected fate of the Christian who witnesses to Christ as commanded. Ezekiel's vision of hope is offered only to those who also seek out persecution. Ezekiel's message of comfort has been inverted, delayed and spiritualized into a heavenly reward for those who enter the world of suffering John creates. This fate and the authority of the prophet who announces it are verified and guaranteed by prophetic tradition into which John is shown to be called, and by the presence of Christ in the witness of the text. The contexts of the two texts, Revelation and Second Ezekiel, are different, and this may be reflected in their use of texts from the Hebrew Bible such as Ezekiel. However, both offer subversive readings of Ezekiel which reflect their marginalized position in their societies, and their need to construct an alternative, destabilized and yet comforting world into which their readers may enter. Aspects of postmodern literary theory have yielded new insights into the intertextual relationship between Revelation, its context and its reading of the Hebrew Bible.

Part II
DECONSTRUCTION

Chapter 4

READING THE *CONFESSIONS* DECONSTRUCTIVELY

Readings of Hogg's *The Private Memoirs and Confessions of a Justified Sinner* and of the text of the Bible have in common a diversity and a lack of resolution, despite the attempts of many readers to offer a definitive interpretation. In the context of postmodern literary criticism, assumptions about the stable and closed nature of both texts are under fierce debate. Given that postmodern literary theory developed at least in part as a reaction to traditional readings of texts that take the notions of intentionality and stability for granted, in this chapter such traditional readings of the *Confessions* will be discussed and their assumptions exposed. A brief description of postmodernism will then be given, followed by a more extended discussion of deconstruction, which is perhaps the best known literary critical manifestation of postmodernism. Pippin's (1994) radical, deconstructive reading of Revelation will be considered as a comparison with the readings of Hogg already discussed, and in light of this an alternative, deconstructive reading of the *Confessions* will be offered.

Traditional Readings of the Confessions

The anonymous reviewer of Hogg's *Confessions* in the *Westminster Review* of 1824 regretted that its author had not done better than 'in uselessly and disgustingly abusing his imagination, to invent wicked tricks for a mongrel devil, and blasphemous lucubrations for an insane fanatic' (p. 562). Ever since, there have been critics of the text who have sought to recover the workings of Hogg's imagination and thus to discover the way in which the text 'ought' to be read. For the 1824 reviewer, the author handles the form of the novel 'clumsily' (p. 560), and creates a devil-figure with neither the sublimity or nor the grotesque characteristics that might interest the reader. Furthermore, the author loses his reader's sympathy by inconsistently shifting from a supernatural to a psychological explanation of events. Since Gide's introduction to the Cresset edition of the text in 1947, attempts have been made to redeem Hogg from these 'faults', and to identify intended meanings that prove these reviewer's interpretations to be mistaken.

Much of the critical work carried out on the *Confessions* has depended on the assumption that Hogg's intentions in his writing are available and informative, even if they were unconscious on his part. Most critics implicitly assume that a deliberate contract has been created in the text between author and reader which is recoverable, definite and final. The text is difficult to understand, but a key to its meaning must exist. Once that is discovered, the text's difficulties and ambiguities will make sense and dissolve, and the reasons for the creation of the many interpretative difficulties will be made clear.[1] Within this interpretative context the *Confessions* has variously been understood as a discrediting of fanatical antinomianism, or organized religion in general (Wain 1983; Bligh 1984), as the product of Hogg's Christian faith and knowledge of the Bible (Campbell 1972a and b, 1988a and b, whose work was discussed in Chapter 2), as the reflection of Hogg's own split or outcast personality (Gide 1947; Carey 1969), or as a text with deliberately dual, mutually exclusive interpretative possibilities which the reader must choose between (Gifford 1976; Groves 1988). In the following chapter, these interpretations are discussed in greater detail. Does it remain convincing to argue, in the light of deconstructive thought, that an intended meaning of texts such as Hogg's *Confessions* exists and is recoverable?

In his introduction to the 1983 Penguin edition of the *Confessions*, Wain defines the novel as 'a study in fanaticism' (p. 12). To understand that Hogg's object is to discredit the doctrine of antinomianism is to understand the novel. The modern reader misses the significance of many of the historical details that Hogg incorporates in the text, such as the division between the Tories and the Whigs, represented by the Colwans and the Wringhims respectively, and the exile of John Drummond, first Earl of Melfort whom Hogg portrays as the scapegoat in the

---

1.   Bloedé's assertions about the relationship between meaning in the novel and Hogg's intentions and experience are typical. For her, the *Confessions* is 'more than satire; it is the exteriorisation of Hogg's own conflicts and a projection of those unconscious feelings of guilt and unworthiness...it was the most personal thing he was ever to write' (1966: 186).

murder of George, and who was in fact forced to live abroad. However, the purpose of these details is to create a prosaic and realistic frame for Hogg's tale of demon possession. Within this context, the devil is convincingly portrayed against the background of the contemporary literal belief in the devil as a tangible person and in the influence of the supernatural generally. Robert is a victim of his own fanatical belief in predestination. Whereas 'low' and theologically unsophisticated characters such as Arabella Logan and Bell Calvert are portrayed as human and loving, Robert and his parents are shown to be obsessed, lacking in human compassion and open to the advances of the devil. Wain argues that although sympathetic characters such as George meet harsh ends, their fate is less severe than Robert's descent into hell. The novel grips the reader because its theme, the dangers of fanaticism, is timeless.

Bligh offers an extended version of Wain's book in his 1984 article 'The Doctrinal Premises of Hogg's *Confessions of a Justified Sinner*'. In Bligh's view, Hogg's purpose is to reveal the dangers inherent in antinomianism, and his narrative technique involves controlling the readers' response so that they come to hate antinomianism but pity its adherents. Combining the isolated antinomian preaching of Paul in Romans 6 and 8 with the popular belief that the devil is able to impersonate humans, Hogg in the pathetic figure of Robert tries to warn followers of this doctrine of the dangers of their error. Robert believes his eternal destiny is fixed, leaving him easy prey for the devil, who knows antinomianism is false but propagates it for his own ends. The positive alternative Hogg offers is George's state of happiness as he sits on Arthur's Seat, thinking kindly of Robert and in harmony with nature and God. At the end, Bligh suggests, Robert is portrayed as realizing the meaning of Gil-Martin's double-talk that no human will ever harm him: it will be supernatural forces that lead him to his damnation. By including Robert's own confessions alongside the Editor's account, the reader is drawn to pity Robert, while rejecting the doctrine he will not relinquish. However, on the last page of the novel, Hogg reveals his uneasiness with his work. Fearing it will lead the reader into believing the superstition that the devil is able to possess individuals, which he himself did not accept, Hogg calls the veracity of his account into question. Despite his attempts to create a sense of historicity, he suggests that the author of the *Confessions* section was a 'religious maniac' and that 'with the present generation, it will not go down, that a man should be daily tempted by the Devil, in the semblance of a fellow creature' (1824: 208). In this way, Bligh suggests, the indeterminacy and lack of resolution in the final section of the novel is to be explained. Speaking through the Editor, Hogg manipulates the reader into making one particular interpretation, and brings about a final closure.

There are significant parallels to be drawn between the readings of Hogg's *Confessions* by Wain, Bligh and Campbell, and the conventional reading of the Bible in post-Reformation Scotland as discussed in Chapter 2. For both, the text under discussion is privileged, stable and univocal. Its single meaning is to be found by the ideal reader. The writers of the Bible and Hogg himself are understood to have intended a message in their work, and although this may have been lost through time, accredited readers are allowed to attempt to recover and restore it. For critics such as Wain, Bligh and Campbell, Hogg as author has the right to expect his readers to treat his text with respect, and to make an effort to discover his partially-concealed purpose for writing. Each section of the novel must reflect and elucidate the rest. After reading the novel, the reader is expected to think and act differently from before, either by rejecting fanaticism (Wain and Bligh), or by considering their own spiritual state and guarding against spiritual pride (Campbell). For these readers, the message and meaning of the text is fixed and stable for all time, because of the continuing presence and influence of its author. The aim of these literary critics is to establish a connection between their reading and the reading of the ideal reader, who, for example, is familiar with the biblical text, or tempted by the doctrine of extreme predestination. They read Hogg's text as a stable entity, and speak of the need for readers to become familiar with it in order to understand it. For them, the first reading is not as valid as the tenth.[2] Readers in the twentieth century may not apply anachronistic insights to the text: the role of the critic of the *Confessions*, like the role of the reader of the Bible in the seventeenth and eighteenth centuries, is to restore and preserve the text by recovering the intention and message of the author. In this way, both texts retain their authority. For these and other modern readers of Hogg's work, the *Confessions* has taken on many of the characteristics of a sacred text.

In the work of the three critics of the *Confessions* discussed so far, as in the writings of Boston, Chalmers and Thomson, the text's meaning is

---

2.   Groves (1988: 120), another modern critic, whose work is considered below, laments that '[f]ew readers have given the *Confessions* the careful re-reading it deserves'.

recoverable, fixed and stable. This meaning is to be discovered by considering the intention of the author and the possible role of the original reader. For other critics of the *Confessions*, such as Gide, Carey, Gifford and Groves, although the intention of the author may still be important, the emphasis is placed on applying insights from modern psychology or on considering the role of the general reader in the creation of meaning. These readings highlight the contradictions in the text, rather than its unity.

For Gide (1947), the novel makes sense as a psychological exploration of Robert Wringhim's consciousness, which also reveals something of the state of mind of the reader. There is no need for the reader to resort to a supernatural explanation of events: Gil-Martin is no more than 'the exteriorized development of our own desires, of our pride, of our most secret thoughts' (1947: xv). If Robert reflects the dark side of one's consciousness, open to indoctrination by dogmas such as antinomianism, George represents Hogg's ideal inner man. George is a 'charming representative of normal humanity, spontaneous, gay, rich in possibilities and in no wise encumbered with religious preoccupations' (p. xiii). The novel 'works' by drawing the reader at first towards Gil-Martin as a benevolent and flattering friend, and then gradually revealing that he is the devil. The readers' task is to make this discovery themselves, while recognizing those elements in their own psyche which are attracted to Gil-Martin and all that he stands for. Hogg's novel, then, is a sophisticated psychological analysis of humanity's response to its own internal darkness.

Carey (1969) also considers that psychology holds the key to the novel's meaning, but in addition he indirectly refutes much of Gide's analysis. As Carey points out, the Editor's narrative does not present an objective account of Robert's life which might be relied upon as a means of understanding the Confessions section. The Editor is as prejudiced as Robert, and his sympathy for both the Laird and George is misplaced. Gide's ideal man may be read as a rowdy drunk who slanders his mother. The Laird on his wedding night is a figure to be reviled rather than sympathized with. Significantly, Hogg distances himself from the Editor by refusing to participate in the grave-robbing scene. Far from being a dependable commentator on the facts or events, the Editor is merely a collector and annotator of traditions, who admits to not understanding the pamphlet he finds at the grave and publishes (1824: 206-207). Responding to the uncertainties and ambiguities in the novel, Carey comments that it 'remains indecisive about whether the devil was a delusion or an objective figure' (1969: xiv). Gide had chosen not to highlight the tensions between the two accounts, and had misread or ignored the times in the narrative when characters other than Robert are described as seeing his companion (for example, when Bell Calvert and Miss Logan go to Dalcastle to identify George's murderer [1824: 67]). Carey, however, finds in these tensions a key to Hogg's personality which opens up the meaning of the novel.

Carey explains the novel as the work of Hogg the outcast and split personality. Hogg's interest in the outcast, represented by Robert, who from birth is disowned by the person he believes to be his father, or by Bell Calvert, whipped and then banished from her home, and supremely by Gil-Martin, the 'primal outcast' (1969: xvii), stems from his own feelings of exclusion from Edinburgh literary society. The notion of the existence of a second self, which both George and Robert feel so strongly, may have stemmed from the appearance of articles written in Hogg's name in the *Noctes Ambrosianae* in 1822 at a time when he was shunned by the Blackwood establishment. Hogg's divided attitude towards the portrayal and existence of Gil-Martin may be paralleled in his troubled and ambivalent relationship with the author of these articles, Professor Wilson. Finally, Carey suggests that Robert and George should be read as representations of the two sides of Hogg's character: like George, he was eager to be liked in every society, and yet like Robert he could be suspicious, awkward and difficult. Hogg's character and unique background and situation in the literary world of his day, Carey suggests, account for many of the conflicting aspects of the text. Although none of these points is developed extensively by Carey, they are offered as a way of helping the reader to understand the meaning of the novel.

Gifford (1976) argues that Hogg intentionally creates a text that allows dual, mutually exclusive interpretations. Hogg's purpose is to force the reader to choose between belief in supernatural intervention and scepticism. Gil-Martin may be read either as a creation of Robert's diseased mind, or as the real instrument of punishment of Robert the sinner. For Gifford, this dualism is a reflection of the dualism within Hogg's life and work. After 1810, when Hogg left the Borders to become a man of letters in the capital, there existed within him two selves: the Ettrick Hogg and the Edinburgh Hogg. The existence of these two selves generated the crisis of identity and confidence which was necessary for the creation of the *Confessions*.

According to Gifford, Hogg experienced Robert's feelings of exclusion and uncertainty. Onto this character, Hogg projected his own feelings of unworthiness and guilt. In the novel, he offers the reader three different patterns of experience. In the first section, the Editor's narrative, the subject matter is presented in an apparently rational and objective way, and corresponds to the psyche of the Edinburgh Hogg. This changes in the Confessions section, in which the subjective and supernatural are highlighted, a reflection of the Ettrick Hogg. In the third part the claims of the first two parts are weighed up, new evidence is produced, but no final resolution is offered. It is equally possible to read Robert as the helpless victim of his own *alter ego*, an increasingly unreliable witness of events who finally can no longer live with the fulfillment of his own repressed desires; or as the culpable follower of the devil, making his own moral choices and in the end doomed to damnation. Gifford suggests that the reader enjoys the novel because of the bewilderment it invokes. He accepts that his critical unravelling of the conflicting elements of the plot that has led to the conclusion that dual, mutually exclusive interpretations are intended, may spoil the reader's enjoyment of the tensions. However, he comments:

> in terms of fully understanding both Hogg's great ingenuity...and in terms of placing the novel at its crucial point in Hogg's development, I feel that the dualistic complexity must be unravelled to see how clearly Hogg wished to run with both the hares and the hounds (1976: 179).

The reader's task is to choose between the interpretations.

Like Gifford, Groves (1988) finds parallels between the conflicts and uncertainties in Hogg's life and the different perspectives offered in the *Confessions*.[3] Also like Gifford, Groves attempts to untangle these perspectives and to find meaning in their apparent contradictions. The Editor figure is based on John Wilson, whose obtuseness and prejudice is satirized by the similarities drawn between him and Robert Wringhim. Both are shown to attempt to tame chaos, the Editor employing the rhetoric of deism and empiricism, Robert the certainty of narrow Calvinism. Both embark on journeys that descend into confusion. The theme of the novel, Groves suggests, is the relativity of the human self

---

3.   Groves (1988: 115) asserts that '[b]y gradually unveiling the pride, prejudices, and obtuseness of...[the] "editor", Hogg will enjoy a gleeful revenge on the critics, academics, and editors who dominated the literary world of the 1820s'.

as a function of its time, nature and society. Both the Editor and Robert are trapped in the dogma of their time. Both offer readings that are both mutually exclusive and incomplete.

However, Groves argues for a quite different role for the reader. Whereas the Editor and Robert are 'prisoners of language, victims of the closed systems of discourse they blindly impose upon reality' (1988: 123), '[a] good reader will approach the *Confessions* as a work of art, finding form and meaning in the web of words, rather than becoming trapped in that web like the narrators' (1988: 124). Hogg offers his readers this possibility in two ways: in his use of puns and *double entendre*, and in the portrayal of a wider fellowship and community open to the Editor and Robert. Robert is a victim of his own words and the words of Gil-Martin. When he fails to realize the double meaning of his speech or the speech of Gil-Martin (for example, he says he was 'quite captivated' (1824: 96) on his first meeting with Gil-Martin, and he fails to hear the latent meaning in Gil-Martin's declaration that 'It is *my* Bible, Sir' [1824: 101]), he indicates his narrow vision, fragmented personality and lack of self-knowledge. However, when these puns are recognized by the reader, the difference between Robert's partial outlook and Hogg's mature and complex vision is highlighted. According to Groves, the language games Hogg plays 'convey a joyful intuition of unity underneath the surface of language and the surface of life' (1988: 122), which the reader is invited to share. A further expression of Hogg's belief in underlying wholeness is the movement from individualistic certainty to increased involvement in community which the Editor and Robert undergo. Both go on a long, confusing journey in disguise. In the course of the journey, Robert loses his religious certainty and the Editor, unable to come to a logical conclusion, loses his rationalistic certainty. However, in their confusion, both increase their involvement in the communities they turn to for help: they are at the mercy of the shepherds and farmers of Ettrick. In this increased involvement, Groves finds evidence of an implied affirmation of a social vision. For Groves, although the text seems indeterminate and incomplete, in fact the reader is offered a vision of potential unity:

> at the end Hogg finds subtle ways of pointing the reader on the path of escape, the upward path towards the recovery of personal wholeness and spiritual rebirth through the necessary acceptance of the oneness of humanity (1988: 120).

However, this reading fails to account for the negative aspects of the social vision offered in the text: it is apparent that neither the Editor nor Robert gains support from his encounters with other members of society. Indeed, following his escape from Dalcastle, Robert is hounded out of every community he tries to enter, and the Editor is rejected by the sheep-farmer Hogg whom he approaches for help. There is little of Groves's potential unity to be found in Robert's or the Editor's experiences of community.

Gide, Carey, Gifford and Groves highlight and confront the instability of the text. However, like Wain and Bligh or Boston and Thomson, they assume that these instabilities are both intentional on the part of the author, and resolvable by the alert reader. They suggest that they are that alert reader, for whom the chaos is never complete. Once Hogg's strategy has been perceived, the purpose of the text's surface complexity will be laid bare. For these readers, the text and the intention of the author, whether conscious or sub-conscious, are closely related and recoverable, and exist independently of any reading of them.

Reading Deconstructively

Many readers would want to push the instability of the texts under consideration much further than the critics discussed in the previous section. From the perspective of much postmodern critical theory, and particularly of deconstruction, the convoluted and contradictory theories to explain the text offered by Boston, Chalmers, Thomson and literary critics such as Groves or Carey are indicative of a futile attempt to control any text. The Bible, Fisher's *Marrow*, Hogg's *Confessions* and the 'Chaldee Manuscript' are all endlessly ambiguous and resistant to closure. Many postmodern critical theories deny that the intention of the author is recoverable, relevant or privileged. Instead, meaning is created by each reader of the text: there is no ideal reader whom critics may aspire to understand, and no independently existing meaning of the text to be interpreted objectively. Some of the general tenets of postmodernism were discussed in my introductory chapter. Here some of the ways that postmodern critical theories challenge the readings of Hogg's *Confessions* which have already been discussed are highlighted.

> The text is a weapon against time, oblivion and the trickery of speech, which is so easily taken back, altered, denied. The notion of the text is historically linked to a whole world of institutions: the law, the Church,

literature, education. The text is a moral object: it is the written in so far
as the written participates in the social contract. It subjects us, and
demands that we observe and respect it, but in return it marks language
with an inestimable attribute which it does not possess in its essence:
security (Barthes 1981: 32).

The conventions of much nineteenth-century fiction present a ready-
made world corresponding to the world of the reader. The fictional
world is easily comprehended, straightforwardly constructed and the
motives of the characters objectively explained. Furthermore, the realism of such fiction, and traditional literary criticism of it, tends to retain
an implicit commitment to the world as it exists and as it is convention-
ally structured and represented. It often offers a reassuring sense of
completeness in the fictional world created. The world and the text are
both assumed to exist objectively and independently as objects of analysis.[4] According to this view, the text is a sealed and complete unit of
signs which demands both restoration if its meaning is lost or changed,
and interpretation within determinate limits. In much contemporary
biblical studies, textual criticism and philological study have been
employed in an attempt to restore the text to its original state, and historical criticism has been applied to discover more about the world to
which the text is assumed to refer. The biblical text, once restored as far
as possible, and interpreted with the guidance of any historical information available, is commonly understood to function objectively as a
window on the world in which it was created. The goal of historical
objectivity may have replaced the doctrinal concerns of the eighteenth
and nineteenth centuries, but the assumptions of biblical critics throughout the period have remained very similar. Since the 1824 reviewer, the
same assumptions have on the whole been made by critics of Hogg's
Confessions.

However, in postmodern literary critical terms the text may no longer
be considered as a fixed and independent entity existing in relation to
an objective and analysable world. The relationship between the signifier and the signified is understood to be arbitrary rather than given.
Meaning is assigned to words more on the basis of their difference from
other words than on the basis of any intrinsic value. The text is denied
any substantial presence: the text is deemed to exist in the transitory

4.   See Stevenson (1992: 216-23) for a discussion of the way in which modernist fiction begins to question such a view of the function and form of the literary
text.

interplay with and difference from other texts. Meaning is never fully present: it is always in the process of forming and reforming in an endless swirl of incomplete interpretations. In the words of Derrida:

> language itself is menaced in its very life, helpless, adrift in the threat of limitlessness, brought back to its own finitude at the very moment when its limits seem to disappear, when it ceases to be self-assured, contained, and guaranteed by the infinite signified which seemed to exceed it (1976: 6).

Postmodern literary theory and what Lyotard (1984) has called the 'postmodern condition' are of course closely related. McHale (1987) defines postmodernism as a time of ontological plurality and instability arising from the epistemological uncertainty of modernism. Questions that dominate the time are concerned with the nature of the existence of self(ves), the world and the text. For Habermas postmodernism is characterized by an acknowledgement of the dissolution of the exemplary past and of the necessity to create the normative out of itself. He argues that 'a present that understands itself from the horizon of the modern age as the actuality of the most recent period has to recapitulate the break brought about with the past as a *continuous renewal*' (1987: 7). The old rules of philosophy and art now appear 'as a means to deceive, to seduce and to reassure which makes it impossible for them to be "true"' (Lyotard 1984: 74). The conventions of realism are recognised as conventions rather than as truths. In the continuous process of breaking with the past and its rules, postmodernism is anxious and seeks self-reassurance at the same time as it realizes it can only formulate new rules on the basis of the divisions it has created. Its self-perception is that of being 'cast back upon itself without any possibility of escape' (Habermas 1987: 7). This sense of anxiety and entrapment is a feature of postmodern literary theory, which recognizes that the reader as interpreter is always irretrievably 'in' the world. The text does not exist outwith the reader, but equally the reader is never free from the local, temporary structures of the world which operate without reference to final or objective causes. There is no reading which is not 'framed' by a subjective, transitory lens.

Postmodernism is a difficult and diverse notion to discuss and define, not least because of its inherent resistance to the concepts of stable definition and meaning. Discussing specific, postmodern literary theories, as they may be applied to readings of particular texts, is easier. In Chapters 2 and 3, the literary critical notions of marginalization and ex-centricity were discussed as helpful perspectives from which to read the *Confessions* and Revelation. Deconstruction offers a different perspective, from which the inconsistencies and illogicalities of other readings are ruthlessly exposed. A summary of the history and a discussion of the application of deconstruction are offered in the following section.

Deconstruction is post-structuralist in that it is a reaction against structuralism. It refuses to accept that structure is 'given' or objectively 'there' in the text. Instead it questions the assumption that a text's structure of meaning corresponds to the mental pattern that determines the limit of its intelligibility. There is no deep relationship between the theory and the systems of meaning that theory proposes to analyse. In deconstruction, structuralism's assumed correspondence between the mind, meaning and the concept of the method is suspended. The inadequacy and provisionality of structuralism's terms are acknowledged, and instead of a quest for truth or origins, deconstruction launches itself into an encounter with the text which recognizes the free play of meaning. The practice of deconstruction involves a suspension of the view that language exists to communicate meaning, and its purpose is to find out what happens when philosophical and literary conventions are either inverted or disregarded.

However, Derrida's deconstruction does not demand that rigorous argument and consistency are abandoned. Instead it consistently and rigorously seeks out the obscure yet inescapable logic by which a text deconstructs its own most rooted assumptions. Deconstructon involves a dismantling of a text's conceptual oppositions followed by a reinscribing of them within a different order of signification. It is a seeking out of the blindspots or moments of contradiction where a text involuntarily betrays a tension between what it means to say and what it is constrained to say. Deconstruction seizes on a text's apparently insignificant details, such as asides, footnotes and metaphors, which traditional criticism tends to ignore, and discovers that at these margins of the text there are unsettling forces at work. It reveals not a rich inexhaustible multiplicity of sense attaching to certain privileged literary themes, but an endless displacement of meaning, continually baffling and frustrating the desire for an assurance of thematic unity. However, deconstruction should not be considered a method or concept of reading with its own rules and technique. As Norris comments, 'it is precisely this idea—this assumption that meaning can always be grasped in the form of some proper, self-identical concept, that Derrida is most determinedly out to deconstruct' (1987: 19). To make deconstruction an idea or concept rather than an activity is to do what Derrida seeks always to reject.

In *Of Grammatology* (published in French in 1967 and translated into English in 1976), Derrida offers detailed discussion of the activity of deconstruction which, he argues, involves an acknowledgement and rejection of the traditional, and misguided, affirmation of speech over writing in Western philosophy. Derrida explains that the traditional notion of the book highlights this priority.[5] Books are taken to exist as self-enclosed systems of meaning and reference. Their signifiers all point back toward a 'transcendental signified' or source of authentic and unitary truth. It is the author's sovereign presence that holds the book's writing within proper bounds. Acceptance of these limits gives the book its integrity of purpose and theme. To question the author of the book is to challenge the priority of speech over writing, and presence over absence:

> The good writing has therefore always been *comprehended*...within a totality, and enveloped in a volume or book. The idea of a book is the idea of a totality, finite or infinite, of the signifier; this totality of the signifier cannot be a totality, unless a totality constituted by the signifier pre-exists it, supervises its inscriptions and its signs, and is independent of it in its ideality (Derrida 1976: 18).

If speaking has the value of positive truth, because of its contiguity to the source, then writing is a perfect example of Derrida's notion of

---

5.   This point depends upon the distinction Derrida finds between the notions of 'good' and 'bad' writing implied in Western philosophy. Derrida (1976: 16-17) points out that Paul makes a distinction between the writing of the letter, which kills, and the Spirit, which makes alive (2 Cor. 3.6): writing as a metaphor has both a good and a bad aspect. Similarly, a distinction is made between literary and critical language, resting on the belief that literature embodies an authentic or self-possessed plenitude of meaning. For Derrida, this is a sign of Western prejudice which tries to reduce writing, or the free play of language, to a stable meaning that is equated with the character of speech. In the case of speech there is assumed to be a perfect fit between meaning, intention and utterance, guaranteed by the presence of the speaker. As a result of the distrust of textuality embedded in Western philosophy, literary texts have been granted the status of self-authenticating meaning and truth. Derrida suggest that this myth is best exploded by breaking down the barriers between literary, critical and philosophical texts, and by reading all texts for symptoms of their conceptual limits rather than their interpretative insights.

supplementarity.[6] It is an accessory, twice removed from the source and therefore prey to dangerous misinterpretations and misunderstandings.[7] However, using the logic of the supplement, Derrida seeks to show that it is impossible to conceptualize language without recourse to the metaphor of writing: writing is inscribed at the source even of texts which assert the priority of speech. As Derrida demonstrates, the supplement has two meanings. It is either an optional feature, in which case speech could be understood as a self-sufficient entity, with writing as an aid to communication; or it is something that is required to complete or fulfil some existing lack, in which case writing is a precondition of language in general. Derrida argues that writing is indeed a necessary supplement without which speech could scarcely be conceived. It is an example of an apparently secondary or derivative term that has a central role in determining an entire structure of assumptions. From within traditional philosophy, the voice of the source and truth is threatened by this understanding of language, with the result that 'a feared writing must be cancelled because it erases the presence of the self-same within speech' (Derrida 1976: 270). *Of Grammatology* demonstrates that this reversal, or return of the repressed in the form of the privileging of speech over writing, is not an accident but a necessity inscribed in the very being of all metaphysical thinking.

Derrida seeks to show that there is no necessary bond between sound and sense, although such a privileged bond is assumed by Western philosophy. Because of this assumed relationship, most philosophies are phonocentric, viewing writing either as a secondary but useful transcription of spoken sounds, or as an alien, parasitic threat, an order of signs working to destroy the natural relationship between sound, meaning and truth. Having made this observation, Derrida considers the work of Saussure, who argued that linguistics can only become a genuine science when it regards language 'synchronically' as a network of inter-related sounds and meanings. Derrida takes this argument to its logical conclusion with reference to a science of writing: if language is

6. Derrida argues that writing is 'the supplement *par excellence* since it marks the point where the supplement proposes itself as supplement of supplement, sign of sign, *taking the place* of a speech already significant' (1976: 281).

7. In Chapter 1 of *Of Grammatology* (1976: 6-26) Derrida offers various examples of traditional Western philosophies that explicitly or implicitly privilege speech over writing, such as Christianity and Platonism.

always a system of differential signs, its meaning subsisting in structures of relationships and not in an ideal correspondence between sound and sense, then the classical definition of writing applies to every form of language, whether written or spoken. If it is accepted that writing can signify without the necessity of a present or even identified sender or recipient, then the possibility of the complete absence of a sender or recipient (or presence) from the scene of reading is a structural feature of any writing. It is this feature of writing which, for Derrida, is a precondition of language in general. Writing is the constant, defining supplement of all language because the sign never finds its adequate referent: all language is in a constant state of unfulfilled meaning. Derrida comments that 'from the moment that there is meaning there are nothing but signs. We think only in signs' (1976: 50). In contrast, to think logocentrically, as Western philosophy has traditionally done, is to dream of a 'transcendental signified'. It is to believe in meaning that exists beyond the differential play of language. Deconstruction is a perpetual reminder, in opposition to such dreaming, that meaning is always the sign of a sign: even thought cannot escape the logic of this endless supplementarity. Writing is involved in the origin of language since that origin cannot be conceived without the acknowledgement of the differential nature of signs, and of the absence of a defining presence.

Derrida is aware that such statements about the precedence of writing are completely counter-intuitive. He seeks to show that the classical idea of writing as the sign of a sign exceeds the bounds of its proper and restricted application. All philosophy and reflection on language and thought are caught up in a play of graphic concepts and metaphors which restore the desire for presence. It is with these metaphors and concepts that deconstruction begins. It locates and highlights the stress points where writing resists any attempt to be reduced to a univocal truth. It pays meticulous attention to the letter of the text, or the apparently marginal details that yield implications that the philosophy ignores in order to preserve its own integrity. By insisting on a vigorous literalism of the text, deconstruction demonstrates that subjects such as philosophy, linguistics and social anthropology are based on a covert ideology of the voice, or self-presence, which has not been read with sufficient detail. Writing in Derrida's wider sense is metaphorically whatever eludes, opposes or subverts this discourse of logocentric reason.

In Chapter 2 of *Of Grammatology*, Derrida discusses the work of the linguist Saussure as an example of the logocentrism deconstruction reveals. He argues that Saussure denounces writing[8] because of its unsettling effect on the logic of his argument. Saussure uses 'voice' as a metaphor of truth and authenticity compared to the secondary and help-less writing: speaking offers a link between sound and sense whereas writing destroys this ideal of pure self-presence, intruding between intention and meaning. Norris (1991: 28) comments that writing for Saussure 'occupies a promiscuous public realm where authority is sac-rificed to the vagaries and whims of textual "dissemination"'. Saussure wishes to maintain the notion of the differential nature of language without contradicting his own premise about the natural bond between sound and sense. He seeks therefore to exclude writing from the field of general linguistics, but nevertheless exploits it as a means of support for his own argument, for example where he uses it metaphorically as a type-case of language in general.[9] Derrida deconstructs this incon-sistency to show that even in the work of Saussure, writing (or 'arche-writing', as Derrida sometimes calls it) is a precondition of all possible knowledge.[10] Writing is related to the element of signifying difference which Saussure thought essential to the working of language. Writing is the free play or element of undecidability within every system of

8.   Derrida (1976: 30, 31) quotes from Saussure's *Course in General Linguis-tics*: 'Language and writing are two distinct systems of signs; the second *exists for the sole purpose of representing* the first' (italics added by Derrida, [Saussure 1974: 23]).

9.   Derrida (1976: 52) cites Saussure's explanation of phonic difference as a condition of linguistic value which depends on the example of writing: 'Since an identical state of affairs is observable in writing, another system of signs, we shall use writing to draw some comparisons that will clarify the whole issue' (Saussure 1974: 119).

10. In Chapter 3 of Part II of *Of Grammatology* (1976: 165-94), Derrida makes a similar claim about the work of Rousseau, author of *Essay on the Origin of Lan-guages* (1967), who deplores writing over speech, but depends on writing as means of guaranteeing the reality of his own past experience. Writing for Rousseau has a supplementary power that makes his experiences real by setting them down for oth-ers to read. Derrida seeks to show that there are blindspots in Rousseau's narrative produced by a supplementary logic that suspends or qualifies any recourse he makes to the idea of origin. Rousseau declares what he wishes to say, but says that which he does not wish to say. Derrida comments that 'Rousseau's discourse lets itself be constrained by a complexity which always has the form of a supplement of or from the origin. Its declared intention is not annulled by this but rather *inscribed* within a system which it no longer dominates' (1976: 243).

communication. Oral language is best defined as a generalized writing, the effects of which are disguised by an illusory metaphysic of origin or presence. If, because of this, writing is shown to precede and articulate all our working notions of philosophy, history and science, Derrida asks how can writing be merely one object of knowledge among others? Instead, he argues that thought is deluded if it believes it can comprehend the nature of writing from a stand-point outside or above the field commanded by writing.[11]

Deconstruction, then, is not just a kind of irresponsible play with words. Rather it is a rigorous thinking through of the problems thrown up by philosophy's forgetfulness of its own written or textual nature. It is an abandonment of nostalgic thoughts of the centre, and an acceptance that there is no limit to the range of interpretative options. Instead of a centre or a determined meaning, there is

> the joyous affirmation of the play of the world and of the innocence of becoming, the affirmation of a world of signs without fault, without truth, and without origin, which is offered to an active interpretation (Derrida 1976: 292).

What then are the features of a deconstructive reading of a text? What effect does this activity of the late twentieth century have on literary and biblical criticism? While it would be contrary to the spirit of deconstruction to suggest stable rules that every critic should follow, there are common although variable features of such readings that may be observed. By ruthlessly reading literally, deconstruction demonstrates that a text in the end defies its own logic and confesses what it denies. Texts are allowed to reveal that their referentiality fails, they are endlessly indecisive. The notion of aporia is invoked: a paradox created from within which, once encountered, cannot be rationalized. Indeed, a deconstructive reading is one in which particular attention is paid to textual features that are apparently insignificant or resistant to meaning. Deconstruction is suspicious of readings that try to explain the instabilities or difficulties in a text. Furthermore, a deconstructive critic is aware that his or her reading is never final or completed, and that their interpretation may in its turn be subject to a reading that reveals its inner divisions and contradictions. As the biblical critic Moore

---

11. As Norris (1991: 22) comments, deconstruction stresses that 'there is no language so vigilant or self-aware that it can effectively escape the conditions placed upon thought by its own prehistory and ruling metaphysic'.

comments, such a reading does not lead 'deeper into the heart of the text, but deeper into the heart of reading' (1989: 170).

The work of all of the critics of Hogg considered so far make assumptions about the stability of the text which deconstruction rejects. For Carey (1969), Gifford (1976) and Groves (1985), all ambiguities in the *Confessions* are intentional and explicable. The reader is expected to realize that it is Hogg's split personality which explains the mutually exclusive accounts of the Editor and of Robert (Carey). They should recognize that it is Hogg's intention to force them to decide between a belief in the supernatural and scepticism towards it (Gifford). Or, they should be led to share Hogg's belief in the underlying unity of the world: in contrast to Robert, the reader is privileged to recognize the double-talk of Gil-Martin and to understand that wholeness comes from integration into the wider community (Groves). By giving the personality and circumstances of the author a defining place, or presence, in the creation of meaning, these critics have done to the text exactly what Barthes[12] warned against doing. They have 'impose[d] a limit on that text,...furnish[ed] it with a final signified,...close[d] the writing' (1984: 147). The futility of this move is foreshadowed in their disagreement with one another, which supports another of Barthes's observations: that a book is 'only a tissue of signs, an imitation that is lost, infinitely deferred' (p. 147). The striking lack of unanimity in the study of the *Confessions* suggests that it is an ideal text with which to explore deconstructive reading. Readings of it so far discussed exemplify a third statement from Barthes, that 'A text's unity lies not in its origin but in its destination' (1984: 148). It will be argued that Carey and the others have imposed a unity on the *Confessions* which exists only in their reading of it. This unity is not supported by the text and may not be deduced from the intention of the author.

Postmodern Responses to Hogg's Confessions

Two critics who have taken a less traditional approach to the work of Hogg are Petrie (1992) and Redekop (1985). A consideration of their articles will form the basis of a more thoroughly deconstructive reading

12. Barthes, originally a structuralist literary critic (see, for example, his 1953 work) shows clear signs of Derrida's influence. In *S/Z* (1974), he renounces the reductive method of structuralist narratology and celebrates instead the plural, 'writerly' text.

of the *Confessions*. Redekop speaks the language of postmodern literary criticism, and affirms that Hogg's novel satisfies the contemporary
reader's demand for indeterminacy. The reader she discusses is pictured
in a modern difficulty: buried in the text, trying to escape through
understanding, and yet mocked by the text (in its portrayal of Gil-Martin and Robert as splitters of hairs but also of George, who is incapable
of interpretation and falls victim to Robert) for the attempt. The suicide's grave, Redekop suggests (1985: 161), is a metaphor for the
enclosure of the text. The 'odor of mortality' (p. 161) which comes
from the grave and its occupant during the various grave-robbing occasions mocks the robber/interpreters' attempts to discover the truth on
the basis of the evidence of a rotting corpse. However, Redekop resists
a reading that stops in a circle of nihilistic scepticism and that simply
accepts that the reader's desire for gaps to be filled will not be fulfilled.
Instead she argues that Hogg's 'parodies of dead books [should be
seen] as a static negative against which we may see a positive, dynamic
affirmation of scripture' (1985: 173).

The model in which Redekop suggests the reader is expected to find
meaning is the biblical parable. In the reader's search for a witness with
prophetic authority, Penpunt's story, the 'Auchtermuchty Tale' (1824:
162-66), within Robert's narrative offers an alternative and more
oblique response to gaps in the narrative. In the Tale, Robin Ruthven
saves the overly-pious people of Auchtermuchty from being beguiled
by the preaching of the devil in disguise. A feature of parables such as
the Tale is their need to be completed by interpretation and their
assumption of a larger level of meaning that cannot be reduced to narrative sequence. The moral of Penpunt's story, the need to become an
insider like Robin, without becoming like Robert, and to exercise their
freedom of interpretation (in this case by recognizing and applying the
Golden Rule [Mt. 22.39 etc.]), is one which the reader is called on to
practise and apply within the text. Common sense and a recognition of
belonging to a tradition that is greater than any single member should
act as correctives. The people of Auchtermuchty fail to apply the first of
these correctives, and Robert fails to apply the second, by refusing to
accept Penpunt's story as a counterbalance to what he believes to be
divine revelation.

For Redekop, Hogg's appearance in the novel also offers the reader
an escape-route from indeterminacy. By symbolically dying into his
fiction, Hogg identifies himself with the buried figure of Robert. Hogg

guides the reader to Robert's grave and offers the reader the possibility of resurrection through judgment of Robert's doctrine and yet sympathy for his mistakes. By forgiving Robert, the reader banishes the ghost of Gil-Martin and works towards a Jerusalem of which the last judgment of antinomianism is a parody. The novel's final affirmation of collective humanity and of the values of love and forgiveness reaches out to embrace the community of readers. Redekop (1985: 182) comments that 'It does so by offering the process of misreading itself (the failure to fill the blanks) as an experience of mutual fallibility and by intimating (through a more oblique response to blanks) a prophetic level which makes of us one congregation'.

In summary, then, Redekop argues that the reader is offered no escape into answers by the text of the *Confessions*. However, the Auchtermuchty Tale and the appearance of Hogg, the shepherd-creator, offer the reader some help, and oral tradition and biblical narrative provide a reference to a world outside the text. The reader is given a chance to break out of the cycle of indeterminacy if, after many mis-readings, they recognize these clues and are able to pity Robert for not recognizing them.

Redekop's argument has a distinctly deconstructive flavour, although ultimately it depends on finding stability in the intention of the author[13] and in the text and message of the Bible.[14] Her argument loses its strength if authorial intention and the concept of the Bible as a privileged text are questioned. Deconstructive critics begin from a position of scepticism towards both. Petrie (1992) is one of the few critics of Hogg who has attempted such a radical reading of the text. Using an extended (presumably fictitious) example from a modern perspective,[15] he seeks to show that Robert should be read as mad rather than bad. Robert is in a state of 'paranoid hysteria' (p. 61) rather than mortal sin, and this should have implications for the amount of sympathy he is

---

13. Redekop (1985: 164) states that '[t]he peculiar hybrid of genres that constitutes *A Justified Sinner* derives from the tension in Hogg between the conventions of oral tradition and those of printed narrative'.

14. Redekop (1985: 176) argues that 'unless the reader is a privileged participant in [biblical] tradition, the gaps following scriptural allusions will remain inert and the prophetic truth will be dumb'. For Redekop, the 'gaps' in the narrative are in the shape of a stable, definable biblical tradition.

15. Petrie (1992) constructs an elaborate story about being falsely accused of several murders, and the psychological effect this has on him.

shown by his readers. Petrie suggests that the *Confessions* throws readers into such a state of emotional anxiety that they make mistakes in their readings that then appear in their work on the text. Their prejudices and fears have been imported into their reading of the text. He offers several examples of these misreadings, including the reader anxious to consign Robert to hell as a sinner. As Petrie points out, the basis for the assumption that Robert is damned comes from the end of the novel in which the Editor asserts that Robert committed the act which, 'according to the tenets he embraced... consigned his memory to everlasting detestation' (1824: 208). It is according to Robert's beliefs that he is consigned to hell, and there is no reason for the reader necessarily to embrace this doctrine. For Petrie, this desire of the reader to judge and condemn Robert as a sinner beyond redemption leads away from the most obvious reaction to a suicide, which is pity. Another example of such misreading is the attempt of a critic to establish a category of secure, privileged readers using the fallacious insights offered by biographical details about the author. As has been discussed, this covers the work of many of the critics of Hogg, who argue that as Hogg knew his Bible, he must have been a Christian and must have expected his readers to respond to biblical allusions in a particular way. For Petrie, Hogg (and Robert) has been unlucky in his readers. Because offering sympathy and then empathy to a madman threatens the sanity of the reader, the reader chooses to judge him as a sinner, rather than as a mad criminal whose condition might have been provoked by his environment and might be retrieved by greater understanding and pity. Petrie offers a new way of reading the *Confessions* which recognizes the influence of the culture of the critic and cuts itself loose from the restrictions of authorial intention. These are two of the marks of a deconstructive approach.

Lumsden's work, discussed in detail in Chapter 2, applies postmodern literary critical thought to Hogg's text, although it continues to make assumptions about Hogg's intentions and the bearing of his historical setting on his work. Lumsden relies on assumptions about Hogg's own religious beliefs, and our ability to discover them, in order to read the *Confessions* as a warning against rigid systems such as antinomianism. She takes Hogg's writing on the dangers of religious wrangling in his Lay Sermons as evidence that his intention in the *Confessions* was to satirize the disputatiousness of Robert Wringhim senior. However, such an argument ignores the fact that Hogg was entering the religious debate, with a firmly held view-point and intention, by writing the novel. He must be judged to be engaging in the very activity he seeks to condemn. Lumsden may also be criticized for her certainty that characters such as George and Blanchard are sympathetic characters who carry the voice and view of the author. It could equally be argued that it is the Editor's prejudiced sympathy which lies with George and his father, and that Hogg's sympathy towards these characters is difficult to reconstruct. George could be read as an aimless, dissolute young man who spends his time playing games, drinking and whoring with his friends, and who violently assaults his brother. Carey (1969) had noted that the Laird is the only character in the novel, apart from Gil-Martin, who refuses to pray (1824: 4). Certainly the shocking and disturbing nature of the Laird's actions towards his bride on his wedding night are glossed over by the Editor (1824: 6-7). The scene offers an early example of the ways in which the Editor's prejudices lead to a warped account. His sympathy for the Colwans may be far removed from that of Hogg. Petrie (1992) has also offered an argument against reading Blanchard as a positive character in the text. Lumsden had suggested that Blanchard's theology involved a more flexible theological system than Wringhim's. Blanchard preached that morality was an evolving grammar that had to be worked out in a variety of contexts, and which demanded everyone take responsibility for their actions. Wringhim preached that God had already determined each person's eternal fate: Hogg's purpose was to argue that this way leads to possession. However, Petrie argues that Blanchard's preaching is simply Wringhim's inverted. Wringhim had preached that everything is predestined, so no one is to blame for anything they do. Blanchard's philosophy disregards any extenuating circumstances behind any action, and loads all responsibility onto an individual. As he says, '[i]t was every man's own blame if he was not saved' (1824: 110), regardless of his upbringing or his psychological state. Blanchard's preaching is as inflexible as Wringhim's, and as harsh. Lumsden argues that evidence from other works by Hogg, such as his short story 'Sound Morality' (1982d), suggests that Hogg believed human compassion, which adapts itself to different situations, to be a more flexible and moral way of life than Wringhim's predestination. That may have been Hogg's own belief: but Blanchard need not be read as embracing such a belief.

Lumsden also suggests that Robert is given opportunities to embrace the more flexible grammar of characters such as Blanchard, and to turn from the system of his parents. One such example is the appearance of the White Lady as Robert prepares to kill George on Arthur's Seat. The White Lady offers Robert grace and a chance to escape the ensnarement of Gil-Martin. However, I suggest that this reading sits very uncomfortably with the actual text. The woman's 'still small voice' offers 'derision and chiding' (1824: 129) rather than the guidance and encouragement God gives Elijah in 1 Kings 19. Her 'severity' appals Robert, and her words are scarcely those of a ministering angel of grace. She asks how Robert dares to lift his eyes to heaven with such purposes in his heart: Robert had already told us he was about to ask direction from above. It seems scarcely likely that this figure of vengeance is an answer to his unformed prayer, as she implies he had no right to seek guidance. Her ultimatum, to escape and save his soul, or 'farewell forever', cannot be read as a word from God, as it denies all New Testament teaching about the offer of grace to all who repent. This creature suggests that if Robert carries out the planned act, he will have no possibility of later repentance. Given his state of mind, this represents the unrelenting teaching of Blanchard, rather than a word of grace. Lumsden's sympathetic reading of the *Lady in White*, and her assumption that this reading represents Hogg's view, is not ultimately convincing. Her use of the postmodern idea of the ex-centric opens up new possibilities for reading Hogg's work, as was demonstrated in Chapter 2, but her dependence on assumptions about Hogg's sympathies, which the text does not always support, is problematic.

Deconstructive Approaches to Revelation, Carlyle and Hogg: The View from the Abyss

Deconstructive readings of both the *Confessions* and the Bible are rare although their number is increasing.[16] For both texts, such an enterprise involves questioning similar assumptions about textual unity, origin and status. In their respective fields, both texts occupy an important place. With the publication of the Qumran texts, there has been an increased interest in apocalyptic in biblical studies,[17] and, as the millennium

16. See Chapter 1 for a discussion of the influence of deconstruction on readings of the Bible, such as the Bible and Culture Collective's (1995).

17. At the annual British New Testament Conference, a new seminar group on the topic of Revelation has been set up in response to demand from participants in the conference.

approaches, Revelation is eagerly read for clues about the end of the world.[18] Within the field of Scottish Literature, Hogg's *Confessions* has a central role. Its absence from the syllabus of a First Year university course would surely be commented upon.[19] The Hogg Society, based at Stirling University, regularly holds conferences and publishes papers on Hogg's work. The meaning of both texts, the *Confessions* and Revelation, is disputed but important to large and diverse bodies of readers. The status each text enjoys has arguably prevented or resisted the postmodern and deconstructive readings to which other texts have been subjected. In much of the critical work on both the *Confessions* and Revelation, authorial intention remains sovereign. The search for the meaning of both texts has intrigued many readers, and is most often accompanied by a firm conviction that an answer to the difficulties is to be found in the historical context of the text allied to the author's real or perceived psychological or spiritual state. Commentators on Revelation such as Bauckham (1993a), Fiorenza (1985) and Thompson (1990) are as wedded to these apparently fixed points of interpretation as are Campbell (1972a; 1988b), Carey (1969) or Groves (1985) (or, ultimately, Redekop [1985] or Lumsden [1992]). However, in contrast, Pippin (1994) offers a deconstructive reading of Revelation that challenges the validity and usefulness of traditional historical–critical assumptions, and which in turn offers new possibilities for reading the *Confessions*.

Pippin[20] chooses the concept of the abyss as the entry-point into a fragmented reading of Revelation. She comments that:

> The abyss is a postmodern site because it is a site of conflict and struggle and chaos—the center that collapses... The abyss represents what in postmodernism is the unpresentable, the indeterminate, the fragmented, the self-less and the depth-less (1994: 252).

In the apparently perfect new world described in the visions of Revelation, chaos continues at the edges of the new creation. Death and Hades have been thrown into the lake of fire (20.14), and within the

---

18. A most extreme example comes from 1993 when members of David Koresh's group, the Branch Davidian Sect, apparently burned themselves alive at their 'Ranch Apocalypse' in Waco, Texas.

19. Campbell (1988b: 94) remarks that the *Confessions* 'is now widely accepted as a masterpiece of Scottish fiction'.

20. Pippin's extended work on Revelation, (1992), will be discussed in Chapter 5.

New Jerusalem the blessed are welcomed, but remaining '[o]utside are the dogs and sorcerers and fornicators and murderers and idolaters, and everyone who loves and practises falsehood' (Rev. 22.15). In Rev. 21.4, 'the former things have passed away', and yet in ch. 22 the angel tells John that the evildoer is still to be allowed still to do evil, and the filthy still to be filthy (v. 11). The continuing presence of the abyss in the landscape of utopia, the home of the horrifying and torturing locusts (9.5-6) and of the beast who kills the witnesses in ch. 11, threatens the order and victory of God which the text struggles to portray. Although the city of God may be measured (21.15-17), the abyss is bottomless, deferring the closure of the text, and avoiding the control of the author. As Pippin asks, 'Is creation really new if chaos still abides outside the garden gates? Why does this breach, this rupture, this gaping hole remain in the textual landscape?' (1994: 251).

Most readings of Revelation, like most readings of the *Confessions*, attempt to fill the chaos of the text with ordered meaning. Postmodern literary critical readings such as Pippin's allow chaos to have prece-dence, and to create its own space and disorder. Instead of privileging the final order of the end of time and God's victory over evil's forces, Pippin argues that 'the new Jerusalem as an ordered space is decentred by the well of chaos' (1994: 253). Intertextually, the ἄβυσσος (Rev. 20.1-3) is the mouth of hell,[21] its dangerous depths filled with monsters and serpents (Ps. 42.7), into which those to be punished are thrown to be tortured: 'there are wheels of fire, and men and women hung thereon by the power of their whirling. Those in the pit burn' (*Apoc. Pet.* 12). Its originlessness relates to the Derridean idea that there is no source or origin to meaning: in 1 En. 21.7 the abyss is 'full of great pillars of fire which were made to fall; neither its extent nor its size could I see, nor could I see its source'. The presence of this postmodern icon of gaping absence in the text of Revelation invites speculation.

Pippin asserts that 'the abyss is what one sees when one sees the Other' (1994: 263). The Other of the Apocalypse's abyss is the horrible and profane, the ultimate threat, which is the body of the female.[22] The

21. 'Then when the well was opened there came up immediately a disagreeable and very evil smell which surpassed all the punishments. And I looked in to the well and saw fiery masses on all sides, and the narrowness of the well at its mouth was such that it was only able to take a single man' (*Apoc. Paul* 32).

22. In Sedgwick's (1985) reading of the *Confessions*, the female is equally regarded as Other in the text. In the Editor's narrative, during the tennis match,

woman's body is sacrificed throughout the text (see the personification and destruction of Babylon in ch. 18, or the judgment of the harlot in 19.1-3): yet in the abyss a womb-like space remains, a 'chasm of devouring horrors' (p. 263) which seduces the reader who both fears and desires it. Demons enter the abyss, while only the purified enter the Bride, the New Jerusalem, therefore the abyss must be controlled by lock and key (9.1; 20.1-3). As Pippin comments, '[w]hat remains is the [female] murmur, the rupture that the presence of the abyss places in the text' (p. 261).

The visions of John apparently portray a world of imposed order, in an attempt to ignore or control the murmur from the abyss. However, represented in the narrative of Revelation is a desire for primordial creation, a new birth signalled by the Edenic tree and waters of life in the New Jerusalem (22.1-2). History repeats itself and the presence of the originless and boundless abyss represents the creative and disruptive power of the female, the echo of the formless void out of which the world was first created in Genesis. The presence of the abyss affects the stability of both the New Jerusalem and the text itself. Its existence on the boundaries of the heavenly city continually threatens the city with recreation from within its depths. Its surplus erotic power defies interpretation or meaning and denies the text the status of sacred constancy. The city and the text that describes it are left in ruins. There is no end to the process of interpretation and exegesis: the historical-critical approach to the text requires a grounding in meaning, which the abyss denies, 'for to stand in the abyss is to stand no place' (Pippin 1992: 264).

For Pippin, the abyss has offered a perspective from which to read Revelation deconstructively. I suggest that the presence of the pit of damnation in the *Confessions* offers a similar perspective from which to read that text. There are several striking similarities on a formal level

Robert submits to a feminization of his character in order to get close to George, the more powerful and prestigious man. His nosebleed corresponds to the emblem of specifically female powerlessness that occurs in eighteenth-century novels at moments of sexual threat against women. 'The tools for advancement he perceives himself possessing are those belonging to the castrated, to the visibly and even disgustingly powerless' (p. 102). The oppression of women in the context of male transactive desire is equally telling: the treatment of the Laird's wife is described without comment by the Editor, as acceptable behaviour. It is the relationships between men, both homophiliac and homophobic, which are of interest.

between Revelation and the *Confessions*. Both use a combination of
genres (Revelation the apocalypse and the letter; the *Confessions* the
'objective' report and the 'subjective' memoir). Both claim to have a
didactic or moral aim, and the ending of both invokes a curse on anyone
who changes the text that is handed down to them. Both, then, envisage
their readership extending across time, and attempt to control the
interpretations to which they are subjected. In fact, both texts have been
read in multiple and contradictory ways since their creation. Their
didactic claims have been undermined by their complexity and elusive-
ness. Pippin argues that the presence of the abyss has created this instability in Revelation. It has forced upon the reader the question of how
the indescribable is to be described. I argue below that the presence of
the boundless and sourceless chasm of hell in Hogg's text may be read
as creating the same indeterminacy, and as inviting similarly startling
interpretations.

> Truth, unveiling, illumination are no longer decided in the appropriation
> of the truth of being, but are cast into its bottomless abyss as non-truth,
> veiling and dissimulation (Derrida 1979: 119).

> All was wrapt in a chaos of confusion and darkness (Hogg 1824: 47).

> It was beyond description, conception, or the soul of man to bear (Hogg
> 1824: 183).

In the *Confessions*, the threat of the pit is omni-present. As George
communes with nature on Arthur's Seat, apparently in a blessed state,
he sees the 'wee ghost of the rainbow'. The Editor describes the scene:

> the cloud of haze lying dense in that deep dell that separates the hill from
> the rocks of Salisbury, and the dull shadow of the hill mingling with that
> cloud, made the dell a pit of darkness. On that shadowy cloud was the
> lovely rainbow formed (Hogg 1824: 32-33).

The dark void exists under every beautiful and blessed thing. The
Editor finds its horror unspeakable (in the fight outside the pub, the
Whig party breathe vengeance on the 'heirs of d_n_t_n' [p. 23]), but
allows its darkness to threaten the world he as Editor creates. Characters on all sides threaten the others with eternal destruction. Wringhim
Senior tells the adulterous Laird he has come to 'save him from the
jaws of destruction' (p. 11), although the young Robert is taught to pray
'that his father might be carried quick into hell' (p. 15). In the presence
of his brother and his friends, Robert is described as 'an object to all of
the uttermost disgust' (p. 19), and George considers him his 'polluted

brother' (p. 20): his place is assigned to the boundary where the
unwanted and horrible are kept at a (safe?) distance. In his own narrative, Robert is persuaded that he has been 'plucked as a brand out of the
burning' (p. 93), although Blanchard warns that the creed of his father
and of Gil-Martin 'carries damnation on the very front of it' (p. 107).
Hell, although greatly feared, is invoked by all. Whoever is considered
the Other is assigned there with rabid certainty. For the characters in the
novel Hell is the place where the Other originally belongs and where
the Other will without doubt return.

To each character, including each narrator, hell has a different
meaning corresponding to his or her understanding of the Other.[23] To
Robert, Miss Logan is a 'hag of the pit!' (p. 73): the expression is intelligible in view of his professed antipathy towards women. The Editor's
hell, to which he consigns Robert's memory and name, is 'everlasting
detestation' (1824: 208): the Editor's popularism (he pleads he is
'blameless' in bringing discredit to the Church (p. 207) and confesses
not to understand the pamphlet he has produced for readers who must
also find it opaque [1824: 208]) creates a hell out of the state of being
unpopular. This unstable pervasion of the gaping void of hell engulfs
the presence of God in the text. In this world in which the pits of hell
break through and underlie everything, all positive influences are
threatened. Wringhim Senior speaks of the church in terms of the action
of a gaping hole: 'all earthly bonds and fellowships are absorbed and
swallowed up in the holy community of the Reformed Church' (p. 11).

Miss Logan longs for God to begin the eternal punishment even
before the wicked die, stating that 'if the Almighty do not hurl them
[George's murderers] down, blasted with shame and confusion, there is

23. Jackson suggests that 'over the course of the nineteenth century, fantasies
structured around dualism...reveal the *internal* origin of the other'. The demonic is
a manifestation of unconscious desire rather than a supernatural figure. In novels
such as Hogg's *Confessions* and Mary Shelley's *Frankenstein* 'themes of the "I"
and the "not-I" interact strangely, expressing difficulties of knowledge (of the "I")
(introducing problems of *vision*) and of guilt, over desire (relation to the "not-I")
articulated in the narrative (introducing problems of *discourse*), the two intert-
wining with each other' (1981: 55). The issues of duality and of the relationship
with the internal Other are clearly demonstrated and explored in Robert's relationship with Gil-Martin, which, as Jackson argues, has a corresponding effect on
Robert's psyche and on his and our ability to understand the discourse of his world.
I suggest that the issue of the Other in the *Confessions* affects several of the characters, and not just Robert, and adds to the unstable nature of the text.

no hope of retribution in this life' (p. 65). In fact, for all its rhetoric of after-death judgment and punishment, the text strongly implies that hell exists in the present world. The physical landscape, and the landscape of the mind are the depths of damnation. Robert prepares to kill George on Arthur's Seat:

> I thought of the awful thing of plunging a fellow creature from the top of a cliff into the dark and misty void below—of his being dashed to pieces on the protruding rocks, and of hearing his shrieks as he descended the cloud, and beheld the shagged points on which he was to alight. Then I thought of plunging a soul so abruptly into hell, or, at the best, sending it to hover on the confines of that burning abyss (p. 131).

For Robert, the world he surveys and inhabits, and the other-world he is obsessed with collapse into the 'dark and misty void'. Hell also seeps into his consciousness. Once he is forced to leave Dalcastle, Robert experiences the terrors of a mental hell in which his own identity has become Other to him. He writes, 'I was become a terror to myself; or rather, my body and soul were become terrors to each other... I shuddered at my own image and likeness' (p. 186). For Robert, his creation in the 'image and likeness' of God (Gen. 1.26) is an experience of hell. In the abyss, the identity of a loving God is swallowed up. If Robert is his reflection, God's reality is the Other, whom the apparently 'good' characters, such as Blanchard and the Laird, loathe. The Editor asserts that '[i]t is the controller of Nature alone, that can bring light out of darkness, and order out of confusion' (p. 46), and yet it is his experience, and the reader's, that very little in the way of revelation is offered. In the text, the presence of the abyss is not balanced by the presence of God. The identity of God, the existence of heaven, and the hope of revelation and meaning are radically undermined by the encroaching power of the indescribable pit of damnation.

The perspective of the abyss offered Pippin a new, deconstructive way to read Revelation, and in the last section I have begun to consider Hogg's *Confessions* from the same perspective. Before taking this reading further, it will be useful to attempt a similar reading of another nineteenth-century text, in order to show that Hogg's *Confessions* is not an isolated and unusual text which alone responds well to such a deconstructive reading. Thomas Carlyle's first major work, *Sartor Resartus* (1833, all quotations taken from the 1987 World's Classics edition), is very different from Hogg's *Confessions*, although both works share certain features in common. The texts were written within a decade of each other by Scots from similarly disadvantaged backgrounds. Both texts are structurally and stylistically complex and resistant to closure, relying on mediating editors and demanding considerable effort on the part of the reader to make sense of the material mediated to them. *Sartor Resartus* received much the same critical response both from its contemporary readers and from twentieth-century critics as the *Confessions*: bewilderment at first, and then a need to explain and account for the text's difficulties. A short consideration of the history of the interpretation of *Sartor Resartus*, and a deconstructive reading of the destabilizing effect of the abyss on the text, are offered below as a demonstration of the way in which deconstruction highlights the inadequacies of traditional criticism and the indeterminacies of all texts.

In 1830 Carlyle wrote a long article entitled 'Thoughts on Clothes' which he submitted for publication *Fraser's Magazine* but then withdrew. He expanded it into a novel, *Sartor Resartus*, and in 1831 took it to London to find a publisher. Unsuccessful in this, he re-submitted it in 1833 to *Fraser's Magazine* for serial publication. Later in the century, once it was published as a novel, *Sartor Resartus* was very popular (in their Introduction to the 1987 edition, McSweeney and Sabor refer to it as 'secular scripture for the Victorians' [p. viii]), but initially readers were perplexed and critical. Leigh Hunt commented to Carlyle that he was 'mystified enough when your *Sartor Resartus* first appeared, to take it for a satire on 'Germanick[?ism]'...[although it] also nevertheless appeared...to intimate a number of serious and deep things in it' (Sanders 1963: 464). John Stuart Mill, otherwise sympathetic towards Carlyle and his views, asked why he could not have been more direct (see Mineka 1963: 176, cited in Baker, 1986: 225 n. 14).

As in Hogg's *Confessions*, the multi-levelled narrative structure and style of *Sartor Resartus* confused its readers. The materials of the novel, a work by the German philosopher Diogenes Teufelsdröckh, *Die Kleider, ihr Werden und Wirken*, and a chaotic collection of biographical and other documents by and about Teufelsdröckh, are transmitted to the reader by an editor. The Editor has a personal and professional interest in the philosopher and his work, having made his acquaintance while in Germany, and is keen to transmit his ideas in a way which British readers will comprehend. The Editor comments that part of his endeavour is '[t]o bring what order we can out of this Chaos' (Carlyle 1833: 27). The only access the reader has to either the philosophical work or the fragmentary material is through the quotations the Editor selects, and the interpretative comments he makes. The Editor is not a neutral presenter of the material at his disposal, and at times he freely expresses his criticism, confusion or ambivalence towards the ideas expressed in Teufelsdröckh's work. Of the philosophy the Editor asks, 'Is it of a truth leading us into beatific Asphodel meadows, or the yellow-burning of a Hell-on-earth?' (p. 55). Because only the Editor's perspective is available, readers must come to their own conclusions and possibly decide to distance themselves from that perspective.

The complex relationship between the philosophy itself, the biographical details (which the Editor offers in order to elucidate the philosophy) and the Editor's (imperfect) understanding of either form the content of the novel and the task of the reader. In the same way that the *Confessions* has been approached, modern critics have sought to explain the novel's difficulties by appealing to the author's assumed intention or to some other discernible 'key'. In the introduction to his study of the novel, Tennyson asserts that:

> [t]he questions that persist in plaguing the literary critic of *Sartor* are those posed so early in the career of that remarkable work. What kind of plan holds the whole work together and what is the key to the idiosyncratic style? Laying aside the answers that there is no discernible plan and that the style was adopted merely for shock effect, let us consider two means of coming to genuinely illuminating answers to these questions (1965: 6-7).

Tennyson's two means are to compare *Sartor* with Carlyle's earlier work, tracing the patterns and concerns already visible, and then to offer a critical analysis of the work itself, 'with an eye toward discerning a pattern to the organisation and a logic to the style' (1965: 8). In the second of these two approaches, the role of the Editor is pivotal and deliberate. He is 'a normative voice in the presentation of the strange material. At the same time the Editor is an actor in the drama of the dissemination of Teufelsdröckh's views to England' (1965: 176). The Editor is a 'figure in the larger novelistic structure and…a bridge to the materials of Teufelsdröckh and the clothes philosophy' (p. 183). The Editor's problem of creating order out of the chaos given to him is the reader's problem too. Although initially unsure about Teufelsdröckh and his philosophy, in the end he confesses his admiration for the man and his work. For Tennyson, the Editor reveals Carlyle's intention to the reader, and enables the reader to accept and understand a philosophy very different from the traditional British empiricism. The Editor is a commentator on the philosophical movement of Teufelsdröckh's (and Carlyle's) ideas. The creative procedure of the novel is paralleled by the critical procedure embodied in the Editor. Carlyle offers both the poetic insight of the clothes metaphor and a critical commentary on that insight. With the Editor, the reader experiences the clothes metaphor as art but also examines it as a critic. Because he was unable to trust the readers he was addressing to understand and apply his philosophical message, Carlyle provided a reader within the work as an example and interpreter. Tennyson argues that Carlyle's message to the age, that the material world should be seen as a window on the transcendental and divine, is shown to be both preached and applied in the same novel. The Editor functions as an important character in the drama, but is also the ideal reader of Carlyle's philosophy. When actual readers (such as Tennyson) read the Editor as an idealized version of themselves, they are enabled to read Carlyle, and *Sartor Resartus*, in the intended way.

A more recent commentator on the novel (Baker 1986: 218) argues with Tennyson that 'Carlyle's purpose in writing *Sartor Resartus* is to convert British readers to the Clothes Philosophy'. However, for Baker, the Editor's role in the carrying out of this intention is not simply to lead the reader into gradual agreement with Teufelsdröckh's views. In this reading the Editor's scepticism rather than his growing acceptance and understanding is central. Against all conventional methods of persuasive logic, Carlyle uses irony as his method of bringing about the reader's understanding. He wants his readers to discover for themselves the open secret of his philosophy which will lead them to perceive their surroundings in a completely new way. Baker comments that 'to this purpose Carlyle creates the multi-form ironies which play with the allusion of the surface appearance of the world about him' (1986: 222). Carlyle's first step in the process of guiding the reader into enlightenment through ironic play with the meaning of symbols is to throw the reader's normal perception of the world into confusion. In the apparent chaos of Teufelsdröckh's examples of things which have lost their meaning (such as the sham aprons of clergy costumes [1833: 35]), the reader is expected to begin to question whether or not any object is authentic. The confusion of Carlyle's contemporaries, argues Baker, 'was due to Carlyle's intentional disruption of the expectations of his British audience's naive realism' (1986: 225). The Editor has a role as guide through the confusion: he has mastered Teufelsdröckh's philosophy and acts as a sign that other English readers may do the same.

When he confesses ignorance, his dissimulation is Socratic rather than actual. His pretence of disagreeing with Teufelsdröckh is designed to shock readers into rethinking their views. The Editor follows Teufelsdröckh's method and is an equal participant in the irony. When he apparently scolds Teufelsdröckh for the opinions expressed in the conclusion of 'The World Out of Clothes' (1833: 46), and seems to be taking the view of the conservative British audience, he is in fact participating in the professor's method of shocking the reader through capriciousness, and is having fun with the possible interpretations of stripping humanity of clothes. He admits as much, and makes Carlyle's method transparent:

> The Professor knows full well what he is saying; and both thou and we, in our haste, do him wrong. The truth is, Teufelsdröckh, though a Sansculottist, is no Adamite (1833: 47).

Teufelsdröckh plays with the nature of things' appearance, while the Editor plays with the nature of Teufelsdröckh's ironic appearance. The Editor adds his own ironies to the ironies of Teufelsdröckh's writing, forcing readers to sort out the different strands of irony in order to teach them how to discriminate between real and sham symbols. In the contributions of both the Editor and Teufelsdröckh, Carlyle's aim is to show the reader how to see.

Central to Baker's argument is that Carlyle uses irony to make his point. No system of beliefs can do justice to the complexity and chaos of existence, but it is important to try to make sense of the universe, therefore it is wrong to have no system of belief. Through the text Carlyle wants his readers to gain the experience of comparing the surface meaning of things with their ideal, but from within this romantic vision he ironically sees the inadequacy of suggesting that finite existence is an experience of God's infinity. The Editor's doubts as expressed in the text are in accord with the views of Teufelsdröckh in that they are a recognition of the inadequacy of any philosophy. The Editor and the reader realize with the Professor that any expression of the ideal in the actual is flawed.

For both Tennyson and Baker, Carlyle's intention and method are recoverable. Once recovered, this knowledge makes the difficult text of *Sartor Resartus* comprehensible and closed. Baker reads and interprets the ambivalence of the Editor more sensitively than Tennyson, but both assume that the Editor's role in the text is to guide the reader and that Teufelsdröckh's Philosophy of Clothes is one shared by Carlyle. The complexity and depth of the text supports many other approaches. As a parallel or 'control' discussion to the deconstructive readings of the *Confessions* already offered, I briefly consider some of the ways that chaos threatens the assumed stability of traditional readings and interpretations of *Sartor Resartus*, and in particular its use of the Bible.

The Bible is rarely mentioned directly in the novel, although many biblical images and parallels are drawn. In 'The Everlasting Yea' section, Teufelsdröckh warns against arguing over the issue of the 'Plenary Inspiration' of Scripture. He suggests:

> try rather to get a little even Partial Inspiration, each of you for himself. One Bible I know, of whose Plenary Inspiration doubt is not so much as possible; nay with my own eyes I saw the God's-Hand writing it: thereof all other Bibles are but leaves,—say, in Picture-Writing to assist the weaker faculty (1833: 147).

Extreme subjectivity and the superiority of experience are the hermeneutical principles Teufelsdröckh follows and recommends. In the text, the motif of creation is prevalent and is treated largely according to these principles. The Editor and the philosopher are both God-figures who interpret their role as one of creating out of the chaos that threatens to overwhelm them. As he surveys the paper bags of material, the Editor describes his task as 'endeavouring to evolve printed creation out of a German printed and written chaos' (1833: 62). However, the creation that results is hardly less threatening or comprehensible than the chaos from which it is saved. In the endeavour, which most readers would agree is only partially completed, the Editor's self, as he predicted, is 'swallowed up' (p. 62) into the creation. His self is 'sucked' into the whirlpool which is the professor's mind (p. 221). The creation itself is described as a 'Hell-gate Bridge over Chaos' (p. 155): in contrast to the mighty and threatening power of chaos, his creation is a flimsy structure that leads people from the apparent safety of their self-understanding into 'underground humours, and intricate sardonic rogueries, wheel-within-wheel, [which] defy all reckoning' (p. 153). This 'god' and his 'creation' are highly unstable and scarcely to be distinguished from the confusion of the paper bags of fragments.

Teufelsdröckh and his creation are equally threatened by the chaos of the pre-existent abyss. In his description of the human experiences he undergoes, his psyche is assailed by the forces of darkness. At the death of his adopted father, '[t]he dark boundless Abyss, that lies under our feet, had yawned open' (p. 82); and having been rejected by the woman he loves, 'thick curtains of Night rushed over his soul...through the ruins as of a shivered Universe, was he falling, falling, falling towards the Abyss' (p. 113). Although he describes his conversion as a waking from 'heavy dreams' to 'a new heaven and a new Earth' (p. 142), the new creation of the vision of Revelation, the chaos of his earlier life has not disappeared:

> Wheresoever two or three Living Men are gathered together, there is Society; or there it will be, with its cunning mechanisms and stupendous structures, over-spreading this little globe, and reaching upwards to Heaven and downwards to Gehenna: for always, under one or the other figure, has it two authentic Revelations, of a God and of a Devil; the Pulpit, namely, and the Gallows (p. 179).

The centrality of the figure of the Phoenix to Teufelsdröckh's creation, his philosophy, equally holds within itself both positive and negative forces: 'In that Fire-whirlwind, Creation and Destruction proceed together' (p. 184). Creativity is presented as inherently unstable. Chaos is both a devouring pit and the pregnant womb from which creation emerges. As the Editor muses, it may have been 'in Monmouth Street, at the bottom of our own English "ink-sea"', that Teufelsdröckh's philosophy 'first took being, and shot forth its salient point in his soul,—as in Chaos did the Egg of Eros, one day to be hatched into a Universe!' (1833: 184). In Carlyle's text the ambiguities of the biblical picture of creation, of creation out of the formless darkness of the deep (Gen. 1.2), are explored and subverted from the romantic perspective of subjective experience. At a deeper level, the presence of chaos threatens to overwhelm both the text of the Bible, and *Sartor Resartus* itself. I suggest, then, that Revelation, Hogg's *Confessions* and Carlyle's *Sartor Resartus* may all be read from the deconstructive perspective of the abyss.

In Chapter 2, it was suggested that biblical intertextuality in the *Confessions* may be read as a deliberate, historically-rooted strategy of the author to illuminate his text and to draw his reader into participating in the creation of meaning in ex-centric but still expected ways. It has been argued here, however, that in a deconstructive context the presence of the pit of damnation in texts such as the *Confessions* and *Sartor Resartus* completely destabilizes and deprivileges all previously-held views about God and the Bible. Many of Hogg's commentators have assumed that the Bible was for Hogg and remains for modern readers a stable, sacred and privileged text. What happens to the *Confessions* when chaos and indeterminacy are allowed precedence to create their own space and disorder, as they were in my reading of *Sartor Resartus*? In the following section, I return to the *Confessions* to continue my reading of the view from the abyss.

Campbell's (1972a) interpretation of Robert's vision of the golden weapons has already been discussed in Chapter 2. The reader is expected to realize that Robert interprets the experience as an echo of Peter's vision described in Acts 11. Having made this move, the reader understands afresh Robert's blinding spiritual pride, which leads him to believe he is an apostle with a mission as elevated as that of Peter. In fact the purpose of the vision is to give Robert a chance to turn on Gil-Martin. Gil-Martin himself realizes this, and drags Robert away before he has a chance to consider the meaning of the vision any further. For Campbell, then, although this is not highlighted by him, the reader is expected to take the perspective of the devil, against the evidence of the narrator and the similarities of the vision to Peter's vision in Acts 11. There seems to be no alternative to the two possible and equally disturbing views: the vision is either an echo of Peter's vision, which encourages Robert to kill Blanchard; or it is a divine yet deceiving shadow of that vision which in fact very obliquely offers Robert the opportunity to turn on Gil-Martin. It may be that Gil-Martin's response, to drag Robert away from this threatening apparition, is the sensible one, and his assertion that Robert was 'dreaming' (Hogg 1834:112) is a word of comfort. The God of the abyss may indeed be more constant than the God of such deceptive visions. As Gil-Martin assures Robert, 'doubt thou not, that he whom *thou* servest, will be ever at thy right and left hand, to direct and assist thee' (p. 112).

The vision itself encourages a reading from the perspective of the abyss. The 'cloudy veil' that Robert looks 'up into' (pp. 112-13) is like the mist hovering over the mouth of a deep ravine. This blinding, dim vapour is Robert's (and Campbell's) heaven. Moses had to wear a veil to prevent the Israelites from being blinded by the glory of the presence of God which continued to shine from his face (Exod. 34.29-35). Here heaven is a 'veil' (p. 112) which causes Robert's blindness and through which golden weapons are pointed at him. The veil is a tapestry ('the dim tapestry of the firmament' [p. 113]). When Robert has tried to find God, he has seen only the reverse side of the tapestry without realizing it, and the chance to discern whether a pattern exists at all has been denied to him. This same veil has blinded generations of critics who have failed to see that God, revelation and meaning are destabilized by the abyss which underlies everything in the world of the text.

In this destabilized world, intertextual echoes of the Bible affect a reading of the *Confessions* and are then reflected back into a reading of the biblical text itself, altered and subverted. The relationship between Robert and George affects a reading of the biblical brothers Cain and Abel. Mrs Calvert is given the words which implicitly introduce the idea of the story of Cain and Abel in the Editor's account: 'if there is an earthly crime... for the due punishment of which the Almighty might be supposed to subvert the order of nature, it is fratricide' (p. 75). Aspects of the biblical story and of the events described in the novel are closely correlated: in place of the field in Genesis 4, there is the Arthur's Seat of the attempted murder, and the 'green' where the murder actually takes place; the strange idea of sin lying at Cain's door (Gen. 4.7) finds its correspondence in Robert's fruitless struggle against sin; and the crying out of Abel's blood from the ground, and God's sentence of homelessness on Cain accords with Robert's flight from the night terrors. Gil-Martin's assurance 'that no human hand shall ever henceforth be able to injure your life' (p. 135) echoes the deterrent function of God's promise to take savage revenge on anyone who comes across Cain wandering the earth and slays him (Gen. 4.15). This close patterning of the two stories portrays Robert as a figure trapped in a strangely cruel prewritten script, without the free will to escape. Robert's strange and isolated upbringing at least contributes to his adult failings. The difference between his character and George's is the result of factors as much out of the control of either as the reason behind God's acceptance of Abel's offering rather than Cain's. The final section of the text leaves the reader with the impression that Robert is at the mercy of those who, after him, choose to publish his 'little book' along with their own interpretation of it. Precisely because the Editor prints Robert's narrative along with his own, Robert's 'memory and his name' are consigned 'to everlasting detestation' (Hogg 1834: 208). Just as Robert reveals himself to be trapped in a fatal relationship with the figure of Gil-Martin so that his killing of George (and others) becomes inevitable, so also he has no control in the end over his own story.[24] He has a role to play in

---

24. Fenwick (1988) argues that despite Hogg's attempt to use 'mystery and self-contradiction to disguise the determinism of an author's control over his narrative, so that Robert may appear to be operating "freely" within the confines of Hogg's plot' (p. 61), his carefully constructed plot 'is undercut by an examination of the sinner's motives which allows the reader to see him either as a madman driven by

the retelling of the story of Cain and Abel, and he follows it exactly. And, although, unlike Cain, his own record of events has been preserved, like Cain his own story is read first in the words of a narrator who claims omniscience. Both have suffered at the hands of their readers: Robert in the interpretations that label him either damned or mad; and Cain in the readings of his story found in the New Testament, where he is described as 'of the evil one' and motivated by 'evil' (1 Jn 3.12). From the perspective of the abyss, and in the absence of a benevolent and stable God, both may be read as victims of groundlessness, confused by the lack of response from the God they trust, rather than culpable evildoers. The significant difference between the stories of Cain and Robert is that Robert is offered an opportunity to escape the hell of his existence and to enter into the bliss of non-being. Gil-Martin saves him from the terrors of the night by changing Cain's script and disclosing the (unrevealed and unmentionable) prayer which enables Robert to face the absence of God. Only then is he able to face and bring about his own death. His final act of worship is directed to the sun, the antithesis of the darkness of the pit: its 'glorious orb' (1834: 196) will be the last thing Robert expects to see.

In Hogg's earlier text, *The Three Perils of Man* (1822), something equally subversive happens to the Bible. The intrusive, self-reflexive comments of the narrator about the fictionality of his tale, and specifically his role in the creation of meaning, reflect on all stories and all attempts at story-telling. In this text, when the narrator describes the processes through which the tale has come, having been 'taken down' from the manuscript of an old Curate, Isaac, and given to the 'present Editor' (1822: 2) by someone who lived in Isaac's area, the modern reader thinks of the tortuous process of transmission of biblical texts such as the Gospels. When the Editor comments on the problem of 'so many truths, that any body may see it was scarcely possible to get them all narrated in their proper places' (p. 190), and invokes the image of a

---

his psychotic delusion or as a being warped by heredity and environment and therefore incapable of exercising free will' (1988: 68). For Fenwick, Hogg's interest in Robert's psychology prevents him from sustaining his intended attempt to explore the paradox of Providence and free will. The character of Robert he has created is incapable of repentance, and because of this, Robert's fate at the hands of Hogg's God is fixed. Fenwick is unusual in reading Robert in a sympathetic light, but she does not go so far as to argue that Gil-Martin saves Robert from the fate of a cruel and inflexible God, which is the argument of this Chapter.

waggoner who must take some of his load to the top of a hill and then
return to the bottom to bring the rest, the fractured relationship between
any event and its translation into story is highlighted. The Editor's self-
conscious comment (p. 290) questioning how the curate could have
been told details about a meeting between Michael Scott and his three
pages, Prig, Prim and Pricker, since none of the other characters had
heard it, parallels modern questions about the authority of sources in
the Gospels which purport to describe the feelings or words of Jesus
while he was at a distance from the disciples. One such example is his
prayer on Gethsemane, given in some detail although the disciples are
apparently out of earshot, and asleep (see Lk. 22.39-46). The Editor's
presence tempts the reader to wonder if his tale, and other similar tales,
have any relationship to the events they claim to describe.

In the story-telling contest held to decide which of the imprisoned
and starving group is to be killed and eaten by the others, the tale told
by the poet offers more specific parallels with a biblical story. In the
story, three young girls are saved from torture and death at the hands of
the pagan invading force by a cosmic figure, are led to a cave and sleep
there apparently overnight. When they awake, one of them ventures out
to find food, and discovers that years have passed, their land is free, and
that they are thought to have been translated into heaven. On their
return from quasi-death and resurrection, they re-enter society and live
devoutly until their deaths many years later. Biblical stories of resurrection, such as the dry bones vision in Ezekiel 37, the revivification of the
two witnesses in Revelation 11, and Jesus' own resurrection echo in the
text, although these girls are translated from apparent death into normal
life, rather than into a heavenly existence. The raising of Lazarus is
clearly echoed in the story, but perhaps the closest similarity is with
Jesus' resurrection: like him their 'rebirth' is spent in mediating God to
humanity. The poet describes their time being spent 'in acts of holiness', '[i]n curing of the sick, clothing the naked, ministering to all in
want and wretchedness, and speaking peace unto poor wandering and
benighted souls' (1822: 315). The messianic symbolism is clear. However, the interesting thing about this tale is the reaction it provokes from
those who hear it. The friar judges it 'a legend of purity and holiness',
in which 'the words of truth are contained', whether it is 'truth' or
'fiction' (p. 316). Unsurprisingly, the Master calls it 'the most diffuse
and extravagant, and silly legend that was ever invented by a votary of
a silly and inconsistent creed'. Tam Craik agrees the tale is 'nought but

a string of bombastical nonsense', and the Laird of Peatstacknowe judges it to be 'a' show but nae substance'. When Delany expresses her delight in the story, the friar assures her 'there are many more sublime and more wonderful in thy little book', his translated Bible. The poet's tale is itself a translation of a biblical story into a new time and context. The friar has himself highlighted its fictionality, and Tam and the Laird, following the disdain of the Master, point out its suspiciously nonsensical nature. In *Perils of Man*, the Bible is often mentioned as an object, but its contents are rarely quoted or alluded to except in the incongruous speech of the friar. In the poet's tale, a central biblical theme is explored, but it is either unrecognized or misunderstood by its audience, except the cleric, who understands that all of the Bible may be read as fairytale, and the warlock, who must denounce it. Out of its context from within the pages of the friar's black book, biblical themes have no relevance to the lives of the characters. The Bible belongs in the confusion of fact and fiction, magic and reality, which characterize all tales, including *Perils of Man* itself.

This same confusion finally overwhelms Robert Wringhim. As he describes towards the end of his account, Robert realizes the meaninglessness of his past and future life, and longs for escape:

> Thus was I sojourning in the midst of a chaos of confusion. I looked back on my bypast life with pain, as one looks back on a perilous journey, in which he has attained his end, without gaining any advantage either to himself, or others; and I looked forward, as on a darksome waste, full of repulsive and terrific shapes, pitfalls and precipices, to which there was no definite bourne, and from which I turned in disgust (1824: 150).

However, Gil-Martin reveals to the reader and to Robert that there is nowhere to turn in life from the 'darksome waste'. In Hogg's poem 'The First Sermon' (1874b: 351-52) a preacher confronts this 'hell', and like Robert, cannot live with what he encounters. The young man flounders as he preaches:

> In every line his countenance bespoke
> The loss of recollection; all within
> Became a blank—a chaos of confusion,
> Producing nought but agony of soul.
>
> ...[He] seized a pair
> Of strong plough-bridal reins, and hang'd himself (p. 352).

The callous narrator laughs over his dinner, and suggests the solution is for young ministers to carry a written sermon in their Bible in case of emergencies. The response of the congregation is more sympathetic: 'There was neither laugh/ Nor titter; but a soften'd sorrow/ Pourtrayed in every face.' The existential fear of internal nothingness unites them with the young man. A glimpse of the opposite of the affirmation of hope in meaning, hell, chaos, 'a blank', is too awful to contemplate. Death offers the only escape. In the *Confessions*, as here and in *Perils of Man*, the Bible is a 'chaos of confusion': either a cacophony of different and contradictory elements, or a silent text with no meaning at all. The preached word is a word of deception rather than an expression of truth. Robert is every reader both of the *Confessions* and of the Bible. The ever-present abyss destabilizes his and our understanding of the meaning of the texts, taking away the grounding of either in certainty. Robert, like us, is the victim of the interpretations of others, and is confused by the multiplicity of possibilities. Both texts are open to interpretations that deny what the texts seem to be affirming. In the case of the *Confessions*, Robert's culpability is seriously in question in a world where the saving presence of God is absent and the devouring pit of darkness absorbs all. Gil-Martin may be read as a hero who leads Robert away from the hell of existence, rather than as a corrupting influence who leads him into damnation.

The Bible, much of Hogg's work, and Carlyle's *Sartor Resartus* are difficult texts that respond well, on a textual level, to a deconstructive reading sensitive to their ambiguities, aporias and lack of closure. However, such deconstructive readings of all of these texts, but particularly of the Bible, are by their nature disturbing and destructive of all previously-held certainties. Some of the implications of these readings will be explored in the following chapter.

Chapter 5

READING REVELATION DECONSTRUCTIVELY

When we read Revelation, we feel at once there are meanings behind
meanings... When all is explained and expounded and commented upon,
still there remains a curious fitful, half-spurious and half splendid wonder in the work (Lawrence 1931: 47-48).

[Revelation] is the one great poem which the first Christian age produced, it is a single and living unity from end to end, and it contains a
whole world of spiritual imagery to be entered into and possessed (Farrer
1949: 6).

John is a sort of time traveller who is able to break loose of his prison on
Patmos to explore future worlds, while the horror of his present world is
forever seeping into the future visions of hope and vice versa. There is
no escaping chaos in the Apocalypse. Chaos is everywhere, past, present
and future (Pippin 1994: 259).

In Chapter 4, various traditional readings of Hogg's *Confessions* were
considered from a postmodern, specifically deconstructive perspective.
Their inadequacies, and the insights offered by Pippin's (1994) deconstructive reading of Revelation, led to a new reading of the *Confessions*.
In this chapter, readings of Revelation are central. As Chapter 3
demonstrated, the Apocalypse of John, like Hogg's *Confessions*, has
been interpreted in many different ways. Its unity has been questioned
by source critics, such as Charles (1920), and defended by those who
find common themes, concerns and idioms throughout the text, such as
Bauckham (1993a and b). Its meaning has been sought in its structure,[1]
its use of the Hebrew Bible or of themes common to other apocalyptic
writings,[2] or in the historical context in which it was written.[3] The

---

1.   Farrer (1949; 1964), whose work is considered in the second section of this
chapter, is the best example of a reader who finds the meaning of Revelation in the
text's structure.

2.   Moyise's (1995) work on the intertextuality of Revelation covers both the

dangerous idea that its meaning might be unstable, unrecoverable or dependent on the reader, is generally resisted,[4] in the way that the same idea is generally rejected by scholars of Hogg, as was argued in Chapter 4. Instead, complicated explanations of the text's difficulties and inconsistencies are advanced.

In this chapter, two explanations of Revelation's difficulties are discussed and their weaknesses are exposed from a deconstructive perspective. The two have been chosen because they offer interpretations from a literary critical point of view: although their viewpoints are different, they both make assumptions about the text, the author and the reader against which postmodern literary theory, and in particular deconstruction, developed as a reaction. Their interpretations, although not in the mainstream of New Testament studies, offer ways to understand the force behind deconstruction. D.H. Lawrence's discussion of Revelation (1931) is the work of a novelist with a particular experience of the Bible, writing before the Second World War. Lawrence reads Revelation as a multi-layered text, and aims to unpeel the layers to reveal the power of the original, pagan myth. Farrer's commentary on Revelation (1949) is a biblical scholar's interpretation of a particular aspect of the text, but is informed by some of the literary critical concerns of its time. Farrer reads Revelation as the creative work of an individual, and aims to recover the multiplicity of patterns woven into and behind the text. Following a discussion of these interpretations, Pippin's extended work on the rhetoric of gender in Revelation (1992), will be considered for the further insights it offers into a deconstructive reading of the text. My own reading of Revelation from a deconstructive perspective, and a discussion of the implications of this reading, will then be offered.

Hebrew Bible and selected Qumran texts. Caird's (1966) commentary is a more standard consideration of Revelation as a Christian reinterpretation of ideas and images from the Hebrew Bible.

3.   Thompson (1990) and Fiorenza (1985) are two commentators among many for whom a reconstruction of the historical context of the text has an important hermeneutical role.

4.   Caird, for example, asserts that 'whatever else [John] may have intended, he cannot have set out to mystify... If only we can learn to put ourselves in the place of those Asiatic Christians, we may expect to find that John has said exactly what he means and that he is his own best interpreter' (1966: 3).

D.H. *Lawrence's* Apocalypse

In 1923 Lawrence reviewed John Oman's reconstruction of Revelation, *Book of Revelation*. In the same year he was approached by the painter and mystic Frederick Carter, who had produced a work about the symbolism of Revelation. Although Lawrence was more interested in the psychology of the symbolism than in astrology, which was Carter's preoccupation, he read the text enthusiastically. In 1929 he wrote two introductions to Carter's revised version of his original text, *The Dragon of Revelation*. Neither essay was appended to Carter's book, which was eventually published in 1931. One, the shorter text, was published posthumously as an independent piece in *The London Mercury* in July 1930, and the other was published as *Apocalypse* in 1931. It was the last work of any length that Lawrence wrote.

Lawrence argues that Revelation is a multi-layered text, which has gone through many reworkings and revisions. The earliest layer is a pagan text describing the initiation of a follower of one of the mystery religions. One or more Jewish writer(s) brought this text into line with Hebrew Scripture and added apocalyptic references. John of Patmos revised it again and turned it into a Christian work according to his own understanding of the Gospel. Yet more Christian scribes reworked it into a text orthodox enough to be included in the canon of the New Testament. Lawrence's main aim in *Apocalypse* is to uncover the original form of the text, and to rescue it from what he considered were the damaging accretions of Christianity. He seeks to show the ways in which a healthy, pagan vision of the cosmos has been obscured by the unnatural system that Christianity had become by the time of John of Patmos. For Lawrence, the main characteristic of the myth is its vitality and potency: it is concerned with the living experience of contact with the cosmos, rather than with the promise of life after death. The image of the woman clothed with the sun, who appears briefly in ch. 12, is the original focus of the whole myth. She is the cosmic mother totally alien to the Jewish and Christian traditions. She brings about the renewal and salvation of the world, in contrast to the hope of the annihilation of the world that is dominant in the apocalyptic and Christian sections of the text. Accordingly Revelation depicts her being driven out into the desert, and concentrates on her evil aspect, the whore of Babylon, in chs. 17 and 18. The woman clothed with the sun only survives in the text because she has been uneasily transformed into the Virgin Mary

giving birth to the Messiah. Lawrence argues that this female figure in
her original form represents all we have lost in the world: elemental
contact with the life of the sun and the moon, which the pagan
mythologies celebrated, has been banished to the wilderness. In Revelation as we have it, the original text's life-affirming message of renewal
is overwhelmed by an expectation of the end of the world, in which
only the chosen will be rewarded. However, by stripping away the
additional layers, the modern reader may find in Revelation a manual
that points the way to the symbolic liberation of the self, an idea that is
developed further below.

Apocalypse is a work that oscillates uneasily between criticism and
prophecy, and between close reading of the text and sweeping assertion.
Although a slim volume it has a sprawling, repetitive feel. Lawrence's
book that the text has gone through several reworkings is not unique,
nor is his apparent ability to reconstruct the content and meaning of
each layer.[5] What is more original is his enthusiasm for and commitment to the pagan and pantheistic mythology he uncovers in the text.
Lawrence is a novelist with a mission to persuade and involve his
readership. In this he differs from most literary or biblical critics, from
whom an attempt to retain scholarly distance from the text and from the
reader is usually expected (although not always achieved). What particular insights does Lawrence's work bring to the text, and is he, like
more conventional critics, wedded to the pursuit of fixed meaning and
interpretation?

An example of Lawrence's method is to be found in his discussion
and description of the various horses in Revelation. Noting the horse's
dominance in the text, he places it in its context in humanity's consciousness, asserting that '[f]ar, far back in our dark soul the horse
prances... As a symbol he roams the dark underworld meadows of the
soul. He stamps and threshes in the dark fields of your soul and mine'
(1931b: 101). The four horses of Rev. 6.1-8, argues Lawrence, are survivors from the earliest pagan text. In this scene, which describes the

---

5.   Charles offers a concise history of various redactional and source-critical
interpretations from the last quarter of the nineteenth century (1913: 59-75). In her
introduction to the 1995 edition of Lawrence's *Apocalypse*, Kalnins (1995: 15)
notes that when, in 1929, Carter suggested that he and Lawrence collaborate on a
new book about the Apocalypse, Lawrence agreed and ordered an impressive list of
books from a London bookseller. The list included Charles's *A Critical and Exegetical Commentary on the Revelation of St John* (1920).

opening of the first four seals, the different colours of the horses, white, red, black and pale (green?), are symbolic of different aspects of humanity. To explain this, more details are needed about Lawrence's overall understanding of the original myth underpinning the text of Revelation as we have it.

For Lawrence, the original myth is a symbolic account, probably in the form of an initiation rite into one of the mystery religions, of how to attain inner harmony as well as a sense of living connection with the greater universe. The document showed how the psyche of the individual could relate to and interpret the objective, material universe and how it could understand the subjective, inner world. The integration of spirit and body, imagination and reason, involved a process of rebirth or renewal. This section (6.1-8) originally described the seven centres of the individual's consciousness, which must be conquered and transformed before the old may be reborn as the new man:

> The famous book of the seven seals in this place is the body of man: of a man: of Adam: of any man: and the seven seals are the seven centres or gates of his dynamic consciousness. We are witnessing the opening and conquest of the great psychic centres of the human body (1931b: 101).

Lawrence's imagination had been stimulated by James Pryse's *The Apocalypse Unsealed* (1910).[6] Pryse had written that in Revelation the opening of the seven seals represents the liberation of a latent power in the self. By awakening the seven principal nerve centres of the spine, each of which is a centre of psychic energy, a life-improving energy is released. The horses of 6.1-8, for Lawrence, represent the four physical or dynamic selves or centres of energy that must be conquered on earth before the new self may be revealed. The remaining three seals are the three divine or spiritual natures of a person, the first two of which, the soul and the spirit, must be divested in the underworld. The last, for Lawrence, is the 'living I', 'a stark flame which, on the new day, is clothed anew and successively by the spiritual body, the soul-body, and then the garment of flesh, with its fourfold terrestrial natures' (1931b: 104).

---

6.   Pryse shared Lawrence's confidence in his own ability to fathom the meaning of Rev., writing in the Preface to *The Apocalypse Unsealed* that 'in the following pages the reader will find the complete solution of the Apocalyptic enigma, with ample proof of the correctness of that solution' (1910: vii). His solution was that Rev. was to be read as a manual of spiritual development rather than as a cryptic history or prophecy.

The colours of the four horses symbolize the old natures of man: the sanguine (white), the choleric (red), the melancholic (black), the phlegmatic (pale). Alternatively, they may represent the four planetary natures of man: jovial, martial, saturnine and mercurial. Lawrence avoids settling on one meaning of the symbolism,[7] but he clearly identifies the force of the imagery of the horses themselves. At the time of Revelation and before, the horse gave man mastery, power and the status of lordship: the owner of a horse, like the Almighty himself, enjoyed the attribute of mastery over another creature. Lawrence argues that the horse is 'the first palpable and throbbing link with the ruddy-glowing Almighty of potency' (1931: 101). The horse is both menacing in its power and, once mastered, an indicator of wealth and position. Only the rich and powerful had a horse. For Lawrence it is 'the symbol of surging potency and power of movement, of action, in man' (p. 102). The post-pagan writers of Revelation had already cut away at the symbolism of the horse, allowing only the first rider to ride forth. Today humanity has lost its contact with the horse as a means of transport and it is no longer part of everyday life, with the result that the very old, resonant symbol of the horse is also being lost and humanity is poorer because of it. As Lawrence comments, 'Man is lost to life and power— an underling and wastrel' (p. 102).

The second occurrence of horses on which Lawrence concentrates is found in a later section of Revelation. He argues that the oldest pagan manuscript ended at ch. 7: what follows is more Jewish than pagan in its insistence on the punishments and woes that are to befall the enemy. The first cycle of the cosmic drama had been the 'death' and regeneration of the individual. In this second cycle it is the less important process of the rebirth of the earth that is described. The two hundred million demon-horsemen of the second woe, which appear out of the abyss at the sixth trumpet-call (9.16-19), have heads like lions and mouths that spout fire, smoke and brimstone. These noxious substances kill a third of humanity. The reader is then somewhat abruptly told that the horses' tails are like serpents, with heads, and it is with these tails that they inflict harm.

Lawrence argues that these horses are creations of the apocalyptic writers, rather than symbols from the pagan past. They are divine instruments of woe, plagues that are the scourges of God on the

---

7. As Lawrence comments, 'Fix the meaning of a symbol, and you have fallen into the commonplace of allegory' (1931: 101).

enemies of his people. The symbolism of the four horses of the first section is not present. To be remnants of the original myth, they ought to be 'the reversed or malevolent powers of the abysmal or underworld waters' (1931b: 111), in the same way that the locusts of ch. 8 had stings in their tails suggesting they were once good but are now in their reversed or hellish aspect. The original, watery nature of this torment is signalled by the origin of the four angels at 9.14: they come from the Euphrates, standing for the abysmal waters under the earth. Instead these horses are fiery creatures from the sulphurous, Jewish hell. A watery torture is not enough. Then, unexpectedly, they have serpent-like, evil tails. Lawrence comments that '[h]ere we are back at the right thing—the horse-bodied serpent-monster of the salty deeps of hell: the powers of the underworld waters seen in their reversed aspect, malevolent, striking a third of men' (p. 111). He reconstructs the process out of which these anomalous creatures came into existence in the text. Two apocalyptic writers worked on the text. The later of the two did not understand the meaning of the sea-monsters, and added magnificent brimstone-spouting horses of his own, possibly because he had seen a volcanic eruption and/or the impressive colours of some eastern cavalry. Lawrence notes that '[t]hat is a true Jewish method' (p. 112). When this writer came back to the old manuscript, he took the serpent tails of the sea-monsters described there, and added them (rather clumsily) to his own horses. The horses of ch. 9, then, offer Lawrence evidence of the process of rewriting and reinterpretation he seeks to strip away.

Lawrence's attempt to reinterpret Revelation involves two processes, as demonstrated by his discussions of horses in the text. He is concerned to uncover the original, pagan myth, the existence of which may be signalled by an awkwardness or incongruity in the text available (as in the description of the horses in Rev. 9.17-19). He also aims to recover the potency of the original imagery for modern humanity, which has lost contact with life because of its corrupting obsession with the material and mechanistic. His discussion about the meaning of the symbol of the horse with reference to Revelation 6 is an attempt to reclaim the symbol for a society that no longer depends on the living, brute power of the horse.

How plausible are Lawrence's reconstructions, and how successful is his rhetoric? Certainly a well-established technique of source-critics is to explain awkward or incongruous consecutive verses as evidence of two different sources having been brought together.[8] It is possible that Lawrence has identified such an example of the careless integration of a pagan source by a Jewish or Christian writer, although other commentators have made sense of these verses in terms of their unity and historical reference. Caird (1966: 122-24), for example, interprets 9.14-19 as the work of a single author making reference both to an apocalyptic tradition found in the Old Testament prophets and to a fear of literal invasion from the north which would have been familiar to first-century Jews and Romans. Beyond the Euphrates lived the Parthians who had in the past defeated both the Romans and the people of Israel, and this text echoes frequent scriptural warnings about an army invading from the north, such as Isa. 14.31, Jer. 1.14-16, Ezek. 26.7. Noting this background, Caird argues for a factual basis for the strange picture of horses wounding with their tails and their mouths: a favourite and terrifying tactic of the mounted archers of the Parthian army was to shoot one volley of arrows as they charged and another over their horses' tails as they withdrew out of the range of their enemy's weapons. However, Caird suggests that these verses do not prophesy a literal invasion of the Parthians. The writer of Revelation is using a nightmare version of a familiar first-century fear to instil in his readers a sense of a more ultimate evil. These satanic horses (their nature is signalled by their serpent-tails) are heirs to the apocalyptic tradition found in Ezekiel 38–39. In these chapters, Ezekiel prophesies that the invasion of Gog from Magog will be the fulfilment of Jeremiah's and others' warning of a foe coming from the north. Ezekiel adapts the tradition, however, by asserting that Gog will come after Israel has been punished for her sins and is restored: Jeremiah had predicted that Israel's historic enemies would be the means by which God would punish Israel in the first place. For Ezekiel, the forces of evil would come from beyond the horizons of the known world to destroy the nations who were living in unsuspecting security. His theological point is that evil has a vast reserve army and no earthly order is ever secure

---

8. A well-known example to which such source criticism is applied is Jn 14.31. Jesus says 'Rise, let us go hence' as though he were about to go out to Gethsemane and face his death, but the discourse with his disciples carries on and it is not until three chapters later that he finally leaves the room. A possible source-critical explanation is that the editor of the Gospel was working with several different manuscripts which he has not completely integrated. Barrett (1978: 454-55) summarizes the other possibilities.

from its attack until God wins the final battle. In Revelation 9, the horses are the demonic and evil forces of Gog. Their invasion is necessary, although limited by God, because the Roman world has tried to find security outwith the truly divine. The message to the church is that the progress of the gospel cannot be expected to produce a steady diminution of the power of Satan. He will continue to have power, although it may be used by God for his purposes, until the final judgment. The horses and the destruction they cause are the demonic consequence of human sin, which God continues to allow his angels to release in a limited way.

Caird finds no evidence either of a clumsy integration of sources or of a pagan sub-stratum to the text. Apocalyptic echoes from Scripture and the historical context of the original reader sufficiently explain the imagery. However, both Caird and Lawrence share this very desire to identify and define the text. In fact the textual incongruity so important to Lawrence's argument is only one of several difficulties in this very slippery text. In vv. 13-17, the relationship between the one who commands the action, the ones commanded, and the carrying out of the action is disjointed, and the basis of the narrator's knowledge is unclear and unexplained. In v. 13, the identity of the speaker is shrouded in mystery: in response to the sixth angel's trumpet call, John hears a disembodied voice from one of the four horns on the golden altar that stands before God (and what difference would it make to this text if the voice was that of Abaddon, the angel of the bottomless pit mentioned only seconds before?). The four angels bound at the Euphrates are released by the sixth angel at the command of this voice, and the narrator tells the reader that these angels had been held ready until this time to kill a third of humanity. Where this knowledge had come from is not explained. In v. 16 the narrative jumps to a description of the myriads of cavalrymen whose horses will in the end carry out the mass destruction. Their relationship to the four angels who were originally entrusted with the task is not explained. Although in v. 17 John goes on to describe the sight, in v. 16 he states that he hears rather than sees the number of the horses (two hundred million). In v. 17 itself, it is as if the horses and their riders are part of a completely different kind of experience for John from the sight of the trumpeters and the other woes. He comments pointedly 'And this is how I saw the horses in my vision', as if what had gone before was something other than visionary. Finally, as Lawrence pointed out, the means by which the horses inflict harm is confused: first it is by the substances coming from the mouths of the horses' lion-heads, and then it is by their serpent-like tails, which have heads, but not necessarily the heads of serpents. This section has the abrupt disjointedness of a fantastic dream, or, in the context of the trumpets and the horrific woes, a nightmare. The scenes change abruptly and without continuity before the eyes of the dreamer. He knows things he has not been told. At times the sense of hearing takes over from the sense of sight as the primary way of experiencing the dream. Different scenes are of different qualities and kinds. Logic and narrative flow are lost. I suggest, then, that at least this section of Revelation may be understood as dream-like fantasy rather than pagan myth or contextually-relevant biblical reinterpretation. It has as many meanings or is as meaningless as a dream. As the literary critic Colin Manlove has written, 'The Bible is not simply the truth: it is a fantastical truth' (1992: 91).[9] Derrida makes a related point about scripture:

> the caesura makes meaning emerge. It does not do so alone, of course; but without interruption—between letters, words, sentences, books—no signification could be awakened. *Assuming* that Nature refuses the *leap*, one can understand why Scripture will never be Nature. It proceeds by leaps alone, which makes it perilous. Death strolls between letters. (1978: 71)

The attempts of Lawrence and Caird to explain this section definitively merely gloss over its internal resistance to closure: their attempts to turn perilous leaps into the permanent safety of bridges are inadequate and misguided. These horses have the power to gallop away from anyone who tries to master them.

In the first example of Lawrence's discussion of horses, in Revelation ch. 6, he admits the deadening effect of assigning one meaning to a symbol ('explanations are our doom' [1931b: 102]). The various explanations for the colours of the four horses he does offer are less than convincing. Lawrence has to offer additional arguments to explain why the first of the four natures of man, the sanguine, should be white, rather than red which he needs to hold back for the choleric. He explains 'But how should sanguine be white?—ah, because the blood was the life itself, the very life: and the very power of life itself was

---

9.   The relationship between fantasy and the Bible is currently a point of debate in biblical studies. The 1992 edition of *Semeia*, edited by Aichele and Pippin, was devoted to fantasy and the Bible. The issue will be returned to in a later section of this chapter.

white, dazzling' (1931b: 102). Lawrence's need to explain the symbolism in this way undermines the force of his argument. However, Caird's interpretation of the four colours is equally arbitrary. Caird explains that 'in John's vision the four colours indicate a difference of commission, and the emergence of each new rider betokens the release of a new disaster on earth: invasion, rebellion, famine, and pestilence' (1966: 79-80). Caird goes on to add that 'the identification of the first and fourth riders with invasion and pestilence, however, requires some justification' (p. 80). In the case of the final horse, according to Caird's scheme, the pale green denotes pestilence. However, the horse's rider's name is 'Death'. To explain this, Caird concludes that the final rider is expected both to symbolize pestilence and to encompass the deadly effect of all four plagues. With regard to the first horse and its rider, Caird rejects interpretations that read this figure as representing the victorious course of the gospel. All four are evil powers which, for a fixed time, are tolerated and used by God. It would be inconsistent to read one of them as a positive force in the world. Instead Caird suggests that the white rider's bow may point to the Parthians, the only mounted archers in the ancient world who, as was discussed above, were a constant threat to Romans and Jews alike. This neat correspondence, however, fails to explain why the first horse, if it indeed represents invasion, should be white. Is it not more satisfying in literary terms to see the colours simply as all-encompassing opposites: the bright shining white contrasting with the dull black; the fiery red with the pale sickly green? Visually, the picture is powerful and vivid, but it also contains within itself its own deconstruction. When the oppositions collapse and the colours are mixed together, the white and the black, the red and the green become undistinguished grey and brown. The symbolic horses lose their identity and become ordinary. The text's power over its readers to dazzle and dismay is tenuous and limited. The readings of Lawrence and Caird allow the might of the horses to dominate: a deconstructive reading takes nothing for granted and does not fear the text.

Although Caird and Lawrence have difficulty in persuading the reader to accept their interpretation of the colours of the four horses, Lawrence's insight into the powerful symbolism of the horse roaming the dark underworld meadows of the soul is highly suggestive. It is the insight of the novelist and poet rather than the biblical critic: Caird does not venture into the wider and deeper meaning of these cosmic figures.

Other novelists and poets express a similar feeling for the power of the symbol. Hogg was well aware of the potency of the symbolism when, in the *Confessions*, he set one of Wringhim's night terrors in a stable. Wringhim and those around him are overcome by the apocalyptic horror of the scene: 'The horses broke loose, and snorting and neighing for terror, raged through the house...[M]ad horses smash[ed] everything before them' (1824: 185). When out of the control of those who thought themselves their masters, horses create a scene of chaos. A foretaste of the despair and horror of divine punishment is experienced by Wringhim and presented to the reader. Its key features are loss of control and the awesome power of an external force. For Wringhim the final judgment is a present reality and stalks him without mercy.

Another significant and obvious example is Edwin Muir's poem 'The Horses', written in 1956. This affirms Lawrence's point: that horses bring humanity contact with the land and with life itself. They may be controlled but mastery over them is never complete. Their presence in our world retains fragments of the mysterious and other-worldly, as if they were

> Dropped in some wilderness of the broken world
> Yet new as if they had come from their own Eden (1911: 226-27, ll. 48, 49).

In Muir's poem, the horse returns to save humanity from the catastrophe of cataclysmic materialism. For Lawrence, modern readers have lost the power of the original symbolism of Revelation because they are in the same dangerous state of consciousness as the characters in 'The Horses' before the disaster happened. Horses are

> ...strange to us
> As fabulous steeds set on an ancient shield
> Or illustrations in a book of knights (ll. 38-40).

With the insight of the novelist/poet Lawrence reminds the reader of the depths of the symbolism of the horse through history. The horses in Revelation 6 and 9 are mighty, menacing, mysterious beasts with the power to destroy or to enable. They echo in the deepest consciousness of the reader as cosmic creatures of huge vitality and potential, although modern humanity is in danger of losing the force of the symbol. All of these insights have been lost in the arid exposition of biblical critics. Whatever may be thought about the overall story he tells about the origin of the text, Lawrence has opened up the potential of the symbol of the horses in Revelation without containing the text or the imagination of the reader. In his introduction to Frederick Carter's book *The Dragon of Apocalypse*, Lawrence commented that while reading the book,

> I was very often smothered in words. And then would come a page, or a chapter, that would release my imagination and give me a whole great sky to move in. For the first time I strode forth into the grand fields of the sky. And it was a real experience, for which I have always been grateful (1931a: 45, 46).

Lawrence's words could easily apply to a reading of his own *Apocalypse*. However, from a deconstructive perspective, Lawrence's reading of Revelation is unconvincing. Despite his warnings about the dangers of explanations of the symbolic, Lawrence's story about the origin, composition and meaning of the text is an undeniable attempt to resolve definitively the text's difficulties. The text's resistance to this attempt is denied. I have sought to show that such denials cannot be sustained once the text's deconstructive elements are allowed precedence.

Austin Farrer's Revelation

In *Apocalypse* Lawrence's aim is to reveal the original myth that has been overlaid and modified by several later editors. For him, Revelation is a composite work: its many complexities and contradictions are evidence of the many hands which have been at work on the finished text. Austin Farrer takes the opposite view. In his book *A Rebirth of Images* (1949) and in his later commentary *The Revelation of St. John the Divine* (1964), he aims to describe the web of imaginative association which, he believes, lies behind the finished surface of the unified, poetic creation that is the text of Revelation as we know it. The writer of Revelation self-consciously sets out to create a prophetic text, guided by the Holy Spirit, which will 'liberate' (1949: 17) the images of the Old Testament. These images, of the sacrificial lamb, of David as the viceroy of God and of Adam as the image of God, were awaiting their rebirth in the Christian context as explanations of Christ's existence. In Revelation, which is the sum of this process of the rebirth of the symbols of the Old Testament, each of these images is connected to the others 'by a delicate web of interrelated significance' (1949: 18). An understanding of this web is possible for the modern reader because of the complexity of the text and because the material from which Revelation was created, the Old Testament, is available to us. Farrer's work is a massively detailed and impressive attempt to recover and explain the symbols, and the transformations they have undergone, in John's inspired visionary creation.

In order to understand Farrer's work it is necessary to recognize that he read Revelation as a poem[10] and that in doing so he used the literary critical tools that were available and fashionable at the time. In his essay 'Inspiration: Poetical and Divine', published in 1963 and reproduced in Conti (1976: 39-53), Farrer argues that the impetus behind the writing of poetry and of scripture may be understood in a similar way. In both poetic and inspired writing, truths are expressed through symbols. For Farrer, God speaks to the prophet through his imagination. The revealing image imposes itself and presents itself as a symbol. The prophet sees the imagined object as something charged with divine significance, although it is not until the symbol grows in his imagination and suggests new applications and encodings that he realizes the extent of its significance. Comparable to the work of a poet, the task of a seer like John is to enflesh the bare bones of the tradition or story available to him. In Revelation, the prophecies of Jesus on the Mount of Olives (Mk 13) and the promises of the Old Testament are the living symbols through which John is called to experience and describe the future mysteries. Farrer argues that the result is a densely-patterned and tightly-controlled text. A poet who follows rules of metre and rhyme may allow these rules to help him discover what he has to say: similarly, John places his revelation under the combined control of many trains of significance. Farrer, who claims to be able to separate out and explicate these trains of significance, comments that 'the miracle is that concrete images of vision, briefly and simply presented, conform at once to so many principles of symbolic sequence' (1963: 50). This response of the prophet's imagination to the initial inspiration by God, who works through the imagination, is parallel to the workings of the poetic mind.

By arguing that Revelation is the creation of an inspired poetic imagination, Farrer justifies the use of literary critical tools to make sense of the text. In the first chapter of *Rebirth*, he states that he will employ a 'known method of poetical analysis' (1949: 20), although he does not identify it by name or by its other advocates. However, in 'On Looking Below the Surface', his Presidential Address to the Oxford Society of Historical Theology in 1959, Farrer refers to the way in

---

10. For Farrer, '[t]he poem is the revelation, and the revelation is the poem' (1949: 313).

which in his biblical criticism he had drawn attention to the parallels between the typological exegesis of Scripture and the poetry-criticism of William Empson and Charles Williams. In this Address, in debate with Helen Gardner, he suggests that, whatever the current situation in literary criticism, much work remains to be done on the interpretation of hidden patterns, undisclosed allusions and wilful ambiguities in the Bible. This method of interpretation is clearly related to the 'verbal analysis' of Empson, whose *Seven Types of Ambiguity* had been published first in 1930 and revised in a second edition in 1949.[11] Empson's interest was in ambiguity, which he defined as 'any verbal nuance, however slight, which gives room for alternative reactions to the same piece of language' (1949: 1). The critic's task is to explain why a poetic work has had an effect on its reader, and one way to do this, for Empson, is to analyse these nuances and the alternative reactions they may provoke. Empson argued that things in a text are not always what they seem and that the words of a poem may connote more than they denote. His method involved close reading and the examination of the different meanings and possible connotations of a word or a phrase. His work provoked hostility from traditional critics, such as Olsen (1952), who accused him of scholarly error and a gross overstatement of the possible meanings of words in their contexts. Farrer's stated aim of uncovering the web of significances, and of probing the meaning of the images and allusions in Revelation correlates closely with Empson's literary endeavours. Like Empson, Farrer was accused by his fellow-critics, such as Manson (1949) and Davies (1950), of, among other things, ignoring the evidence of historical research and of finding a complexity of patterns in the text which could not have been intended by the author. The comparison between Empson's interpretations of literature and Farrer's of the Bible will be reconsidered after a summary is given of Farrer's work on Revelation.

Between the publication of *Rebirth* in 1949 and the writing of the *Commentary* in 1964, Farrer's interpretation of the web of imagery in Revelation changed and much of the detailed patterning of the first book was re-examined. In *Rebirth*, the more ambitious and exciting text, Farrer argues that the key to understanding Revelation is the seven-fold pattern of the creation story in Genesis 1, allied with elements of the creation story in Genesis 2 and the yearly round of Jewish

11. Detweiler and Robbins (1991: 248-52) offer a useful discussion of the reciprocal relationship between New Criticism and biblical studies.

festivals. From Rev. 1.9 to the end of the book, the text may be divided into seven sections that correspond to the six days of creation plus the Sabbath.

The first work of the Genesis story is the generation of elemental light. The first work of Revelation is introduced by the vision of the sevenfold candlestick, and followed by the messages to the seven churches (1.9–3.22). This is a transformation of Zechariah 4, which depicts the candlestick of the Lord alight in Israel. In Revelation Christ has replaced the candlestick of the old covenant with himself and those who derive from him.

The work of the second day in Genesis 1 is the creation of the firmament, dividing the upper waters from the lower and conceived as a curtain between the earthly and the heavenly. John's second week begins with the crossing of this barrier: John goes through a door in heaven, and sees a sea of glass that holds the upper waters (4.1, 6). The drama of the unsealing of the six seals (6.1–7.19) is also a penetration of heavenly things into the world. The unsealing of the scroll and the breaking of the barrier between heaven and earth are combined when the Lamb opens the sixth seal (6.12-17). The sky departs like a rolled-up scroll and heaven threatens to overwhelm the inhabitants of the earth. The unrolling of the scroll and of the sky are both revelations of God.

The third work in Genesis, the creation of the earth, the sea and trees, is preceded in Revelation by the two intrusive visions of ch. 7. These visions are preparatory and anticipatory: they begin with the withholding of the winds on land, sea and tree. The seven-fold pattern itself begins with the blowing of the first trumpet, which brings about the destruction of a third of the earth, trees and grass (8.7), and the second which destroys a third of the sea (8.7-8).

The work of the fourth day is the creation of the various luminaries, which Farrer relates to the series of beast visions in 12.1–14.5. This series begins with several references to heavenly lights: there is a sign in the sky, a woman clothed with the sun and with the moon at her feet appears, and her crown is made of the twelve stars (12.1).

The pouring-out of the vials represents for Farrer the transformation of the work of the fifth day of creation, the creation of birds and water-creatures. The work is introduced in chs. 14 and 15 by the appearance of the Son of Man from the clouds and the angels, bird-like creatures, coming out of the temple in heaven. Those who have already conquered the beast are depicted as standing beside a sea of glass and fire. The vial visions themselves include watery images of life and death: the sea and rivers are turned to blood (16.3-4), and frog-like creatures spring from the mouths of the demonic beasts (16.13-14).

In Genesis the work of the sixth day is the creation of the beasts of the earth and in particular of Adam himself. In Revelation, Adam is represented by the figure of Christ, who in 19.11-16 appears from heaven wearing the name and nature of God. His appearance in the sixth vision awaits its fulfilment in the final vision of the sequence.

The sequence of creation-days began with the Sunday of the resurrection. The sixth day, which represents the millennial reign of Christ, is the other day of Christ, the Friday when he won the victory over principalities and powers and on which he returns to conquer his visible adversaries. The Saturday sabbath is depicted in the visions of chs. 20–21.8. The action that occurs in this section, in contrast to the restful inactivity of the first sabbath in Genesis 1, has to be justified. Farrer does this by redefining the meaning of the sabbath. He argues that '[t]he Sabbaths of God are just as much the eternal repose out of which his action breaks, as they are the eternal repose into which his action resolves' (1949: 70). The events of the sabbath make possible the stunning vision of the bride, the wife of the Lamb, and appearance of the luminary (Christ) in the appended octave-Sunday which makes up the activity of Rev. 21.9–22.5. By the end of Revelation, God and the Lamb are united, representing the temple and the light in the one holy city.

As Farrer admits, the eighth day has no type in the first Genesis story of creation. However, he argues (1949: 75-77) that parallels may be drawn between the vision of the eighth day and the second creation story in Genesis. In the second creation story, creation is carried out in a day, which corresponds to the eighth day detailed in Revelation. In Genesis 2, man is made out of dust and is vivified by the breath of God, which is represented in the final vision of Revelation as the general resurrection. The tree, the river and the precious stones in the garden described in Gen. 2.9-14 reappear in the paradise of Revelation's last vision (21.18-21; 22.1-2). The creation of the woman and her cleaving to the man (Gen. 2.21-24) may be identified with the arrival of the Lamb's bride, the church (Rev. 21.2-3; 9-11). For Farrer, both creation stories in Genesis are fundamental to the details of the structure and content of the book of Revelation.

In the text of Revelation Farrer (1949: 37-58) finds a further seven-fold series corresponding to the seven days of creation and the things brought into being on these days. Within each of the first six divisions representing the days of creation already discussed, Farrer argues for the existence of a further seven-fold pattern. Some of these sevens are obvious and numbered internally, such as the opening of the seven seals (6.1–8.6) or the pouring out of the seven vials (16.1-21), although others, such as the seven last things (19.11–21.8), are only discovered once the overall pattern is realized. Farrer finds several other series of patterns in the text of Revelation, although they cannot all be considered in detail here.[12] As Goulder (1985: 199), Farrer's pupil, remarks of *Rebirth*, 'when we have finished, we are in chastened mood: here is inspiration indeed'.

In the *Commentary* there is a reordering of the patterns, without considerable simplification. The basic six-week series corresponding to the first six days of creation in Genesis 1 is replaced with a four-week pattern (Farrer 1964: 7-19). The four weeks are made up of the four explicitly counted series of sevens: the messages, seals, trumpets and vials. In *Rebirth*, Farrer had identified two other sevenfold series, labelled by him as the seven beast-visions and the seven last things, by counting the occurrence of the phrases 'And I saw' and 'And there was seen'. Later, in the *Commentary*, he was to read the beast-visions as subsidiary parts of the seventh trumpet vision of the third week, and the visions of the last things as subsidiary to the vision of the seventh vial of the fourth week of his new system. The resulting four-fold rather than six-fold series represents for Farrer a half week of weeks, the half week of judgment described in Dan. 9.27. This is the final week of

12. For example, Farrer argues that a further pattern found within the text is based on a year and a half of quarterly Jewish–Christian festivals. The Feast of Dedication is symbolized by the seven lamps of ch. 1. In chs. 4 to 6 the lamb, symbol of Passover, opens the seals of the scroll, representing Pentecost. The seven trumpets of chs. 8 and 9 are taken as symbols of the New Year, and the symbols of wilderness, tabernacling, harvest and vintage in chs. 12 to 14 represent the Feast of Tabernacles. The vision of the seven vials (ch. 16) symbolizes Dedication again, and the appearance of the Bride of Christ in ch. 21 is to be read as the antitype of Esther at Purim. The final vision of ch. 22 represents the final Passover/Pentecost. In addition to these series of patterns, Farrer also finds patterns in the text corresponding to the order of worship in the temple on a single day, and a march round the city taking a year and a half. The gates of the city are the twelve apostles, the twelve tribes and the twelve stones on the High Priest's breastplate.

tribulation, shortened by God for the sake of the Elect. This four-fold series of seven, representing the four days of the half-week of the end-time, is also to be read as an extrapolation of the four-fold scheme of days prophesied by Jesus in Mark 13. On the first day, which has already been revealed, Jesus exhorts his disciples, as he does on the Mount of Olives in Mark 13. This is represented by chs. 1–3 of Revelation, in which Jesus returns to give messages of advice to the seven churches. The second day, of waiting and the beginning-pains of the travail (Mk 13.5-13), are represented in Revelation by the first day of the disclosed apocalypse. The vision of the seven unsealings centres on the waiting of the saints (Rev. 6.10-11). The plagues brought by the horsemen (6.1-7) and the woes accompanying the sixth seal represent the beginning-pains. The vision of the seven trumpets (Rev. 8–11) represents the third day, the day of the Anti-Christ (Mk 13.14-23), which culminates in his usurpation at 11.12-13. The fourth day, the day of Christ (Mk 13.24-27) is represented by the vision of the pouring-out of the seven bowls (Rev. 16–19) and the advent of Christ in 19.11-16. The visions of the end of the world that follow this advent (Rev. 20–22) are to read as sequels to the events of these four days, roughly sketched because they form no part of Jesus' own prophecy on the Mount of Olives detailed in Mark 13.

John had found the framework of the half week already present in Jesus' prophecy of the kingdom of the Anti-Christ in the Markan narrative. He retains it and extends it into a framework for the whole of the time between the preaching of Jesus and the day of judgment. The pattern is continued within the four-fold series of sevens: Farrer argues that each of these four weeks is itself divided into two, forming two half weeks. For example, the first four out of the seven unsealings (the second in the overall four-fold pattern of sevens) are grouped together: only these first four release the four horsemen of 6.1-8. Similarly, in the third set of sevens, the trumpets, only the final three trumpets are accompanied by the judgment of the three woes (8.13–11.19). Farrer concludes that Revelation takes the form of a 'half week' made up of four weeks, and that each of these four weeks are themselves halved.[13]

13. Since *Rebirth*'s six-fold pattern of the new creation has been reconsidered in the *Commentary*, the six quarters of the Jewish–Christian year must also be modified into a single cycle of annual festivals in Farrer's later text. In the *Commentary*, this cycle begins in Revelation with an Easter vision, and moves through Pentecost/Passover in Revelation 4 and 5. Farrer correlates New Year with the

When Farrer's interpretations of Revelation were published, both his method and specific details of his readings were criticized. In his review of *Rebirth* Manson criticizes Farrer's need for explanations of aspects of the text that do not fit his scheme, such as the extra visions that appear outwith a series of seven. Manson comments that '[t]he author is incredibly fertile and ingenious in explanations; but it is the fact that explanations are necessary which shakes our confidence' (1949: 208). There was also, of course, great scepticism about the worth of Farrer's whole approach. Manson argued:

> The more I see of the new method of interpretation, the more arbitrary and uncontrolled it seems to me to be. In particular there is a great deal of exegesis in this book which appears to depend on mere verbal similarity without any real connection in thought (1949: 208).

Like Davies, who labelled Farrer's interpretation as 'too ingenious to be convincing' (1950: 74), Manson suggested that most of Farrer's readings originated in his head rather than in John's. Similar criticisms are levelled at postmodern readings of texts too, of course, but Farrer could scarcely be categorized as a fore-runner of that critical movement. Farrer's certainty sits unconvincingly within postmodern literary critical thought, which has many questions to ask of all interpretations that claim to be definitive. In the first chapter of *Rebirth*, Farrer (1949: 19-22) admits that symbols may have a multiplicity of references or significances; advises that not all of the intricacies he finds were necessarily consciously created by the author; and warns that the original readers would have been unlikely to have understood everything in the text. However, after making these fleeting observations, he confidently outlines a tightly-controlled pattern of meaning with which to explain the complexities of the book. The symbols may be unstable, the author may have been unaware of the full meaning of his writing and the intended reader could not have been expected to grasp the whole meaning. However, Farrer suggests that he has discovered the key to Revelation.

---

trumpet visions and with the events which follow them (chs. 8–9), and Tabernacles with the overcoming of the dragon and the beast from the sea and with the ingathering of the vintage (chs. 12–14). The final feast, Dedication, is represented by the pouring out of the vials (chs. 15–16), which echoes the dedication of the temple dishes in Num. 7.

Farrer and Empson make similarly powerful and startling claims for their readings of texts. For both, to read a text is to elucidate the structuring and meaning–creating action of literary-rhetorical concepts such as ambiguity, analogy, irony and paradox. In his highly critical discussion of Empson's work, Olsen (1952: 45-82) provides the modern reader with an insight into the extent of Empson's influence on Farrer, and the discomfort Empson's method invoked among literary critics of his time. Olsen comments that the proponents of I.A. Richards' and Empson's 'new criticism' believed they had brought new and scientific accuracy into the way texts were treated. Reading a poem involved 'a process of 'inventing reasons' why certain elements [in the poem] should have been selected' (1952: 48). The pleasure of poetry came from the mental activity, or 'puzzling' (p. 48), involved in responding to its ambiguities. The method of the critic was to discuss the 'permutation and combination of all the various 'meanings' of the parts of a given discourse' (p. 48). From the mass of dictionary meanings the critic selects those which satisfy the conditions of ambiguity he or she wishes to promote. Olsen suggests that for Empson the discovery of the main meaning of a text is 'an embarrassing matter' (p. 49) which is resolved by invoking historical and psychological propositions about the poet and the audience. Empson's method involves both 'utter absurdity' (p. 49) by claiming that either a character in the text or the poet means all of the possible meanings of a word, and a machine-like brutality towards all poetic texts. Already the similarities between Farrer's approach and Empson's are obvious: Farrer's method may be defined as the inventing of reasons to explain the selection of different elements of the text of Revelation. The complex and overlapping patterns he finds are certainly the result of puzzling over the permutations and combinations of the many meanings of each element of Revelation. When necessary, historical details about John's Jewish–Christian background, and that of his audience, are invoked as justification of a particular reading, although the question of intention is avoided. In his overwhelming drive to fit all aspects of the text into the multiple layers of significances, Farrer is at times guilty of brutality towards the text and an extreme lack of sensitivity towards what it actually says.[14] However, the correlation between the work of Farrer and Empson will best be seen in an example of Empson's criticism.

14. For an example of this brutality towards the text, see the discussion of Farrer's interpretation of the horses of Rev. 6 below.

Empson's (1949) first chapter deals with the first of his seven types of ambiguity, in which a detail in a text is effective in several ways at once. The closing section of the chapter discusses dramatic irony as an example of this type of ambiguity. Empson comments that dramatic irony is a useful device for his purpose because 'it gives an intelligible way in which the reader can be reminded of the rest of the play while he is reading a single part of it' (1949: 44). He offers an example from *King Lear*. Near the beginning of the play, Cordelia will say nothing to express her love or advance her cause with her father. Lear responds that 'Nothing will come of nothing, speak againe' (1.1.89). In a later scene in the same Act, the Fool sings a nonsense song, and the following conversation takes place:

Kent	This is nothing, foole.
Fool	Then 'tis like the breath of an unfee'd Lawyer, you gave me nothing for't. Can you make no use of nothing, nuncle?
Lear	Why no, Boy.
	Nothing can be made out of nothing.
Fool (to Kent)	Prithee tell him, so much the rent of his land comes to, he will not beleeve a Fool. (1.4.124-30)

Empson argues that although the lines make perfect sense even if the reader makes no connection with the first reference, Lear's meaning is only realized if the distant connection is made:

> that he, rather than Cordelia, was the beggar for love on that occasion; that she might well say *nothing*, if she had known how he would act to her; that, perhaps, it was no fault of his that had spoiled Regan and Goneril, since no upbringing could have *made* anything of them; that these words anyway are the ripe fruit of his experience; and that there is indeed *nothing* that can be made out of him, now that he has become *nothing* by the loss of everything in his world (1949: 46).

Empson argues that most people know the text so well, they do not recognize the effect caused by verbal irony which would be impossible to notice on a first reading or performance. He suggests that the context in which Shakespeare worked may have been responsible for his plays being so rich with such cross-referencing details: the stories of the plays were already owned and used by the company before Shakespeare wrote them up, so he and the actors already knew them well; his versions could be altered for a special court occasion; and a particular member might keep a particular part for a long time. These circumstances would give the actors a detailed knowledge of the text, a keenness for continual additions, an ability to make distant connections and an interest in the words of the minor characters. All this, Empson asserts, Shakespeare assumes in his audience. Empson's role as critic is to uncover the multiple meanings for those readers who are not up to the task.

Empson's reading is certainly ingenious, although the introduction of the upbringing of Regan and Goneril seems unwarranted by the text. It is clear that Farrer follows Empson's method. In both *Rebirth* and the *Commentary* patterns are traced throughout and across the text. Farrer argues that the breadth of meaning is only realized when the patterns he discovers are recognized. The form of Revelation may be explained by its status, nature and context. Its dominant images, from the Old Testament and the teaching of Jesus, were the common property of the early church, just as Shakespeare's plays were based on stories already well-known to his audience. Farrer (1949: 311) imagines John working at his text slowly, building it up an elaborately formal process, so that 'the already written part of his own work becomes formative of the rest, almost as though it were holy scripture'. In the *Commentary* Farrer argues that John is conscious of writing 'a new Ezekiel' (1964: 29), a complex symbolic unity that is both a new canonical prophecy and a dramatic masterpiece. Like Shakespeare, John is given his basic material, and lacks complete control over the production of his text, but expects his finished product to be read and reread with extreme care and interest. Realizing this, like Empson, Farrer claims he is able to interpret and understand the text even more carefully and expertly than its original audience.[15]

In the argument of this book, Farrer's work is of interest because it is an early attempt to make sense of Revelation from a literary perspective, using literary critical theory as a method. In his review of a new American edition of *Rebirth*, Archer argues that 'the book is one of the pioneer literary studies of the New Testament as literature' (1987: 69).

---

15. In *Rebirth*, Farrer asserts that the original readers of Revelation 'without intellectual analysis…would receive the symbols simply for what they were. They would understand what they would understand, and that would be as much as they had time to digest. They would not, of course, understand it all' (1949: 21). In comparison, Farrer, with the method of 'poetical analysis' (p. 20) at his disposal, considers himself in a better position to 'restore and build up an understanding' (p. 20) of the multiplicity of symbols.

As such it is also a good example of a reading that assumes the intentional seamlessness of the text and that seeks to explain all aspects of the text as a unity. Archer's judgment on this is that Farrer's effort is 'a dead-end' (p. 70). To a much greater extent than Lawrence, Farrer defines the meaning of each aspect of the text with minute precision. Farrer's treatment of the horses in Revelation 6 and 9 demonstrates his commitment to an integrated web of significances within the text which extends back into a multitude of Old Testament references. In the *Commentary*, the horses of 6.1-8 are described as part of a pre-conceived design into which John falls. The sword given to the second rider is the first on the traditional list of the Lord's grievous plagues, sword, famine and pestilence, given in Ezek. 6.11. The scales held by the third horseman represent scarcity; the fourth horseman is named 'Death', representing pestilence. Each of the four horsemen also correspond to the four key zodiacal signs. The first rider is associated with the conquering lion, a figure unambiguously presented in the same guise as the Word of God in 19.11-16. The lion is followed by the bull, the beast of slaughter identified as the second rider by the sword he is given. The Man should come next, but, argues Farrer, the constellation of scales, represented by the third horseman, 'is in the very claws of the eagle's zodiacal equivalent, the scorpion' (1964: 98). Instead, man, the sign of Aquarius, presides over the end of the year, aptly symbolized by the death brought by the fourth rider. Caught up in the network of correspondences he has entered into, John, as imagined by Farrer, remembers Ezekiel's alternative list of plagues (Ezek. 14.21) and assigns a fourth plague to the set of four horsemen. Although no plague is evoked by the coming of the first rider, in the summary verse Rev. 6.8, the lion of which the first rider is taken to be a symbol, is interpreted as one of the marauding wild beasts of Ezekiel's later list. Farrer explains the colours of the horses by their reference to Zechariah 6, which are red, black, white and dappled grey. In Zechariah (a 'confused text' [p. 99]) the horsemen and the destruction they bring are distinguished only by the colour of their horses. In Revelation, John rearranges the colours and reinterprets their significance: white represents victory, red slaughter, black famine (corresponding to the blackened faces of victims of famine and scorching drought) and 'livid' in place of dappled grey, a 'forced' (1964: 99) description of pestilence. Farrer characteristically finds further significances between these horses and the horses of 9.12-19, which Lawrence had found so alluring. Each of the later horseman is an intensified antitype of the riders in ch. 6. In ch. 6 there were four horsemen and three of them brought distinct plagues represented by their own colours red, black and livid. In ch. 9 there are four cavalry commanders, each leading vast hosts, each bearing three plagues (fire, smoke and brimstone) and each with breastplates of three colours (fiery, smoke-blue and brimstone-yellow). The riders of ch. 6 are given authority over a quarter of the earth (6.8): the three plagues accompanying the lion-horses of ch. 9 kill a third of humanity (9.18). From ch. 6–9 there has been an intensification of the deadly effects of the horsemen. In Farrer's scheme no detail is insignificant and little of what has gone before fails to reappear in the text. The result is an incredibly dense and utterly convinced reading of a difficult and puzzling text.

Derrida Reads Revelation

From certain postmodern critical perspectives, Farrer's conviction that the patterns he finds were at least in part intended by John is untenable. Even if John did follow the scheme Farrer constructs, the reader is in no position to know or to prove this. The author is no longer to be regarded as the guardian of the meaning of the text. Indeed, deconstruction demands that the illusion of presence or truth 'in' or 'behind' a text, guaranteeing its meaning, is abandoned. In the essay 'Of an Apocalyptic Tone Recently Adopted in Philosophy' (1982), Derrida argues that apocalyptic writing highlights this condition of every scene of writing in general:

> If an apocalypse reveals, it is first the revelation of the apocalypse, the self-presentation of the apocalyptic structure of language, of writing, of the experience of presence, either of the text or of the mark in general: that is, of the divisible dispatch [envoi] for which there is no self-presentation nor assured destination (1982: 87).[16]

Derrida's interest lies in the features of the text of Revelation that fascinated Lawrence and that Farrer ignored: because of the frequent (and often incomprehensible) shiftings of tone, voice and narrator, 'no longer do we know very well who loans his voice and his tone to the other in the Apocalypse; no longer do we know very well who

16. Derrida (1982: 64-65) explores the various meanings of and possibilities for *apokalupto* at the beginning of the essay. Later in the essay, he suggests that the term desires or demands that the apocalyptic discourse is itself demystified or deconstructed in its drive for disclosure and unveiling.

addresses what to whom' (1982: 87). Derrida takes Rev. 1.2-3 as his example, but he could equally have used Rev. 9.13-19, which was discussed above. Revelation is distinctive because

> it leaps from one place of emission to the other...; it goes from one destination, one name, and one tone to the other; it always refers to the name and to the tone of the other that is there but as having been there and before yet coming, no longer being or not yet there in the presence of the *récit* (p. 87).

Derrida has argued that this undecidability of origin and destination is a condition of the structure of all writing, although it is rarely as obvious as it is in the example of Revelation. He suggests here that apocalyptic is 'a transcendental condition of all discourse, of all experience itself, of every mark and trace' (p. 87). This condition of discourse is denied or rejected by both Lawrence and Farrer in their work on Revelation, but their readings of the text fail to account adequately for the indeterminacies highlighted by Derrida.

For deconstruction, such indeterminacies offer the way in to a text. Deconstruction recognizes, with Derrida, that the task of interpretation is 'interminable, because no-one can exhaust the overdeterminations and the indeterminations of the apocalyptic strategems' (1982: 89). But rather than giving up on the task, or embarking upon it for its own sake, Derridean deconstruction is also informed by the complex 'ethico-political motif or motivations of these strategems':

> By its very tone, the mixing of voices, genres and codes, and the breakdown of destinations, apocalyptic discourse can...dismantle the dominant contract or concordat. It is a challenge to the established admissibility of messages and to the enforcement or the maintenance of order of the destination (p. 89).

Revelation designates both the content of what is announced about the end of the world, and at other times the announcement itself, 'the revelatory discourse of the to-come or even of the end of the world rather than what it says, the truth of the revelation rather than the revealed truth' (p. 88). Both the message and its verification come from the same text, introducing 'an immediate tonal duplicity in every apocalyptic voice' (p. 88). John also claims status and truth as a messenger, writing 'under the dictate of the great voice come from behind his back' (1982: 88), and yet denounces (and calls on his readers to denounce)[17] 'all those charged with a historic mission of whom nobody has requested anything and whom nobody has charged or entrusted with anything' (p. 89). It is in the best apocalyptic tradition to denounce the false apocalypses, but Revelation can offer its reader no ground upon which to verify its claims to speak the truth. There are no limits to the demystification that apocalypse demands: this demystification must extend to the text of Revelation itself. In these ways, the text of Revelation deconstructs itself.[18] A deconstructive reading of the text recognizes and highlights these aporias, and accounts for their political or ethical consequences.

In Chapter 4, Pippin's article (1994) on the abyss in Revelation offered such a reading, which in turn opened up a new perspective from which to read Hogg's *Confessions*. Pippin's extended discussion of the role of gender in the rhetoric of Revelation (1992) demonstrates the radical differences between the readings of Lawrence and Farrer, and a deconstructive reading. Her work offers a model for other deconstructive readings.

Tina Pippin Reads Revelation

From the outset, Pippin states that she 'want[s] to play with the polyvalence of the symbols, unanchoring them from any specific historical context' (1992: 16). She notes that in the rhetoric of the text, death and desire are closely linked. There is a tension in the text between desire for life and desire for death: the reader must choose between the Lamb, which will result in death but bring eternal life, and the beast, which will also bring death, but with no hope of life after death. Another central concern in the text is what to do with desire both for power and wealth as symbolized in the body of the Whore of Babylon, and for God's world symbolized in the body of the Bride. To analyse these

---

17. Derrida's example of John's denouncement of false apostles is Rev. 2.1–2.4.

18. Pippin, whose work is considered below, suggests another way in which Revelation deconstructs itself (1992: 88-89). She notes that in Revelation there is a privileging of speech over writing (Derrida's phonocentrism) whenever the voices speak to John and instruct him to write. However, ultimately, writing is privileged over speech. John is told to 'Write this, for these words are trustworthy and true' (21.5), and the curse of God is threatened upon anyone who edits the written word (22.18-19). Thus, 'the "violent hierarchy" of speech/writing is overturned' (1992: 89).

conflicting themes and their theological implications, Pippin uses contemporary deconstructive theory, from a feminist perspective, to discuss the narrative tensions in Revelation.

Pippin argues that the evocative language of Revelation allows an
infinite number of readings. In the end, the utopian vision promised is
not enacted and the text's closure is betrayed: the new heaven and new
earth remain in the realm of desire, just beyond reach (22.10), and thus
never fully definable. As part of her reading, Pippin defines Revelation,
as apocalypse, as an early form of what is now called fantasy literature.
In the world it creates, improbable events become probable. The reader
is caught between the natural and supernatural, and experiences the
cathartic effect of reading about and participating in Revelation's world
where God, unbelievably, liberates all believers. In Revelation's fantasy
world, horror and fear, in response both to monsters met on the way
(12–13) and to the heavenly figures such as the one like the Son of Man
(1.12-17), give way to hope in (but not experience of) God's power to
defeat the evil powers. On the journey, readers' desires for violence
against oppressors and for a utopian society where there is no more
pain or violence, draw them into the text. Although the utopia Revelation describes has not yet occurred.[19] like all fantasy literature the text
illuminates the real world: '[t]he fictional nature of the fantastic desta-
bilises the rational world' (1992: 95). The rhetoric of the text affects the
reality of its readers, and offers them liberation and hope.

However, '[t]he Apocalypse is not a tale for women' (1992: 105).[20]
Reading the text for what it says about gender reveals the nature of the
political and cultural situation of women, and exposes the dominant
male attitudes expressed there. All women in the narrative, from the

19. In the section on Lawrence above, it was argued that sections of Revelation
may be read as descriptions of dreams or nightmares. Here Pippin (1992: 95) suggests that the vision of utopia is comparable to a dream's relationship to reality:
'The dream of utopian reality remains a dream—remains in absence/presence in the
narrative, even though it is God who tells the narrator, "Write this, for these words
are trustworthy and true" (21.5, 22.6)'.

20. Moore (1995) argues that Revelation is a 'male fantasy' (p. 55). Moore
notes the striking similarities between the vision of God offered in Rev. 4.8-11 and
modern descriptions of male body-builders, and suggests on the basis of this that
the God of Revelation is an object of hero worship. Eternal bliss for the writer of
the text is 'an uninterrupted vision of a being who is divine, perfect and hypermasculine' (p. 55). For both Pippin and Moore, Revelation is a text that is alien to a
female reader.

Woman clothed with the sun, to the Whore of Babylon and the Bride, are victims, and their fate is without fail decided by men. The transformation promised and shown in Revelation is only partial: women are excluded from participating in the victory. They are absent from the number of the faithful in 14.4, who are all men (only οἳ μετὰ γυναικῶν οὐκ ἐμολύνθησαν will follow the Lamb and be the first fruits of redemption). Unworthy of this redemption, all females who appear in the text are objects of desire and violence. Evil is associated with the woman and her body, and she is to be desired and feared because of this power. The Whore of Babylon is the archetypal image of the loose woman, seductive but also presented as grotesque. Her erotic power is dangerous, but so too is her independence and egotism. The communal carnival of her death (Rev. 17–18), in which she is stripped, constitutes the 'ultimate misogynist fantasy' (Pippin 1992: 67). Her safe counterpart, the Bride, is a woman defined and controlled by men. She must retain her erotic attractiveness, as a replacement for the Whore and signalled by the wedding imagery (Rev. 21), but her sexuality is limited and outwith her control. Her body exists simply as an object of desire for men: her own desires are not addressed. Indeed, she quickly loses her identity as a woman, and is transposed into the symbolism of the city (Rev. 21.9-10) (p. 21). Under this image, the entrance of the faithful followers through her gates (21.27) reads like a mass rape. The message of the text is that the erotic power of women is dangerous and must be controlled by men if anything positive is to come of it. The erotic female brings either death or birth: she is either the way to God in terms of rebirth into the New Jerusalem; or the way to Satan and death in the abyss. Those females with autonomous power, such as the Whore of Babylon, bring death. Those who are conduits to God are those who are safely defined by men as brides and mothers. There is no woman in the text whose identity is anything other than archetypal or stereotypical, or who has power and control over her own life. From a woman's perspective, safety is only to be found in exile and loneliness. The Woman clothed with the sun, who is taken to this place of safety (Rev. 12.14), has no name and her fate remains undetermined. She is identified only by her role as mother (12.5, 13), and after fulfilling her function she is decentred. Speechless and silenced, except for her cries in childbirth, her safety depends on the activity of others. As an archetype of the text's ideal woman, she sends a powerful message to the female reader.

The utopia of the text is a place where desires are controlled. The unconscious desires of the male reader are revealed but then redirected. Females are not allowed to desire power, and those who do are labelled monsters. There is no affirmation of the female body, desire, autonomy or erotic power. Pippin (1992: 105-107) suggests that the desire of women must be for a different utopia from the one offered in Revelation. In today's world, all desire both for violent destruction of enemies at the hand of God, and for martyrdom, has to be rethought. Women's response to Revelation must be a complete reinterpretation of the meaning of choosing Christ rather than Satan. Certainly the liberation offered by the text cannot be reclaimed by feminists.

Pippin's book is that although Revelation may be a liberating text for some,[21] for women the text always needs deconstruction rather than reconstruction:

> The Apocalypse is a decolonizing literature that turns around and recolonizes. A feminist reading of this text is necessarily deconstructive; the Apocalypse is made up of conflicting readings that cannot be resolved (1992: 56).

However, Pippin does not address in any detail the implications of a deconstructive reading of Revelation from anything other than a feminist perspective. She leaves untouched the many other cultural boundaries set up by the text in terms of systems of opposites such as Christian and non-Christian, outsider or insider. Deconstruction offers a way to read the text that is sensitive to these boundaries as well as to the marginalization of women. In Revelation the process of decolonizaton followed by recolonization which Pippin discovered with reference to women in the text can also be shown to apply to those forced to choose between Christ and Satan, the believer and the non-believer. The rhetoric of the text encourages the reader to make the same choice: a deconstruction of this rhetoric has consequences for the text's claim to

---

21. Pippin (1992: 50) mentions Fiorenza's (1985) work on the cathartic power of Revelation for Christians in oppressed situations, and the readings of Boesak (1987), which find specific hope and comfort in the text for Christians struggling under the regime of apartheid. In his introductory chapter, Boesak writes '[w]hat follows here is biblical exegesis from the underside, reflections on the Apocalypse with the Christian church of today in mind—even more specifically, with the black church of South Africa in mind' (p. 36). For members of this church, Boesak asserts that 'the Apocalypse is an exciting, inspiring, and marvellous book... It is prophetic, historical, contemporary' (pp. 38-39).

the status of Scripture.[22] In the following section the text is read as a nightmarish struggle for control of the believer/reader. Its paradoxical imagery and shifting perspective are considered from a position of scepticism rather than faith, and the power relationships within the text, particularly between Christ and the people with whom he has contact, are highlighted. Central to the discussion will be a consideration of the role of place in the text in the creation and maintenance of boundaries between the believer and the non-believer.

The Nightmare Worlds of Revelation

Revelation is set in a labyrinthine place where doors slam shut and the sound of locks turning echoes in the darkness. Of the eight references to keys in the Bible, four occur in Revelation. Jesus tells John that he has the keys of Death and Hades (ἔχω τὰς κλεῖς τοῦ θανάτου καὶ τοῦ ᾄδου [1.18]); John is told to write to the angel of the church in Philadelphia with the words of the one who has the 'keys of David' (ὁ ἔχων τὴν κλεῖν Δαυίδ [3.7]); the star fallen from heaven is given the key to the shaft of the bottomless abyss (ἐδόθη αὐτῷ ἡ κλεὶς τοῦ φρέατος τῆς ἀβύσσου [9.1]); and in a parallel picture an angel comes from heaven with the (another?) key to the pit, and locks the dragon/serpent/satan figure into it for a thousand years (20.1-3). People, places and symbols travel backwards and forwards through these doors and across boundaries. The New Jerusalem journeys from heaven to earth (ἔδειξέν μοι τὴν πόλιν τὴν ἁγίαν Ἰερουσαλὴμ καταβαίνουσαν ἐκ τοῦ οὐρανοῦ ἀπὸ τοῦ θεοῦ [21.10]). Death, Hades and those whose names are not written in the Book of Life are thrown downwards from heaven into the lake of fire (ἐβλήθη εἰς τὴν λίμνην τοῦ πυρός [20.11-15]). Angels, stars, cities and the damned all make a downward journey, but there is also movement upwards. John sees an open door in heaven, and the Spirit acts as his conduit there (ἀνάβα ὧδε, καὶ δείξω σοι ἃ δεῖ γενέσθαι μετὰ ταῦτα. εὐθέως ἐγενόμην ἐν πνεύματι, καὶ ἰδοὺ θρόνος ἔκειτο ἐν τῷ οὐρανῷ, καὶ ἐπὶ τὸν θρόνον καθήμενος [4.1-2]). The beast ascends from the bottomless pit, through its lockable opening, to make war on the witnesses of God (τὸ θηρίον τὸ ἀναβαῖνον ἐκ τῆς ἀβύσσου ποιήσει μετ' αὐτῶν πόλεμον [11.7]) and the witnesses, having lain dead on the street for three and a half days,

22. As Hassan suggests (1987: 505), one of the features of postmodernism is decanonization, 'a "delegitimation" of the mastercodes in society'.

stand up and go up into heaven on a cloud (ἀνέβησαν εἰς τὸν οὐρανὸν ἐν τῇ νεφέλῃ [11.12]). The woman of ch. 12 is exiled downwards from heaven to the wilderness, and then, with eagle's wings, escapes into the air to avoid the dragon (ἡ γυνὴ ἔφυγεν εἰς τὴν ἔρημον... καὶ ἐδόθησαν τῇ γυναικὶ αἱ δύο πτέρυγες τοῦ ἀετοῦ τοῦ μεγάλου, ἵνα πέτηται εἰς τὴν ἔρημον εἰς τὸν τόπον αὐτῆς [12.6, 14]). In this nightmare, nothing is stable and fixed: the scene changes rapidly from one sphere to another, as does the perspective of the watcher.[23]

At first sight, the figure of Jesus is in control of the boundaries and movement between them. Death and Hades are both described as places to which Jesus has the key, implicitly by virtue of having crossed the boundary from death back to life. Jesus assures John:

μὴ φοβοῦ· ἐγώ εἰμι ὁ πρῶτος καὶ ὁ ἔσχατος καὶ ὁ ζῶν, καὶ ἐγενόμην νεκρὸς καὶ ἰδοὺ ζῶν εἰμι εἰς τοὺς αἰῶνας τῶν αἰώνων καὶ ἔχω τὰς κλεῖς τοῦ θανάτου καὶ τοῦ ᾅδου.

Fear not, I am the first and the last and the living one; I died, and behold I am alive for evermore, and I have the keys of Death and Hades (1.17, 18).

John participates in and mirrors this action by falling at Jesus' feet 'as though dead' (ὡς νεκρός [1.17]) and is revived by the touch of Jesus' right hand. However, the extent of Jesus' control becomes sinister rather than assuring when he tells John to write to the angel of the church in Philadelphia (3.7-8). As holder of the key of David, Jesus claims the ability to open and shut things in an irrevocable way. He sets before the church an open door, which cannot be shut (θύραν ἠνεῳγμένην, ἣν οὐδεὶς δύναται κλεῖσαι αὐτήν). Is this a reward for their steadfastness in the face of difficulty, or a compensation for their lack of power? The connection between the statement about the open door and the acknowledgement of the Philadelphians' weakness is unexplained. Also unclear is where the door leads. Is it a door through which the Philadelphian Christians are to go? Or is it a door which allows others, possibly those of the synagogue of Satan, to reach the Philadelphians? Is it an escape route, and if so, from whom or what; or a way leading to danger, a temptation to be avoided? The open door is an

23. In his exploration of postmodernist fiction, McHale (1987: 37) describes the postmodern condition as 'an anarchic landscape of worlds in the plural', reflecting the plurality of postmodern life. The world of Revelation is equally plural and confusing.

ambiguous, ruptured boundary between the known and the unknown. The reader, like the Philadelphians, is offered no guidance about what is on the other side. However, a further promise involving enclosure is given in v. 12 of the same chapter: Jesus will make those who conquer into a pillar in God's temple, from which they will never leave. The open door of v. 8 has been slammed shut.

The nature of Jesus' control of the boundaries in the text is further questioned by dramatic changes in the way he describes himself and is described by others. A pleasant and gracious image is offered at 3.20. Here Jesus is a guest waiting to be given permission to enter a home. He is either unable or unwilling to force his way in, and depends on the home-owner both to hear him knocking and to open the door. However, at 3.3 he warns the church at Sardis that unless they wake up and repent, he will come to them like a thief (ἥξω ὡς κλέπτης). There is a similar warning interjected in John's vision of the gathering of the hosts at Armageddon. Apparently Jesus interrupts John's narrative to warn that he will come like a thief and that only those who are awake and clothed will be blessed ('Ιδοὺ ἔρχομαι ὡς κλέπτης. μακάριος ὁ γρηγορῶν καὶ τηρῶν τὰ ἱμάτια αὐτοῦ, ἵνα μὴ γυμνὸς περιπατῇ καὶ βλέπωσιν τὴν ἀσχημοσύνην αὐτοῦ [16.15]). A thief is someone who either has no key and must force an entry, or who has acquired a key illegitimately. His coming is unexpected, and unwelcome, as the context implies, but it is also illegal and dishonest. Although Jesus holds so many keys and controls so many doors, he has to threaten to break in to those who are unprepared. In the text there remain some places that resist him. Perhaps the unspecified area beyond the open door which Jesus sets before the Philadelphians at 3.8 is such a place of resistance.

Jesus, then, is a mercurial figure who is door-keeper, jailer, thief and guest in the world of the text. He opens up possibilities, protects, guards and imprisons those of whom he approves. He threatens forcefully to invade the boundaries of those who have forgotten him, and he waits to be admitted into the lives of those who need his presence without realizing it. Jesus is active and involved in all areas in which the vision might intersect with the lives of its readers. Because of his changing nature, his presence is more likely to provoke anxiety than reassurance. Such dream-like anxiety is further provoked in his interjected warning in 16.15: the blessed are those who both stay awake and who keep (τηρῶν) their clothes rather than go naked. At 22.7, a further interjected blessing is offered: the blessed are those who keep (τηρῶν) the words of the prophecy of this book. Nakedness and exposure, common night-marish motifs, are identified with failure to live up to and live by the prophecy detailed in the experience of the text. Those who fail will have nowhere to hide. Jesus' presence in his different guises brings about this threat, rather than offers comfort and relief from it.

Another aspect of there being nowhere to hide in Revelation is that no one escapes being branded by one side or another. Ownership and control are established in the text by naming, marking and sealing. Each person's eternal fate depends on where their name is written, and what is written on them. For salvation, it is vital that your name is written in the book of life (ἄλλο βιβλίον ἠνοίχθη, ὅ ἐστιν τῆς ζωῆς, καὶ ἐκρίθη-σαν οἱ νεκροὶ ἐκ τῶν γεγραμμένων ἐν τοῖς βιβλίοις κατὰ τὰ ἔργα αὐτῶν [20.12]), but your fate may have been sealed from before the foundation of the world (καὶ προσκυνήσουσιν αὐτὸν πάντες οἱ κατοικοῦντες ἐπὶ τῆς γῆς, οὗ οὐ γέγραπται τὸ ὄνομα αὐτοῦ ἐν τῷ βιβλίῳ τῆς ζωῆς τοῦ ἀρνίου τοῦ ἐσφαγμένου ἀπὸ καταβολῆς κόσμου [13.8]). Even those whose names have been included are liable to have their names blotted out of the book: Jesus tells the church at Sardis that they 'still have a few names' (ἀλλὰ ἔχεις ὀλίγα ὀνόματα), and that the names of those who conquer he will not remove from the book (ὁ νικῶν οὕτως περιβαλεῖται ἐν ἱματίοις λευκοῖς καὶ οὐ μὴ ἐξαλείψω τὸ ὄνομα αὐτοῦ ἐκ τῆς βίβλου τῆς ζωῆς [3.4-5]). Presumably those who fail to conquer are blotted out. Another indicator of destiny is the mark carried on the body. In ch. 9 certain individuals have already been given the seal of God on their foreheads, and because of this they escape the torture of the locusts (καὶ ἐρρέθη αὐταῖς ἵνα μὴ ἀδική-σουσιν τὸν χόρτον τῆς γῆς οὐδὲ πᾶν χλωρὸν οὐδὲ πᾶν δένδρον, εἰ μὴ τοὺς ἀνθρώπους οἵτινες οὐκ ἔχουσι τὴν σφραγῖδα τοῦ θεοῦ ἐπὶ τῶν μετώπων [9.4]). The second beast of Rev. 13.16 causes 'all' to be marked on the hand or forehead with the mark which is 'the name of the beast or the number of its name' (τὸ χάραγμα τὸ ὄνομα τοῦ θηρίου ἢ τὸν ἀριθμὸν τοῦ ὀνόματος αὐτοῦ [13.17]). However, differently marked people appear with the Lamb in the next chapter, who have his name and the name of his father written on their foreheads (τὸ ὄνομα αὐτοῦ καὶ τὸ ὄνομα τοῦ πατρὸς αὐτοῦ γεγραμμένον ἐπὶ τῶν μετώπων αὐτῶν [14.1]). These are the redeemed first fruits of humanity. Those who survive to the end to experience the New Jerusalem will all have the Lamb's name on their foreheads. No-one remains intact, unmarked or independent, and the basis upon which each individual receives any mark seems arbitrary. Each person's eternal fate is ultimately outwith their control,[24] and the warnings and admonitions of the figures who are met in the world of the nightmare only heighten the anxiety of the reader.

Names in the text are significant and powerful. Nameless multitudes exist to be tortured, slaughtered or redeemed, but the key figures (except the Woman clothed with the sun) are given or claim many different names. The angel of the pit has a Greek and a Hebrew name (ὄνομα αὐτῷ Ἑβραϊστὶ Ἀβαδδών, καὶ ἐν τῇ Ἑλληνικῇ ὄνομα ἔχει Ἀπολλύων [9.11]), and the serpent is called both Devil and Satan, and also has a title, 'the deceiver of the whole world' (ὁ καλούμενος Διάβολος καὶ ὁ Σατανᾶς, ὁ πλανῶν τὴν οἰκουμένην ὅλην [12.9]). The beast from the sea has an unspecified 'blasphemous name' (ὀνόμα[τα] βλασφημίας) upon its ten heads (13.1). In ch. 19 the figure on the white horse has a similar multiplicity of revealed and hidden names. He is called Faithful and True (πιστὸς καὶ ἀληθινός [19.11]), but he also has a name written upon him that no one knows but himself (ἔχων ὄνομα γεγραμμένον ὃ οὐδεὶς οἶδεν εἰ μὴ αὐτός [19.12]). More names follow: 'his name is called the word of God' (κέκληται τὸ ὄνομα αὐτοῦ ὁ λόγος τοῦ θεοῦ [19.13]), and on his thigh are written the titles 'King of Kings' and 'Lord of Lords' (βασιλεὺς βασιλέων καὶ κύριος κυρίων [19.16]). The need to mark others with your own name to identify and own them may be read as similar to this accumulation of names and titles. Both are aspects of the struggle for control, although the claiming of multiple names also, inevitably, increases diversity and confusion.[25]

24. Derrida (1978: 65), quotes from Jabès' *Le Livre des Questions* (1963: 30): 'And Reb Ilde: "What difference is there between choosing and being chosen when we can do nothing but submit to the choice?"'. Derrida's point is the relationship between the author and his or her text. He argues that 'the poet, in the very experience of his freedom, finds himself both bound to the language and delivered from it by a speech whose master, nonetheless, he himself is'. In Revelation there is a similar tension between choosing and being chosen, ie having no choice.

25. Derrida (1991) discusses the jealousy and resentment of God which leads to the imposition of God's name upon the people. Noting that Babel may be translated both as 'confusion' and as 'the name of God as name of father' (p. 4) (*ba* signifying 'father' and *bel* signifying 'God'), Derrida comments that God, in response to the people building a tower and a city in Genesis 11, 'out of resentment against that unique name and lip of men...imposes his name, his name of father; and with this violent imposition he opens the deconstruction of the tower, as of the universal language; he scatters the genealogical filiation' (p. 4). Because the name given by God

In this context, even the apparently positive titles applied and claimed by God and his representatives on earth may be read as attempts to impose a hierarchy of control. Moore (1995: 31) argues that the description of the adoring multitudes in Rev. 4.8-11 promotes the possibility that the God of Revelation is a projection of an 'embarrassingly muscular being, insatiably hungry for adulation'. I argue that the accumulation of titles throughout the text offers a picture of a God who both demands and claims authority, but whose claims are continually undermined by their number and variety. The picture is one of a fractured God, which is emphasized by the multiplicity of his envoys, and in particular the multiple personalities of the figure on the horse in ch. 19.

In two places, Jesus promises to give new names to those who conquer: at 2.17 he offers a white stone with a secret, new name written on it (δώσω αὐτῷ ψῆφον λευκήν, καὶ ἐπὶ τὴν ψῆφον ὄνομα καινὸν γεγραμμένον ὃ οὐδεὶς οἶδεν εἰ μὴ ὁ λαμβάνων); and at 3.12 he says he will write on those who have become pillars of the temple the name of God, the name of the city of God, that is, the New Jerusalem, and his own new name (ὁ νικῶν ποιήσω αὐτὸν στῦλον ἐν τῷ ναῷ τοῦ θεοῦ μου καὶ ἔξω οὐ μὴ ἐξέλθῃ ἔτι καὶ γράψω ἐπ' αὐτὸν τὸ ὄνομα τοῦ θεοῦ μου καὶ τὸ ὄνομα τῆς πόλεως τοῦ θεοῦ μου, τῆς καινῆς Ἰερουσαλὴμ ἡ καταβαίνουσα ἐκ τοῦ οὐρανοῦ ἀπὸ τοῦ θεοῦ μου, καὶ τὸ ὄνομά μου τὸ καινόν). The owner of a stone is turned to stone, and both are written upon. Things change from one thing into another in a nightmarish way. In the text, God names and claims his own by writing (γράφω), either in a book of life or on the person involved. The exception is at 9.4, where the distinguishing and saving mark is the 'seal' (σφραγίς) of God, an authenticating and literal stamp of approval. In contrast, the beast's sign is an engraved rather than a written mark (χάραγμα), something made, in Acts 17.29, out of the art and imagination of mortals and something that God is not (οὐκ ὀφείλομεν νομίζειν...χαράγματι τέχνης καὶ ἐνθυμήσεως ἀνθρώπου, τὸ θεῖον εἶναι ὅμοιον). God's mark is the written word, and its recipient is a

to the people, and given by God to himself, is divided, signifying 'confusion', 'the war he declares has first raged within his name: divided, bifid, ambivalent, polysemic: God deconstructing' (p. 4). The multiplicity of names claimed by the Christ for himself and of other names given to his enemies, signifies a similar internal deconstruction. Does it also signify a similar resentment of the world and its dealings as was provoked by the building of the tower in Genesis?

cipher, whose task is to authenticate another (as the Corinthian believers are the certification of Paul's apostleship in 1 Cor. 9.2): the beast's is an engraving, turning its recipient into a created, but independent, work of art, a thing of beauty in itself. The beast's mark, which is extended to all classes and ranks of people rather than to a chosen few only, allows normal daily life to continue, in the form of buying and selling (καὶ ἵνα μή τις δύνηται ἀγοράσαι ἢ πωλῆσαι εἰ μὴ ὁ ἔχων τὸ χάραγμα τὸ ὄνομα τοῦ θηρίου ἢ τὸν ἀριθμὸν τοῦ ὀνόματος αὐτοῦ [13.17]). God's mark, which is for the chosen few only, leads to enclosure in stone, perpetual existence in his presence, and exclusion from contact with earthly life (3.12).[26] Little wonder that in contrast to this static, controlled existence, the positive, subversive aspects of the alternative world of the beast and his followers cannot be completely subsumed in the text. These aspects of the alternative world escape the control of the dominant vision.

Revelation is a text of anxiety. The claims of God and of Satan struggle within it. God and the Holy City are apparently victorious, but the alternative vision continues to lurk at the boundaries of the city and the text. More fundamentally still, the appeal of the alternative breaks through, despite the rhetoric of the dominant voice. As Pippin (1992) commented, the anarchy of the destabilizing existence of the Whore of Babylon cannot be resolved in God's New Jerusalem. The life offered to those with the mark of the beast rather than the mark of the chosen remains positive and productive, despite God's attempt to punish and mock. God's offering to those who become written pages in his book, or pillars in his temple, is static in comparison. The note of fear and anxiety in the text comes from the burden and impossibility of choosing between the beast and God, and the danger of choosing against God. However, when the text is read as a nightmare, this burden is lifted. The

26. Moore (1995) argues that the vision of the New Jerusalem given in Rev. 21.1–22.5 is a vision 'of power absolutized' (p. 42), a 'Foucauldian nightmare… [which] represents the absolute displacement of outward subjection, tangible coercion, by inner self-policing, which is now so deeply implanted as to be altogether undistinguishable from freedom' (p. 41). The option presented is a world of torture. For Moore, such a text is scarcely a text of comfort or liberation. Although the emphasis of Moore's deconstructive reading is very different from my own, his observations about the dangerous and disturbing aspects of the text's dominant vision are supportive of my reading.

chaos may be read as part of the world of a dream rather than characteristics of God's word which must either be ignored or explained. Pippin
had defined Revelation as a text that denies liberation to the female, and
had rejected it on these grounds as unreclaimable for women. Reading
the barbarities of Revelation as a nightmare allows all readers to reject
the text as Scripture. It denies the text the privileges and status of God's
Word, and offers all readers the opportunity to construct an alternative
vision of the future that does not involve torture, anxiety and loss of
control and independence. Once the reader wakes up to this possibility,
and the voice of the alternative vision is heard, relief replaces the
anxious world of the bad dream.

Lawrence recognized the potency and importance of the text of
Revelation, and Farrer realised its complexity and depth. Both failed to
allow its competing voices to speak, and silenced those aspects of the
text which undermined or contradicted their own position. Only when
these voices are heard and these aspects of the text are recognized is the
Revelation of John read with integrity in a postmodern world.

Chapter 6

CONCLUSION

Central to the aim of this book has been an exploration of the reading process. In particular, readings of Scripture have been considered, both in the Bible itself, and in the work of James Hogg. Modern readings of Revelation have been compared with readings of Hogg's *Confessions*: readings of the *Confessions* have enabled a more accurate reading of the Bible as literature; and readings of Revelation have highlighted some of the assumptions of privilege that have been made about texts such as the *Confessions*. Two postmodern literary critical perspectives have been discussed, and it has been suggested that the application of these perspectives to readings of all texts, but particularly sacred texts, has profound implications.

There are two methodological conclusions to be drawn from this exploration. The first is raised by comparing the approach taken in Part 1 (Chapters 2 and 3) with the approach taken in Part 2 (Chapters 4 and 5). In Chapters 2 and 3, the concerns and vocabulary of the postmodern notion of marginalization are considered helpful in readings of the *Confessions* and Revelation because of the marginalized position each text occupies in its historical context. The ex-centric situation of both authors leads to texts that are subversive and sceptical of society's dominant master narratives. I argue that in the *Confessions* this is evidenced in the way Hogg uses the Bible. In his work, the dominant principles of preaching from the Bible, as demonstrated in the sermons of Boston, Chalmers and Thomson, are subverted in the language of Robert's father and supremely in the speech of Gil-Martin. All interpretations of the Bible that claim to be doctrinally authoritative and final are shown by Hogg to be inadequate, deceptive and ultimately dangerous. In Revelation, the author is ex-centric both in terms of the State and with regard to the rest of the Christian community. John's purpose is to encourage his readers to see things as they are not: to reject the

State, recognizing it as evil, and to seek out persecution in order to gain reward in heaven. One of the ways this perspective is reinforced is in the writer's use of the Hebrew Bible. A consideration of the way Ezekiel 37 is read in Revelation 11 suggests that the writer identifies the slain in the Ezekiel text with all followers of Christ, who must accept persecution for the sake of their witness to the Gospel. John reinforces his own prophetic status by placing himself within the tradition of prophetic voices stretching from Moses through Ezekiel to Jesus. A subversive reading of the sacred text is also found in Second Ezekiel, in a fragment of the text discovered at Qumran. Here, the text reflects the needs of a community that has chosen physical marginalization and separation from the wider community. The promise of the Ezekiel vision of the restoration of the land to the Israelites has become a prophecy promising the reward of resurrection to those who believe themselves to be the faithful remnant of the people of God. In all of these texts, there is a subversive, critical response to the apparent stabilities of the centre. Without the self-consciousness or relentlessness of a postmodern writer, these writers nevertheless share many of the concerns of postmodern literary theory. For this reason, the postmodern perspective of marginalization, when applied to these texts, illuminates their previously silenced ex-centricities.

In Chapters 4 and 5, Revelation and the *Confessions* are approached in a more radically postmodern way. Some of the modern readings of both texts are considered. The reliance of these readings on a reconstruction of the intentions of the author, and their attempts to explain all aspects of the texts' difficulties on this basis, are debated from the perspective of deconstruction, which questions the availability and validity of this knowledge. Their interpretations are shown not to stand up to the ruthless readings of deconstruction. Alternative readings of the two texts are offered from this deconstructive perspective. It is suggested that the abyss, or pit of damnation, is ever-present in the world of the *Confessions*, destabilizing all perceptions of reality. God, a force for good, is absent in this world: even the apparently 'good' characters commonly assumed to carry the author's sympathy are shown to be as inadequate and as open to alternative readings as all other characters. The Bible, it is argued, is either silent or deceptive, offering no comfort or certainty. In this context, Gil-Martin may be read as a heroic figure who tells Robert the truth about his situation, and offers him the only escape available, which is suicide. When Revelation is read in this way, the text's shifting perspectives and demands may be considered without the need to harmonize or explain them logically. The changing figure of Christ, alternatively the jailer, guest and thief, and the anxiety provoked by the text's insistence that all must be marked or branded, with eternal consequences, allow the text to be read as a description of a nightmare rather than as a vision of the future. The recurrent themes of nakedness, judgment and imprisonment are those of a horrifying dream rather than authoritative Scripture. A deconstructive scepticism towards both the *Confessions'* and Revelation's claims to authority, and awareness of their contradictions and complexity, offers completely new and disturbing ways to consider their meaning, or the implications of their meaninglessness.

Is the approach taken in Part I incompatible with that taken in Part II? If the logic of deconstruction's scepticism towards a fixed, stable and recoverable historical context of a text is acknowledged and accepted, is any reading that allows the writer's context a role in the creation of meaning fatally flawed? Throughout, the aim of this book has been to argue against readings that attempt to close the text, or to prevent its endless ambiguities from working in the imagination of each new reader. All the readings I have offered have been presented simply as possibilities, and as attempts to avoid the most blatant smoothing-over of dissident voices in the texts. If the deconstructive approach becomes one more way of reading a text that denies the validity of all others, it has denied its own premise. Deconstruction does not deny that judgments may still be made on the readings of others: but a deconstructive reading must also allow for the possibility that such judgments are not the only answer. Deconstruction reveals above all that no reading, whether of the author, the original reader or a later interpreter, has the right to the final word about a text's meaning. No hierarchy of interpretations exists. Here, two possible ways of reading Revelation and the *Confessions* have been offered. Both involve the language and ideas developed by the general movement called postmodernism. The latter simply takes those ideas further than the former. One benefit of presenting two postmodern literary critical perspectives in this way in the field of biblical studies is that the shock of the second way is softened by the gentler introduction of the first way. Indeed, my hope is that the approach suggested by Lumsden (1992) and adapted in Part I will enable previously suspicious biblical scholars to begin to consider

positively some of the implications of postmodern literary theory for
biblical studies.

A second methodological issue raised by the book is the validity of
reading a biblical text alongside a text from nineteenth-century Scottish
literature. At first sight, bringing the two texts into contiguity with each
other seems strange and arbitrary. However, the similarities between
the two texts, their shared readings of the Bible and the way they have
been read over time have been suggested as one reason for bringing
them together. Another is the insight gained by doing so. Lumsden's
1992 reading of the *Confessions* enabled a new reading of Revelation.
Pippin's 1992 and 1994 reading of Revelation enabled a new reading of
the *Confessions*. Attempts are often made to 'read the Bible as literature', without a consideration of what it means to read Scripture as if it
were a novel. Such readings exist in a contextual vacuum. Here a context for doing so is offered. By reading Revelation alongside the *Confessions*, the privilege and status of the biblical text is more easily
disregarded. The text may be read more naturally and freely as a whole,
rather than as a collection of short verses and chapters. The implications
for the *Confessions* are harder to define. Perhaps by reading the novel
alongside a biblical text, its status within the canon of Scottish literature
is more easily recognized, and dealt with. In general terms, I have
sought to show that the process of reading is illuminated when two
texts from radically different backgrounds are read and interpreted side
by side.

Conclusions about specific readings of the text flow from the
methodological issues already considered. When Revelation is read in
the context of deconstruction as a deprivileged text, its horror loses its
sting. When its apparent message about the necessity of choosing God
over Satan is deconstructed, the choice loses its eternal implications.
The boundary between the chosen and the lost is blurred, and the mark
of the beast may even be read as a positive sign allowing normal life to
go on, in opposition to the mark of God, which results in eternal incar-
ceration in the pillar of the temple. If Revelation is no longer read as
having any literal or figurative bearing on the future, but as a disjointed,
chaotic nightmare, the anxiety it provokes is put into perspective. If the
text's theological significance is questioned, all that is left is a succes-
sion of violent images. Pippin had suggested that Revelation, although
a text of liberation for some, cannot be reclaimed for women: I have
suggested that Revelation is unreclaimable on a far wider scale.

In contrast, deconstructive readings of the *Confessions* heighten that text's horror. The burden of explanation of every strand and ambiguity in the novel is lifted, but the horror of it is then allowed to stand without any natural or even supernatural explanation. In my readings, the locus of horror is transferred from the realm of life beyond or outwith earthly experience, and placed inescapably within everyday life. When the world of experience is understood to be meaningless and yet endlessly threatening and destabilizing, as Robert discovers, the only escape available is into the nothingness of death. The *Confessions* deconstructed is a text of almost unmanageable fear.

There are several aspects of this book that might be explored further. In particular, the psychological implications of reading Revelation as a description of a nightmare would repay further consideration. No doubt Jung or Freud would have much to say about the meaning of such a dream. Also, in Chapters 4 and 5, the literary critical term 'fantasy' has been used, although the wealth of literature dealing with this notion in fiction (and, to a lesser extent, in the Bible), has not been discussed in any depth. I suggest that more inter-disciplinary work could be done in this area. Finally, the debate about the theological and literary critical implications of postmodern readings continues, and much more remains to be said. Reading texts in the ways I have suggested disturbs and challenges most traditional readings, whether of fiction or of Scripture. However, as I have argued, the implications of postmodernism, in its many forms, cannot be ignored.

APPENDIX 1:
GENESIS RABBAH 19.9 AND 19.10

Based on Neusner's (1987a: 77-79) expansion of Theodor and Aleck's *Midrash Bereshit Rabba: Critical Edition with Notes and Commentary* (1893–1936, I–III).

19.9

1. A. 'And the Lord called to the man and said to him, "Where are you?"' (Gen. 3.9).

    B. [The word for 'where are you' yields the consonants that bear the meaning] 'How has this happened to you?'

    C. [God speaks:] 'Yesterday it was in accord with my plan, and now it is in accord with the plan of the snake. Yesterday it was from one end of the world to the other [that you filled the earth], and now: "Among the trees of the garden" (Gen. 3.8) [you hide out].'

2. A. R. Abbahu in the name of R. Yose b. Haninah: 'It is written: 'But they are like a man [Adam]; they have transgressed the covenant' (Hos. 6.7).

    B. 'They are like a man': specifically, like the first man. [We shall now compare the story of the first man in Eden with the story of Israel in its land.]

    C. '"In the case of the first man, I brought him into the garden of Eden; I commanded him; he violated my commandment; I judged him to be sent away and driven out; but I mourned for him, saying "How..."' [which begins the book of Lamentations, hence stands for a lament, but which, as we saw, also is written with the consonants that also yield 'Where are you'].

    D. 'I brought him into the Garden of Eden.' As it is written: 'And the Lord God took the man and put him into the Garden of Eden' (Gen. 2.15).

    E. 'I commanded him.' As it is written: 'And the Lord God commanded...' (Gen. 2.16).

    F. 'And he violated my commandment.' As it is written: 'Did you eat from the tree concerning which I commanded you?' (Gen. 3.11).

    G. 'I judged him to be sent away.' As it is written: 'And the Lord God sent him from the Garden of Eden' (Gen. 3.23).

    H. 'And I judged him to be driven out.' 'And he drove out the man' (Gen. 3.24).

    I. 'But I mourned for him, saying, "How...."' 'And he said to him, "Where are you?"' (Gen. 3.9), and the word for 'where are you' is written 'How...'

J. 'So too in the case of his descendants, [God continues to speak,] I brought them into the Land of Israel; I commanded them; they violated my commandment; I judged them to be sent out and driven away but I mourned for them, saying, "How…"'

K. 'I brought them into the Land of Israel.' 'And I brought you into the land of Carmel' (Jer. 2.7).

L. 'I commanded them.' 'And you, command the children of Israel' (Lev. 24.2).

M. 'They violated my commandment.' 'Send them away, out of my sight and let them go forth' (Jer. 15.1).

N. '…and driven away.' 'From my house I shall drive them' (Hos. 9.15).

O. 'But I mourned for them, saying, "How…."' 'How has the city sat solitary, that was full of people' (Lam. 1.1).

19.10

1. A. 'And he said, "I heard the sound of you in the garden, and I was afraid, because I was naked, and I hid myself". He said, "Who told you [that you were naked? Have you eaten of the tree of which I commanded you not to eat?"]' (Gen. 3.10-11):

   B. Said R. Levi, 'The matter may be compared to the case of a woman who wanted to borrow a little yeast, who went in to the house of a snake-charmer. She said to her, "What does your husband do with you? [How does he treat you?"]'.

   C. 'She said to her, 'Every sort of kindness does he do with me, except for the case of one jug filled with snakes and scorpions, of which he does not permit me to take charge'.

   D. 'She said to her, 'The reason is that that is where he has all his valuables, and he is planning to marry another woman and to hand them over to her'.

   E. 'What did the wife do? She put her hand into the jug [to find out what was there]. The snakes and scorpions began to bite her. When her husband got home, he heard her crying out. He said to her, "Could you have touched that jug?"'

   F. 'So: 'Have you eaten of the tree of which I commanded you not to eat?' (Gen. 3.11).

APPENDIX 2:
4Q385 SECOND EZEKIEL 2

Text reconstructed and translated by J. Strugnell and D. Dimant, 1988: 45-58.

[וידעו]   ]

] כי אני יהוה] הגוא͏ֹל עמי לתת להם הברית   vacat   1

] ואמרה יהוה] רא͏יֹתֹי רבים מישראל אשר אהבו אֶת שֶמֶך וילכו   2

בדרכ͏ין]   צדק וא[להֹ מתי יהיו והיככה ישתלמו חֶסדם ויאמר יהוה   3

אלי אֹני אֹרֹאֹהֹ את בנֹי ישראל וידעו כי אני יהיה   vacat   4

] ויאמר] בֹן ארם הנבה על העצמות ואֹמרת הֹ ˙˙˙ ̄עֹצם אל עצמו ופרק 5

] אל פרקן וי͏ה]י כן ויאמר שנית הנבא ויעלו עליהם גרים ויקרמו עור 6

] מלמעלה וי͏ה]͏י כן] וֹי͏אֹמֹ͏ר שוב אנבֹא על ארבע רוחות השמים ויפחו רוה[ות 7

] השמים בהם ויחיו]ויֹעֹמֹ͏ד עם רב אנשים ויברכו את יהוה צבאות אש͏ר הים[8

] ו]אמרה יהוה מתי יהיו אלה ויאמר יהוה אל͏י   vacat   [9

]   [˙ים [ו]˙יכֹף עץ ויזקף]   [10

[... and they will know]

(1) [that I am Yahweh] who redeem My people, giving unto them the covenant. *vacat*.

(2) [And I said: 'Yahweh.] I have seen many men from Israel who have loved Thy Name and have walked (3) in the ways of [righteousness; And th]ese (things) when will they *be*, and how will they be recompensed for their loyalty?'

And Yahweh said (4) to me: 'I will cause the children of Israel to *see, and* they shall know that I am Yahweh.' *vacat*.

(5) [And He said:] 'Son of Man, prophesy *over* the bones and say: be ye joined bone to its bone and joint (6) [to its joint'. And it wa]s so.

And He said a second time: 'Prophesy and let sinews come upon them and let them be covered with skin (7) [above'. And it wa]s s[o].

And He said again: 'Prophecy *concerning* the four *winds* of heaven and let the win[ds (8) of heaven] blow [*upon them and they shall revive,*] and a great crowd of people shall stand up, and they shall bless Yahweh Sabaoth wh[o has given them life again.']

(9) [*vacat* And] I said: 'O Yahweh. when shall these things be?' And Yahweh said to m[e   ]

(10) [   ] ... and a tree *shall bend and shall stand erect* [   ]

BIBLIOGRAPHY

Addison, W.
    1936   *The Life and Writings of Thomas Boston of Ettrick* (Edinburgh: Oliver & Boyd).

Aichele, G., and T. Pippin (eds.)
    1992   *Fantasy and the Bible* (Semeia, 60; Atlanta, GA: Scholars Press).

Alexander, J.
    1993   'Hogg in the *Noctes Ambrosianae*', *Studies in Hogg and his World* 4: 37-47.

Alexander, P.
    1984   'Midrash and the Gospels', in C. Tucker (ed.), *Synoptic Studies: The Ampleforth Conferences of 1982–1983* (Sheffield: JSOT Press): 1-18.
    1990   sv 'Midrash', in R. Coggins and J. Houlden (eds.), *A Dictionary of Biblical Interpretation* (London: SCM & Trinity Press International).

Alter, R., and F. Kermode, (eds.)
    1989   *The Literary Guide to the Bible* (London: Fontana).

Altizer, T.
    1982   'History as Apocalypse', in Raschke (ed.) 1982: 147-77.

Anonymous
    1824   Review of Hogg's *Confessions of a Justified Sinner* in *Westminster Review* 2: 560-62.

Archer, L.
    1987   Review of Farrer's *A Rebirth of Images*, in *Christianity and Literature* 37: 69-70.

Ashton, J.
    1994   *Studying John: Approaches to the Fourth Gospel* (Oxford: Clarendon Press).

Auerbach, E.
    1953   *Mimesis: The Representation of Reality in Western Literature* (trans. W Trask; Garden City, NY: Doubleday).

Baker, L.
    1986   'The Open Secret of *Sartor Resartus*: Carlyle's Method of Converting his Reader', *Studies in Philology* 83: 218-35.

Barr, J.
    1983   *Holy Scripture: Canon, Authority, Criticism* (Oxford: Clarendon Press).

Barrett, C.K.
    1978   *The Gospel According to St John: An Introduction with Commentary and Notes on the Greek Text* (London: SPCK, 2nd edn).

Barthes, R.

1953   *Le Degré zéro de l'écriture* (Paris: Editions du Seuil).

1981   'Theory of the Text', in R. Young (ed.), *Untying the Text: A Post-structuralist Reader* (Boston, MA: Routledge & Kegan Paul): 31-47.

1974   *S/Z* (trans. by R Miller; New York: Hill & Wang).

1984   'The Death of the Author', in *idem, Image, Music, Text* (trans. S. Heath; London: Fontana): 142-48.

Bauckham, R.

1991   'A Quotation from 4QSecond Ezekiel in the Apocalypse of Peter', *RevQ* 15: 437-46.

1993a   *The Climax of Prophecy: Studies on the Book of Revelation* (Edinburgh: T. & T. Clark).

1993b   *The Theology of the Book of Revelation* (Cambridge: Cambridge University Press).

Beasley-Murray, G.

1974   *The Book of Revelation* (London: Marshall, Morgan & Scott).

Beckwith, I.

1967   *The Apocalypse of John: Studies in Introduction* (Grand Rapids, MI: Baker Book House [1919]).

Bible and Culture Collective

1995   *The Postmodern Bible* (New Haven: Yale University Press).

Bligh, J.

1984   'The Doctrinal Premises of Hogg's *Confessions of a Justified Sinner*', *Studies in Scottish Literature* 19: 148-64.

Bloedé, B.

1966   'James Hogg's *Private Memoirs and Confessions of a Justified Sinner*: The Genesis of the Double', *Etudes Anglaises* 26: 175-88.

Boesak, A.

1987   *Comfort and Protest: Reflections on the Apocalypse of John of Patmos* (Philadelphia: Westminster Press).

Booth, W.

1961   *The Rhetoric of Fiction* (Harmondsworth: Penguin Books).

Boston, T.

1720   *Human Nature, in its Fourfold State* (Glasgow: J Bryce).

1979   *The Beauties of Boston: A Selection of his Writings* (ed S. M'Millan; Inverness: Christian Focus Publications [1831]).

Bousset, W.

1906   *Die Offenbarung Johannis* (Göttingen: Vandenhoeck & Ruprecht, 6th edn).

Bowers, F.

1959   *Textual and Literary Criticism* (Cambridge: Cambridge University Press).

Boyarin, D.

1990   *Intertextuality and the Reading of Midrash* (Bloomington, IN: Indiana University Press).

Brooke, G.

1992   'Ezekiel in some Qumran and New Testament Texts', in J. Barrera and L. Montaner (eds.), *The Madrid Qumran Congress* (2 vols.; Leiden: E.J. Brill): I, 317-37.

Brown, D.
　　1976　　*James Hogg* (Edinburgh: Ramsay Head Press).
Bruns, G.
　　1989　　'Midrash and Allegory: The Beginnings of Scriptural Interpretation', in
　　　　　　Alter and Kermode (eds.) 1989: 625-46.
Burke, S.
　　1992　　*The Death and Return of the Author: Criticism and Subjectivity*, in
　　　　　　Barthes, Foucault and Derrida (Edinburgh: Edinburgh University Press).
Burleigh, J,
　　1960　　*A Church History of Scotland* (Oxford: Oxford University Press).
Burnett, F.
　　1990　　'Postmodern Biblical Exegesis: The Eve of Historical Criticism', *Semeia*
　　　　　　51: 51-80.

Caird, G,
　　1966　　*A Commentary on the Revelation of St John the Divine* (London: A. & C.
　　　　　　Black).
Campbell, I.
　　1972a　 'Author and Audience in Hogg's *Confessions of a Justified Sinner*', *Scot-
　　　　　　tish Literary News* 2: 66-76.
　　1972b　 'Hogg's *Confessions of a Justified Sinner*', *Liturgical Review* 2: 28-33.
　　1988a　 'The Bible, the Kirk and Scottish Literature', in Wright (ed.) 1988: 110-
　　　　　　27.
　　1988b　 'James Hogg and the Bible', in Wright (ed.) 1988: 94-109.
Campbell, I. (ed.)
　　1979　　*Nineteenth Century Scottish Fiction* (Manchester: Carcanet New Press
　　　　　　Ltd).

Carey, J.
　　1969　　'Introduction' in James Hogg, *The Private Memoirs and Confessions of a
　　　　　　Justified Sinner* (London: Oxford University Press): xi-xxiii.
Carlyle, T.
　　1833　　*Sartor Resartus* (Oxford: Oxford University Press, 1987).
Carter, F.
　　1931　　*The Dragon of Revelation* (London: Harmsworth).
Chalmers, T.
　　1849　　*Institutes of Theology*, I (2 vols.; Edinburgh: T. Constable).
Charles, R.H.,
　　1913　　*Studies in the Apocalypse: Being Lectures Delivered before the University
　　　　　　of London* (Edinburgh: T. & T. Clark).
　　1920　　*A Critical and Exegetical Commentary on The Revelation of St. John*, I (2
　　　　　　vols.; Edinburgh: T. & T. Clark).
Cheyne, A.
　　1983　　*The Transforming of the Kirk: Victorian Scotland's Religious Revolution*
　　　　　　(Edinburgh: St Andrew Press).
Collins, A.Y.
　　1991　　'Review of Thompson's *The Book of Revelation*', *JBL* 110: 748-50.
Collins, J.
　　1992　　'Dead Sea Scrolls', *ABD*, II: 85-101.

Connor, S.
    1989   *Postmodernist Culture: An Introduction to Theories of the Contemporary*
                (Oxford: Basil Blackwell).
Conti, C. (ed.)
    1976   *Interpretation and Belief* (London: SPCK).
Court, J.
    1979   *Myth and History in the Book of Revelation* (London: SPCK).
Culpepper, R.
    1983   *The Anatomy of the Fourth Gospel: A Study in Literary Design* (Phila-
                delphia: Fortress Press).
Davies, M.
    1990   'Literary Criticism', in R. Coggins, and J. Houlden (eds.), *A Dictionary of
                Biblical Interpretation* (London: SCM Press): 402-405.
Davies, W.D.
    1950   Review of Farrer's *A Rebirth of Images* in *Congregational Quarterly* 28:
                73-74.
Davis, C.
    1982   'The Theological Career of Historical Criticism of the Bible', *Cross
                Currents* 32: 267-84.
De Groot, H.
    1990   'The Imperilled Reader in *The Three Perils of Man*', in *Studies in Hogg
                and his World* 1: 114-25.
Derrida, J.
    1966   'Structure, Sign and Play in the Discourse of the Human Sciences', in
                idem, 1978: 278-95.
    1976   *Of Grammatology* (trans. G.C. Spivak; Baltimore: The Johns Hopkins
                University Press).
    1977   'Signature Event Contex' (trans. S. Weber and J. Mehlman) *Glyph* I: 172-
                97.
    1978   'Edmond Jabès and the Question of the Book', in *idem*, 1978: 64-78.
    1978   *Writing and Difference* (trans. A Bass; London: Routledge & Kegan Paul).
    1979   *Spurs: Nietzsche's Styles* (trans. B Harlow; Chicago: University of Chi-
                cago Press).
    1982   'Of an Apocalyptic Tone Recently Adopted in Philosophy', *Semeia* 23:
                63-97.
    1991   'Des Tours de Babel' (trans. J. Graham), *Semeia* 54: 3-34.
    1995   *The Gift of Death* (trans. D Wills; Chicago: University of Chicago Press).
Detweiler, R. (ed.)
    1982   *Derrida and Biblical Studies* (Semeia, 23; Atlanta: Scholars Press)
Detweiler, R., and V. Robbins
    1991   'From New Criticism to Poststructuralism: Twentieth-century Hermeneu-
                tics', in Prickett 1991: 225-80.
Dimant, D., and J. Strugnell
    1990   'The Merkabah Vision in Second Ezekiel (4Q385 4)', *RevQ* 14: 331-48.
Dimant, D.
    1992a   'Histoire et apocalyptique à Qoumrân: nouvelles perspectives', *Canal-
                infos* 9: 14-22.

1992b   *New Light from Qumran on the Jewish Pseudepigrapha–4Q390*, in
             J. Barrera and L. Montaner (eds.), *The Madrid Qumran Congress* (2 vols.;
             Leiden: E.J. Brill): II, 405-48.

Docherty, T. (ed.)
1993   *Postmodernism: A Reader* (New York: Columbia University Press).

Draisma, S. (ed.)
1989   *Intertextuality in Biblical Writings: Essays in Honour of Bas van Iersel*
             (Kampen: Kok).

Eichrodt, W.
1970   *Ezekiel: A Commentary* (trans. C Quinn; London: SCM Press).

Eisenman, R., and M. Wise
1992   *The Dead Sea Scrolls Uncovered* (Harmondsworth: Penguin Books).

Empson, W.
1949   *Seven Types of Ambiguity* (London: Chatto & Windus, 2nd edn).

Enright, W.
1968   'Preaching and Theology in Scotland in the Nineteenth Century: A Study
             of the Context and the Content of the Evangelical Sermon' (PhD Thesis,
             University of Edinburgh).

Evans, C., and J. Sanders (eds.)
1993   *Paul and the Scriptures of Israel* (Sheffield: JSOT Press).

Farrer, A.
1949   *A Rebirth of Images: The Making of St John's Apocalypse* (Westminster:
             Dacre Press).
1951   *A Study in St Mark* (London: A. & C. Black).
1959   *On Looking Below the Surface*, in Conti (ed.) 1976: 54-65.
1963   *Inspiration: Poetical and Divine*, in Conti (ed.) 1976: 39-53.
1964   *The Revelation of St John the Divine* (Oxford: Clarendon Press).

Fenwick, J.
1988   'Psychological and Narrative Determinism in James Hogg's *The Private
             Memoirs and Confessions of a Justified Sinner*', *Scottish Literary Journal*
             15: 61-69.

Ferguson, S.
1982   'The Teaching of the Confession', in A. Heron (ed.), *The Westminster
             Confession in the Church Today* (Edinburgh: St Andrew Press): 28-39.

Fielding, P.
1996   *Writing and Orality: Nationality, Culture and 19th Century Scottish Fic-
             tion* (Oxford: Oxford University Press).

Fiorenza, E.S.
1985   *The Book of Revelation: Justice and Judgement* (Philadelphia: Fortress
             Press).

Fisch, H.
1986   'The Hermeneutic Quest in Robinson Crusoe', in Hartman and Budick
             1986: 195-212.

Fish, S.
1980   *Is There a Text in This Class?: The Authority of Interpretative Commun-
             ities* (Cambridge, MA: Harvard University Press).
1989   *Doing What Comes Naturally: Change, Rhetoric, and the Practice of
             Theory in Literary and Legal Studies* (Oxford: Clarendon Press).

Fishbane, M.
    1986   'Inner Bible Exegesis: Types and Strategies of Interpretation in Ancient
                Israel', in Hartman and Budick 1986: 19-37.
    1988   'Use, Authority and Interpretation of Mikra at Qumran', in M. Mulder
                (ed.), *Mikra: Text, Translation, Reading and Interpretation of the Hebrew
                Bible in Ancient Judaism and Early Christianity* (Assen: Van Gorcum):
                339-77.
Fisher, E.
    1728   *The Marrow of Modern Divinity* (edited with notes by T. Boston; Edin-
                burgh: J. & D. Collie).
Ford, J.M.
    1975   *Revelation* (Garden City, NY: Doubleday).
Fowler, R.
    1991   *Let the Reader Understand: Reader Response Criticism and the Gospel of
                Mark* (Minneapolis: Fortress Press).
Freund, E.
    1987   *The Return of the Reader: Reader-response Criticism* (London: Methuen).
Freyne, S.
    1989   *Reading Hebrews and Revelation Intertextually*, in Draisma (ed.) 1989:
                83-93.
Frye, N.
    1964   *The Educated Imagination* (Bloomington, IN: Indiana University Press).
Funk, R.W.
    1988   *The Poetics of Biblical Narrative* (Sonoma, CA: Polebridge Press).
Gabel, G., and C. Wheeler
    1986   *The Bible as Literature: An Introduction* (New York: Oxford University
                Press).
García Martínez, F.
    1994   *The Dead Sea Scrolls* (trans. W Watson; Leiden: E.J. Brill).
Gide, A.
    1947   'Introduction', in James Hogg, *The Private Memoirs and Confessions of a
                Justified Sinner* (London: Cresset Press): ix-xvi.
Gifford, D.
    1976   *James Hogg* (Edinburgh: Ramsay Head Press).
    1989   'Introduction to Hogg's *The Three Perils of Man: War, Women and
                Witchcraft*' (Edinburgh: Scottish Academic Press).
Gifford, D. (ed.)
    1988   *The History of Scottish Literature*, III (4 vols.; Aberdeen: Aberdeen Uni-
                versity Press).
Green, W.S.
    1993   'Doing the Text's Work for it: Richard Hays on Paul's use of Scripture',
                in Evans and Sanders (eds.) 1993: 58-63.
Goulder, M.
    1985   'Farrer the Biblical Scholar', in P. Curtis (ed.) *A Hawk Among Sparrows:
                A Biography of Austin Farrer* (London: SPCK): 192-212.
Groves, D.
    1985   'James Hogg as Romantic Writer', in Hughes 1983: 1-10.

1986	'Blake, Thomas Boston, and the Fourfold Vision', *Blake: An Illustrated Quarterly* 19: 142.
1988	*James Hogg: The Growth of a Writer* (Edinburgh: Scottish Academic Press).

Habermas, J.

1987   *The Philosophical Discourse of Modernity* (trans. F. Lawrence; Cambridge: Polity Press).

Handelman, S.

1982   *The Slayers of Moses: The Emergence of Rabbinic Interpretation in Modern Literary Theory* (Albany: State University of New York Press).

Hart, K.

1991   'The Poetics of the Negative', in Prickett 1991: 281-340.

Hartman, G., and S. Budick

1986   *Midrash and Literature* (New Haven: Yale University Press).

Hassan, I.

1987   *The Postmodern Turn: Essays in Postmodern Theory and Culture* (Lincoln, OH: Ohio State University Press.)

Hawthorn, J.

1993   *Unlocking the Text: Fundamental Issues in Literary Theory* (London: Edward Arnold).

Hays, R.

1989   *Echoes of Scripture in the Letters of Paul* (New Haven: Yale University Press).

1993   'On the Rebound: A Response to Critiques of *Echoes of Scripture in the Letters of Paul*', in Evans and Sanders (eds.) 1993: 70-96.

Henderson, G. (ed.)

1937   *The Scots Confession 1560* (Edinburgh: Church of Scotland Committee on Publications).

Hewitt, D., J. Alexander, P. Garside, C. Lamont, D. Mack and G. Wood

1996   *The Edinburgh Edition of the Waverley Novels: A Guide for Editors* (Edinburgh: Edinburgh Edition of the Waverley Novels).

Hogg, James

1817   'An Ancient Chaldee Manuscript', *Blackwood's Magazine* 2: 89-96.

1822   *The Three Perils of Man: War, Woman and Witchcraft* (Edinburgh: Scottish Academic Press, 1989 edn).

1824   *The Private Memoirs and Confessions of a Justified Sinner* (Edinburgh: Canongate, 1991 edn).

1830   'A Letter from Yarrow—The Scottish Psalmody Defended', in W. Tennant and J. Hogg, *et al.* 1830: 25-32.

1832   'Statistics of Selkirkshire', in *Prize-Essays and Transactions of the Highland Society of Scotland*, IX (Edinburgh: Blackwood): 281-306.

1834   *A Series of Lay Sermons on Good Principles and Good Breeding* (London: James Fraser).

1874a   *The Works of the Ettrick Shepherd: Tales*, I (ed. T. Thomson; London: Blackie & Son).

1874b   'The First Sermon', in Hogg 1874a: 351-52.

1874c   'Odd Characters', in Hogg 1874a: 407-412.

1874d   'The Mysterious Bride', in Hogg 1874a: 453-58.

1874e   *The Works of the Ettrick Shepherd: Poems and Ballads*, II (ed. T Thomson; London: Blackie & Son).

1874f   'The Pedlar', in Hogg 1874e: 64-67.

1982   *Selected Stories and Sketches* (ed. D Mack; Edinburgh: Scottish Academic Press).

1982a   'Storms', in Hogg 1982: 1-21.

1982b   'George Dobson's Expedition to Hell', in Hogg 1982: 41-49.

1982c   'Tibby Hyslop's Dream', in Hogg 1982: 50-70.

1982d   'Sound Morality', in Hogg 1982: 121-32.

Holladay, W. (ed.)

1988   *A Concise Hebrew and Aramaic Lexicon of the Old Testament* (Based on the First, Second and Third Editions of the *Koehler–Baumgartner Lexicon in Veteris Testamenti Libros*) (Leiden: E.J. Brill).

Hollander, J.

1981   *The Figure of Echo: A Mode of Allusion in Milton and After* (Berkeley, CA: University of California Press).

Horgan, M.

1979   *Pesharim: Qumran Interpretations of Biblical Books* (Washington: Catholic Biblical Association of America).

Hughes, G. (ed.)

1983   *Papers given at the Second James Hogg Society Conference (Edinburgh, 1985)* (Aberdeen: Association for Scottish Literary Studies).

Hughes, G.

1983   'The Importance of the Periodical Environment in Hogg's Work for *Chambers's Edinburgh Journal*', in Hughes (ed.) 1983: 40-48.

Hutcheon, L.

1988   *A Poetics of Postmodernism: History, Theory, Fiction* (London: Routledge).

Iser, W.

1974   *The Implied Reader: Patterns of Communication in Prose Fiction from Bunyan to Beckett* (Baltimore: The Johns Hopkins University Press).

1978   *The Act of Reading: A Theory of Aesthetic Response* (Baltimore: The Johns Hopkins University Press).

Jabès, E.

1963   *Le Livre des Questions* (Paris: Gallimard).

Jackson, R.

1981   *Fantasy: The Literature of Subversion* (London: Methuen).

Jasper, D.

1987   *The New Testament and the Literary Imagination* (London: Macmillan).

1989   *The Study of Literature and Religion: An Introduction* (London: Macmillan).

Jasper, D. (ed.)

1984   *Images of Belief in Literature* (London: Macmillan).

Jasper, D., and T. Wright (eds.)

1989   *The Critical Spirit and the Will to Believe: Essays in Nineteenth Century Literature and Religion* (London: Macmillan).

Jenkins, F.

1972   *The Old Testament in the Book of Revelation* (Grand Rapids: Eerdmans).

Jones, B
   1992   *The Emperor Domitian* (London: Routledge).

Jones, D.
   1988   'Double Jeopardy and the Chameleon Art in James Hogg's *Justified Sinner*', *Studies in Scottish Literature* 23: 164-85.

Kalnins, M.
   1995   'Introduction to Lawrence's *Apocalypse and the Writings on Revelation*' (Harmondsworth: Penguin Books).

Kermode, F.
   1979   *The Genesis of Secrecy: On the Interpretation of Narrative* (Cambridge, MA: Harvard University Press).
   1983   *Essays on Fiction 1971–1982* (London: Routledge & Kegan Paul).
   1983a   'Instances of Interpretation', in *idem* 1983: 168-84.
   1983b   'Prologue', in *idem*, 1983: 1-32.
   1985   *Forms of Attention* (Chicago: University of Chicago Press).
   1986   'The Argument about Canons', in F. McConnell (ed.), *The Bible and the Narrative Tradition* (New York: Oxford University Press): 78-96.
   1990   *Poetry, Narrative, History* (Oxford: Basil Blackwell).

Kiddle, M.
   1940   *The Revelation of St John* (London: Hodder & Stoughton).

Kilian, J.
   1989   *Form and Style in Theological Texts* (Pretoria: University of South Africa, 2nd edn).

Kister, M.
   1990   'Barnabas 12.1; 4.3 and 4QSecond Ezekiel', *RB* 97: 63-67.

Kister, M., and E. Qimron
   1992   'Observations on 4QSecond Ezekiel (4Q385 2-3)', *RevQ* 15: 595-602.

Knox, J.
   1855   *The Works of John Knox*, IV (6 vols.; ed. D. Laing; Edinburgh: Wodrow Society).

Koehler, L., and W. Baumgartner
   1990   *Hebräisches und aramäisches Lexicon zum Alten Testament* (Leiden: E.J. Brill, 3rd edn).

Kristeva, J.
   1986   'Word, Dialogue, and Novel' (trans. A Jardine, T. Gora and L. Rondiez), in T. Moi (ed.), *The Kristeva Reader* (Oxford: Basil Blackwell): 30-57.

Kümmel, W.
   1975   *Introduction to the New Testament* (trans. H.C.Kee; London: SCM Press, 17th edn)

Lawrence, D.H.
   1931a   'Introduction to *The Dragon of the Apocalypse* by Frederick Carter', in Lawrence 1931b: 45-56.
   1931b   *Apocalypse and the Writings on Revelation* (Harmondsworth: Penguin Books, 1995 edn).

Lumsden, A.
   1992   'Travelling Hopefully: Postmodern Thought and the Fictional Practice of Walter Scott, James Hogg and Robert Louis Stevenson' (PhD thesis, University of Edinburgh).

Lyotard, J.-F.
    1984   *The Postmodern Condition: A Report on Knowledge* (trans. G. Benning-
                ton and B. Massumi; Manchester: Manchester University Press).
Mack, B.
    1988   *A Myth of Innocence: Mark and Christian Origins* (Philadelphia: Fortress
                Press).
Mack, D.
    1970   'Hogg's Religion and *The Confessions of a Justified Sinner*', *Studies in
                Scottish Literature* 7: 272-75.
MacQueen, J.
    1989   *The Rise of the Scottish Novel* (Edinburgh: Scottish Academic Press).
Malbon, E.S., and E. McKnight (eds.)
    1994   *The New Literary Criticism and the New Testament* (Sheffield: Sheffield
                Academic Press).
Manlove, C.
    1992   *The Bible in Fantasy* (Semeia, 60; Atlanta, GA: Scholars Press): 91-110.
Manson, T.W.
    1949   Review of *A Rebirth of Images*, in *JTS* 50: 207-208.
Martin, W.
    1986   *Recent Theories of Narrative* (Ithaca, NY: Cornell University Press).
McGann, J.
    1983   *A Critique of Modern Textual Criticism* (Chicago: University of Chicago
                Press).
McHale, B.
    1987   *Postmodernist Fiction* (London: Methuen).
McKeating, H.
    1993   *Ezekiel* (Sheffield: JSOT Press).
McSweeney, K., and P. Sabor
    1987   'Introduction' in T. Carlyle, *Sartor Resartus* (Oxford: Oxford University
                Press): vii-xxxiii.
Mergenthal, S.
    1990   *James Hogg: Selbstbild und Bild: Zur Rezeption des 'Ettrick Shepherd'*
                (Frankfurt am Main: Peter Lang).
    1991   'James Hogg's *Lay Sermons* and the Essay Tradition', *Studies in Hogg
                and his World* 2: 64-71.
Miller, K.
    1985   *Doubles: Studies in Literary History* (Oxford: Oxford University Press).
Mlakuzhyil, G.
    1987   *The Christocentric Literary Structure of the Fourth Gospel* (Rome:
                Pontifical Biblical Institute. Press).
Moore, S.
    1989   *Literary Criticism and the Gospels: The Theoretical Challenge* (New
                Haven: Yale University Press).
    1991   *The Gospel of the Book* (Semeia, 54; Atlanta, GA: Scholars Press): 159-
                96.
    1992   *Mark and Luke in Poststructuralist Perspective: Jesus Begins to Write*
                (New Haven: Yale University Press).

| | 1994 | *Poststructuralism and the New Testament: Derrida and Foucault at the Foot of the Cross* (Minneapolis: Fortress Press). |

1994   *Poststructuralism and the New Testament: Derrida and Foucault at the Foot of the Cross* (Minneapolis: Fortress Press).

1995   'The Beatific Vision as a Posing Exhibition: Revelation's Hypermasculine Deity', *JSNT* 18: 27-55.

Moyise, S.

1995   *The Old Testament in the Book of Revelation* (Sheffield: Sheffield Academic Press).

Muir, E.

1991   'The Horses', in P. Butter (ed.), *The Complete Poems of Edwin Muir* (Aberdeen: Association for Scottish Literary Studies): 226-27.

Murphy, P.

1993   *Poetry as an Occupation and an Art in Britain, 1760–1830* (Cambridge: Cambridge University Press).

Neusner, J.

1987a   *Christian Faith and the Bible of Judaism: The Judaic Encounter with Scripture* (Grand Rapids: Eerdmans).

1987b   *What is Midrash?* (Philadelphia: Fortress Press).

Newton, K.M. (ed.)

1988   *Twentieth Century Literary Theory: A Reader* (London: Macmillan).

Norris, C.

1987   *Derrida* (London: Fontana).

1991   *Deconstruction: Theory and Practice* (London: Routledge, 2nd edn).

Oliphant, M.

1897   *Annals of a Publishing House: William Blackwood and his Sons, their Magazine and Friends*, I (2 vols.; Edinburgh: Blackwood, 2nd edn).

Olsen, E.

1952   'William Empson, Contemporary Criticism, and Poetic Diction', in R. Crane (ed.), *Critics and Criticism: Ancient and Modern* (Chicago: University of Chicago Press): 45-82.

Oman, J.

1923   *Book of Revelation* (Cambridge: Cambridge University Press.)

O'Neill, J.C.

1991   'The Man from Heaven: SibOr 5.256-259', *JSP* 9: 87-102.

Parker, H.

1984   *Flawed Texts and Verbal Icons: Literary Authority and American Fiction* (Evanston, IL: Northwestern University Press).

Parsons, C.

1989   'The Parodic Background of the "Chaldee Manuscript"', *Studies in Scottish Literature* 24: 221-25.

Petersen, N.

1985   *Rediscovering Paul: Philemon and the Sociology of Paul's Narrative World* (Philadelphia: Fortress Press).

Petrie, D.

1992   'The Sinner Versus the Scholar: Two Exemplary Models of Mis-remembering and Mis-taking Signs in Relation the Hogg's *Justified Sinner*', *Studies in Hogg and his World* 3: 57-67.

Phillips, G.
  1990   'Exegesis as Critical Praxis: Reclaiming History and Text from a Post-modern Perspective', *Semeia* 51: 7-49.
Phillips, G. (ed.)
  1990   *Poststructuralist Criticism and the Bible: Text/History/Discourse* (Semeia, 51; Atlanta, GA: Scholars Press).
Philonenko, M.
  1993–94   'Un arbre se courbera et se redressera (4Q385 2 9-10)', *RHPR* 73: 401-404.
Pippin, T.
  1992   *Death and Desire: The Rhetoric of Gender in the Apocalypse of John* (Louisville, KY: Westminster/John Knox Press).
  1994   'Peering into the Abyss: A Postmodern Reading of the Biblical Bottom-less Pit', in Malbon and McKnight (eds.) 1994: 251-68.
Powell, M.
  1993   *What is Narrative Criticism?: A New Approach to the Bible* (London: SPCK).
Prickett, S.
  1986   *Words and the Word: Language, Poetics, and Biblical Interpretation* (Cambridge: Cambridge University Press).
  1989   *Biblical Criticism and the Nineteenth Century Novel*, in Jasper and Wright (eds.) 1989: 1-22.
  1991   *Reading the Text: Biblical Criticism and Literary Theory* (Oxford: Basil Blackwell).
Prickett, S., and R. Barnes
  1991   *The Bible* (Cambridge: Cambridge University Press).
Pryse, J.
  1910   *The Apocalypse Unsealed* (London: Watkins).
Puech, E.
  1992   'Une apocalypse messianique (*4Q521*)', *RevQ* 15: 475-519.
  1994   'L'image de l'arbre en 4QDeutéro-Ézéchiel (4Q385 2, 9-10)', *RevQ* 16: 429-40.
Raschke, C.
  1982   'The Deconstruction of God', in Raschke (ed.) 1982: 1-33.
Raschke, C. (ed.)
  1982   *Deconstruction and Theology* (New York: Crossroad).
Rousseau, J.J.
  1967   *Essay on the Origin of Languages* (trans. J. Moran; New York: F. Unger).
Redekop, M.
  1985   'Beyond Closure: Buried Alive with Hogg's *Justified Sinner*', *English Literary History* 52: 159-84.
Riffaterre, M.
  1990   'Compulsory Reader Response: The Intertextual Drive', in Worton and Still (eds.) 1990: 56-78.
Roloff, J.
  1993   *Revelation: A Continental Commentary* (trans. J. Alsup; Minneapolis: Fortress Press).

Royle, T.
　　1980　　*Precipitous City: The Story of Literary* (Edinburgh: Mainsteam Publishing).
Russell, D.
　　1993　　Review of Pippin's *Death and Desire*, *ExpTim* 104: 281-82.
Safrai, S.
　　1987　　'Oral Torah', in S. Safrai (ed.), *The Literature of the Sages* (Assen: Van Gorcum): 35-120.
Sanders, C.
　　1963　　'The Correspondence and Friendship of Thomas Carlyle and Leigh Hunt: The Early Years', *BJRL* 45.2: 439-85.
Saussure, F.
　　1974　　*Course in General Linguistics* (trans. W. Baskin; London: Fontana).
Scharlemann, R.
　　1982　　'The Being of God when God Is not Being God: Deconstructing the History of Theism', in Raschke (ed.) 1982: 79-108.
Scott, P
　　1988　　'The Last Purely Scotch Age', in Gifford (ed.) 1988: 13-22.
Searle, J.
　　1977　　'Reiterating the Differences: A Reply to Derrida', *Glyph* I: 198-208.
Sedgwick, E.
　　1985　　*Between Men: English Literature and Male Homosocial Desire* (New York: Columbia University Press).
Selden, R.
　　1989　　*A Reader's Guide to Contemporary Literary Theory* (Hemel Hempstead: Harvester Wheatsheaf, 2nd edn).
Simpson, L.
　　1962　　*James Hogg: A Critical Study* (Edinburgh: Oliver & Boyd).
Smith, N.
　　1980　　*James Hogg* (Boston: Twayne Publishers).
Staley, J.
　　1988　　*The Print's First Kiss: A Rhetorical Investigation of the Implied Reader in the Fourth Gospel* (Atlanta, CA: Scholars Press).
Staten, H.
　　1985　　*Wittgenstein and Derrida* (Oxford: Basil Blackwell).
Stegner, W.
　　1984　　'Romans 9.6-29—A Midrash', *JSNT* 22: 37-52.
Stern, D.
　　1984　　'Moses-cide: Midrash and Contemporary Literary Criticism', *Prooftexts* 4: 193-204.
Sternberg, M.
　　1985　　*The Poetics of Biblical Narrative: Ideological Literature and the Drama of Reading* (Bloomington, IN: Indiana University Press).
Stevenson, R.
　　1992　　*Modernist Fiction: An Introduction* (Hemel Hempstead: Harvester Wheatsheaf).

Strack, H., and G. Stemberger
  1991   *Introduction to the Talmud and Midrash* (trans. H. Bockmuehl; Edinburgh: T. & T. Clark).
Strout, A.
  1946   *The Life and Letters of James Hogg, The Ettrick Shepherd.* I. (*1770–1825*) (Lubbock, TX: Texas Technichal Press).
Strugnell, J., and D. Dimant
  1988   '4Q Second Ezekiel', *RevQ* 13: 45-58.
Sutherland, S.
  1990   'History, Truth and Narrative', in M. Warner (ed.), *The Bible as Rhetoric: Studies in Biblical Persuasion and Credibility* (London: Routledge).
Tennant, W.
  1830   *Remarks on the Scottish Version of the Psalms, with a View to its Amelioration*, in Tennant and Hogg *et al.* (eds.) 1830: 13-25.
Tennant, W., and J. Hogg, *et al.*
  1830   *Critical Remarks on the Psalms of David and their Various English and Latin Versions: Particularly on the Version Now Used in our Scottish Church, with a View to its Emendation* (Edinburgh: Constable & Co.).
Tennyson, G.
  1965   *Sartor Called Resartus: The Genesis, Structure, and Style of Thomas Carlyle's First Major Work* (Princeton, NJ: Princeton University Press).
Thompson, L.
  1990   *The Book of Revelation: Apocalypse and Empire* (Oxford: Oxford University Press).
Thomson, A.
  1825   *Sermons on Hearing the Word Preached* (Edinburgh: William Whyte & Co.).
Tracts on Blackwood's Magazine
  [s.a.]   Edinburgh: Abernethy & Walker.
Vanhoye, A.
  1962   'L'utilisation du livre d'Ezechiel dans l'Apocalypse', *Bib* 43: 436-76.
Vermes, G.
  1970   'Bible and Midrash: Early Old Testament Exegesis', in P. Ackroyd and C. Evans (eds.), *The Cambridge History of the Bible* (3 vols.; Cambridge: Cambridge University Press): I, 199-231.
  1992   'Qumran Forum Miscelanea I', *JJS* 43: 299-305.
  1995   *The Dead Sea Scrolls in English* (Harmondworth: Penguin Books, 4th edn).
Vogelgesang, J.
  1985   'The Interpretation of Ezekiel in the Book of Revelation' (PhD Thesis, Harvard University).
Wagner, S.
  1978   'darash', *TDOT*, III: 293-305.
Wain, J.
  1983   'Introduction', in James Hogg, *The Private Memoirs and Confessions of a Justified Sinner*' (Harmondsworth: Penguin Books): 7-25.

Watson, H.
    1984   'William Tennant, the Ettrick Shepherd and the Psalms of David: A Linguistic Controversy', *Scottish Language* 3: 60-70.

Watson, J.
    1883   *The Pastor of Ettrick: Thomas Boston* (Edinburgh: James Gemmell).

Waugh, P. (ed.)
    1992   *Postmodernism: A Reader* (New York: Edward Arnold).

Wevers, J.
    1969   *Ezekiel: New Century Bible* (London: Nelson).

Wheeler, M.
    1979   *The Art of Allusion in Victorian Fiction* (London: Macmillan).

Wimsatt, W., and M. Beardsley
    1946   'The Intentional Fallacy', *Sewanee Review* 54: 468-88.

Wittgenstein, L.
    1953   *Philosophical Investigations* (trans. G. Anscombe; Oxford: Basil Blackwell).

Wolde, E. van
    1989   'Trendy Intertextuality?', in Draisma (ed.) 1989: 43-49.

Worton, M., and J. Still (eds.)
    1990   *Intertextuality: Theories and Practices* (Manchester: Manchester University Press).

Wright, D. (ed.)
    1988   *The Bible in Scottish Life and Literature* (Edinburgh: St Andrews Press).

Zimmerli, W.
    1983   *Ezekiel 2* (trans. J. Martin; Philadelphia: Fortress Press).

INDEXES

INDEX OF REFERENCES

OLD TESTAMENT

INDEX OF AUTHORS

JOURNAL FOR THE STUDY OF THE NEW TESTAMENT
SUPPLEMENT SERIES